Walter T. Oman
1st Baptist Church

THE ROYAL ROUTE
TO HEAVEN

THE ROYAL ROUTE
TO HEAVEN

Studies in First Corinthians

by ALAN REDPATH

FLEMING H. REVELL COMPANY

Scripture quotations in this book are principally from the King James Version. Those quotations marked RSV are from the *Revised Standard Version of the Bible*, copyrighted 1946 and 1952. Several are from *The New Testament in Modern English* by J. B. Phillips, copyrighted 1959, used by permission of The Macmillan Company and of Geoffrey Bles Ltd.; and from *The Bible: A New Translation* by James Moffatt, copyrighted 1922, 1926, 1935, used by permission of Harper & Brothers. Occasionally the author offers a free translation of the original Scripture or an adaptation of several versions.

FOREWORD

THE CONTENTS OF this book represent the theme of messages preached from the pulpit of Moody Church over a period of several months. They do not claim to be in any sense a scholarly exposition of Paul's first letter to the Corinthian church. Such must be left to a far more gifted pen than mine. My only claim to justify their publication is the attempt to deal with what, in my judgment, is the priority need of the church today and to do so from a heart that has been deeply burdened with the urgency and relevance of the truths contained in these chapters.

If the reader turns to this book for a greater understanding of the doctrines of the faith, he may well be disappointed. If, however, he turns with a hungry heart to which God has revealed the shallowness and ineffectiveness of the church in the world today, it will be my fervent hope he will find in these pages that which will be both food and fire.

We often hear it said that the church of today is at once unique in the wealth of its equipment and in the bankruptcy of its enduement. To recognize this is one thing. To take action about it is quite another, and this is something that can be personally painful and costly. Yet in the light of the judgment seat of Christ, how can we possibly allow things to go on as they are? Words could never express how grateful to God I would be if He could in some way use this volume to bring His people from the byways and blind alleys, along which Satan has driven so many, to commence the triumphant march along the royal route to heaven.

It would be lacking in courtesy were I not to bear testimony to the many hours of work on manuscripts that have been spent both by my beloved wife and Miss Arline Harris, to both of whom I owe a great debt of gratitude, and without whose consecrated efforts this book could never have been published.

Alan Redpath

Moody Memorial Church,
Chicago, Illinois

CONTENTS

PART III DYNAMIC FOR THE JOURNEY

THE ROYAL ROUTE TO HEAVEN

There's a royal route to heaven—
Will you travel it today?
'Tis the path of full surrender
All along the homeward way.
It is yielding every moment
To the blessed Saviour's will,
Seeking only for His glory,
And His purpose to fulfill.

Chorus:

There's a royal route to heaven—
'Tis the way the Saviour trod.
'Tis the path of full surrender
And the deep, sweet peace of God.

There's a royal route to heaven—
They who travel it may know
Peace that passeth understanding
Which the Father doth bestow.
Dead to self and its desires,
Living unto Christ alone,
Finding joy and satisfaction
Which the world has never known.

There's a royal route to heaven—
Which will bring a rich reward
When the last long mile is covered
And we face our loving Lord.
Oh, how small will seem the trials
Of the steep and rugged way
When we stand in His blest presence
At the close of life's brief day.

—Avis B. Christiansen

PART I

Discipline for the Journey

CHAPTER 1

RESOURCES FOR THE JOURNEY

I Corinthians 1:1-9

THE TITLE *The Royal Route to Heaven* implies that there may be other roads leading to the same destination. We find that to be true before we journey far in this first epistle to the young church at Corinth. There is, of course, only one starting point in the Christian life: Calvary, where the sinner meets his Saviour and is ransomed, healed, restored, and forgiven. But beyond that starting point may occur many deviations from the plan of God; in this letter the Apostle Paul warns us of some of them.

It is possible for a Christian to live on a carnal level instead of on a spiritual level. It is possible to walk after the flesh even though we are converted to walk in the Spirit. It is possible to be saved, but to be saved as by fire: one day to stand before the judgment seat of Christ stripped of everything but our soul's salvation. On the other hand, there is a royal route to heaven, and the word "royal" implies sovereignty. In the Christian life, it means placing the crown where it rightly belongs: on the Saviour's brow. That is the main burden of these messages.

I am not interested in getting to heaven by the skin of my teeth, are you? My one desire is to get there by the grace of God, after a useful life in which the purpose of the Lord in saving my soul has been fulfilled.

This Corinthian letter exposes the tragedy of low-level Christian living, and reveals the glory of a journey made under the sovereignty

of Jesus Christ. Before we launch into a detailed study, here is a
telescopic view of the route we are going to follow.

The city of Corinth was a Roman colony on Grecian soil, the seat
of Roman government for the area, and a center of Greek commerce. A proud and wealthy city, it has been called the "Vanity Fair"
of the Roman Empire. Indeed, the word "Corinthian" came to be a
synonym for loose living. These Greeks were notorious for their
shallowness. They loved to argue just for the sake of argument;
they were very proud of their knowledge—in fact, they thought
they knew everything!

In such a place Paul had planted the seed of the gospel. Arriving
there after a shattering experience at Athens, he later declared, "I
determined not to know any thing among you, save Jesus Christ,
and him crucified" (2:2). He stayed in Corinth eighteen months
preaching the gospel (Acts 18:1-18), then he visited there again on
his third missionary journey (Acts 20:2-3). At that time he became
deeply burdened for these converts, and subsequent letters brought
him distressing news of sin in the Corinthian church (1:11).

Now here is a psychological point I would like to underline: in
spite of the sin in their midst, these people had the audacity to write
and ask theological questions of Paul. When people come for spiritual advice, I find they very rarely mention the real root of the
problem. Instead, they will ask a variety of theological questions.
But it is not long, if you know anything of the art of diagnosis,
before you discover that behind the whole thing there is, more
often than not, tragedy. That is exactly what happened with the
church at Corinth.

Therefore Paul did not hurry to answer their questions. Not until
chapter 7 did he say, "Now concerning the matters about which
you wrote" (RSV). In the first six chapters he deals with the situation
that existed in Corinth. He goes right to the root of the trouble first,
before he answers their theological questions.

To analyze this letter briefly, we find that the first eleven chapters
deal with carnality. He exposes the tragedy of their living in sin and
worldliness, and applies the positive remedy of the cross of Jesus
Christ. Then, as if he has had enough of it, he says, "Now, touching
spiritual things" (12:1), and he lifts us up to the tremendous heights
of the gospel of resurrection and life. The last five chapters of this

epistle deal with spirituality, and are constructive. For every aspect of carnality, Paul prescribes the dynamic remedy of the full message of the gospel.

There is a great deal of preaching today that does not follow Paul's example here: preaching the gospel of forgiveness of sins which is not accompanied by preaching on deliverance from s-i-n. That was the whole trouble with the church at Corinth: they knew all about the forgiveness of sins; there was nothing wrong with their theology, but a great deal wrong with their practice. They did not understand the gospel of deliverance from s-i-n, and that is the thrust of Paul's letter to them.

After this brief glimpse of the background, we now commence a more detailed study. We watch how this great missionary preacher approaches a church that is living on such a low level. He might have been indignant; he might have lashed out at them, but we find he doesn't do that. Paul adopts the tactics of the Master Himself, tactics which the Lord would have us all practice in such a situation, I'm sure. He lifts up the believers by reminding them of the glory of their salvation and of the great privileges that are theirs in Christ.

Will you notice with me, therefore, as we come to grips with this epistle, how Paul reminds them of their relationship to God? Then he reviews their equipment for the journey and their resources as Christians traveling this road. He begins by emphasizing his authority: "Paul, called to be an apostle of Jesus Christ through the will of God" (1:1). Although they do not recognize the school from which he came, he reminds them that he is speaking as an apostle, a "sent one," because he is in the will of God.

Then he addresses them as "the church of God which is at Corinth" (1:2). The Greek word *ecclesia* (translated "church") means "called ones," and they were the "called-out of God" in Corinth. They were not to cringe in fear before ungodly people, but to live as those called into the only position of authority any Christians can have in a pagan world: a position of dignity and power in Jesus Christ. He Himself said, "I will give unto thee the keys of the kingdom of heaven: and whatsoever thou shalt bind on earth shall be bound in heaven: and whatsoever thou shalt loose on earth shall be loosed in heaven" (Matthew 16:19).

In the next phrase Paul writes, "to them that are sanctified in

Christ Jesus, called saints," not "called *to be* saints," as we have the
verb inserted in the Authorized Version. This is what they are in
the sight of God, His separated ones, "called saints." In the remaining portion of verse 2 he opens it up to include every one of us:
"with all that in every place call upon the name of Jesus Christ our
Lord, both theirs and ours."

Here they were, God's called-out people in Corinth, and here
we are also, given a flaming message to proclaim, the good news
of redemption in Christ Jesus. Here is the gospel for a city with
all its corruption and licentiousness, vice and ignorance—a gospel
that is completely adequate for every situation when it is intelligently preached and intelligently understood. This letter is addressed not just to a few people in Corinth, a city that is now in
ruins, but to the church of Jesus Christ in any city of the world
in any era of history, even the times in which we live. We are
God's separated, called-out ones to a position of authority, that
is to say, a position in which we are supposed to know what we
believe, to live it and proclaim it. That is the only way through
which others can find the living Christ. We may be called, also, as
was the church at Corinth, to live in a city notorious for its corruption and licentiousness, but that is a sphere in which the church,
by contrast, should shine at its brightest.

"Called out"—that is our relationship to God and His message.
To those who are in that wonderful position the Lord gives resources for the journey that are "abundantly above." You find Paul
listing them for us, beginning in verse 3: "Grace be unto you, and
peace, from God our Father, and from the Lord Jesus Christ. I
thank my God always on your behalf, for the grace of God which
is given you by Jesus Christ." Here the Holy Spirit points out to
us that double spiritual power which, if we understand and appropriate it, will be adequate for everything that we can ever meet
in life. What is it? "Grace and peace" (1:3).

If I asked you to define the word "grace," perhaps you would say,
"It is the undeserved lovingkindness of God which has met us in
our sin and need." Yes, grace is that, but it is far more than that.
It comes, as Paul says here, from God our Father through the Lord
Jesus Christ: God the Father is the source and Jesus Christ is the
channel through whom it comes. Grace, therefore, is His life of

purity and holiness; His death that was sufficient to pay the price
for our sins; and His present ministry by which He imparts the
Holy Spirit today, enabling us to die to sin and live in His power.

It seems to me that "grace" in the New Testament is that which
brings into our lives everything that delights the heart of God.
There is grace to make me like the Master, grace to give me triumph when otherwise I would fail, grace to make me patient where
I would be impatient, grace to enable me to glorify the Lord Jesus
in every situation. Are you concerned about pleasing God today?
Let me remind you that He has already placed within you that
possibility: His life, His character, His Spirit.

The second word, "peace," does not imply laziness or inactivity.
It is movement without friction, creating perfect harmony. It also
means balance and unity which result from every part of your life
being centered upon doing the will of God. These two inner powers God has given to each one of His children. If we are Christians,
therefore, and have begun to travel this royal route to heaven, we
have some tremendous potentials.

Not only have we been given grace and peace, but other wealth,
also. "That in every thing ye are enriched by him, in all utterance,
and in all knowledge" says the Apostle in verse 5. Here we take
a backward look to the moment of our conversion, when we were
enriched. When we came to Jesus Christ, He imparted to our life
spiritual wealth that is going to be revealed "in all utterance and
in all knowledge." We have a message to proclaim, for God has
given us His gospel to preach, His Word to live by, His life to
live out—"all utterance." He has given to us the Holy Spirit, the
great Discerner of truth, by whose wisdom and strength we can
understand and appropriate the grace of God and the riches of our
Lord Jesus Christ—"all knowledge."

We should pause here to remind ourselves that these promises
are to all the church of Jesus Christ. This is the purpose of our salvation; here is the vantage ground that God has gained when He
saved you and me. His convincing argument to the world is the
Christian who is possessed and indwelt by the Spirit of God. It is
only through your life and mine that God can do things in our
neighborhoods that He could not accomplish otherwise. That is
His way of working, the way in which His sovereign purpose is

fulfilled—through a people to whom He has made Himself known, a people who have enlightenment from the Word of God, a people whose very lives demonstrate that the God in whom they believe is alive because He dwells within them.

That possibility should be a very solemn, challenging thought to our hearts: to know that God has a beachhead in us, that He intends to do something with our lives that He would not accomplish apart from His Spirit dwelling with each one of us. Therefore, regardless of the amount of theory or intellectual understanding you may be acquiring, the conclusive argument for His gospel of redemption is your life and mine in the place where God has put us.

Then let me ask you to notice the tremendous privilege that is ours as Christians, which is defined in the ninth verse: "God is faithful, by whom ye were called into the fellowship of his Son Jesus Christ our Lord."

You will recall a verse near the end of this letter, where Paul writes, "Therefore, my beloved brethren, be ye stedfast, unmoveable, always abounding in the work of the Lord, forasmuch as ye know that your labour is not in vain in the Lord" (15:58). Apart from greetings, that is the end of his letter, and it seems as if that verse goes right back to this one in the first chapter: "God is faithful . . . *therefore* be ye stedfast, unmoveable." How can we be steadfast? Because God is faithful, and He has called us into the fellowship of His Son. This is the priceless privilege of the Christian life.

The Greek word for "fellowship" here is *koinonia*, which means having everything in common. It is the thought of communion together, of mutual understanding. We who have been enriched, made wealthy by the grace of God so that our lives may reveal Christ to others, experience this tremendous privilege of having everything in common with our Lord. We are in partnership with Him, if you like.

A partnership is a business relationship, but it is also a family tie. A husband or wife may refer to the other one in their marriage as their "partner," because they have all things in common. At least, that is God's intention; His plan is the sharing of all interests. We have the same thing in our Lord Jesus Christ. Your interests are

His: your mind and its development, your body and its sanctity, purity and holiness, your spirit and its graciousness, tenderness and love. Your concern is to be His glory, the wonder of His person, the majesty and greatness of His power. Your constant ambition should be not only to learn about doctrine, but to know Him. His interests are in your development, your progress, your growth. Your interests are to be in the glory of the sovereignty of Christ.

There should be not only mutual interests, but mutual devotion. How wonderful to know that all the resources of Christ are yours! "In him dwelleth all the fulness of the Godhead bodily. And ye are complete in him" (Colossians 2:9-10). What a breath-taking verse that is! All your resources are His: your personality, your possessions, your abilities, whatever they are. That is the completeness of communion: all He has belongs to you, and all you have (which is so little at best) belongs to Him. That is the response He is seeking from His children.

As we set out on this royal route to heaven, we have the resources of grace and peace; we are enriched in all utterance and in all knowledge; and we are given this great and precious privilege of partnership with Christ. All He has is at your disposal now, and His desire is that all you have should be at His disposal now and always. Are you in that living, vital relationship with the Lord Jesus today?

CHAPTER 2

DIRECTION DECIDES DESTINY

1 Corinthians 1:10-18

IN 1 CORINTHIANS 1:18 the revised versions render more correctly the Greek verbs: they indicate continuous action in the present. "For the preaching of the cross is to them that *are perishing* foolishness; but unto us that *are being saved*, it is the power of God." Here we have two contrasting experiences of life: "being saved," and "perishing." Paul highlights them for us, showing us that neither of them is static, that both suggest movement, a journey along some road. The category to which each one of us belongs is quite clearly defined by our attitude toward the message of the cross: ". . . to them that are perishing, foolishness; but unto us that are being saved, it is the power of God."

In its context, we find this tremendous statement set against a church situation which was full of strife, envy, and a divisive spirit. "I am of Paul," said some. "And I of Apollos," said others, or "And I of Cephas." Still others were saying, "I don't belong to any of them. I am not a denominationalist: I am of Christ" (1:12).

To that Corinthian church, split by this party spirit and demonstrating all the evidences of immaturity, Paul has taken a stand: "I determined not to know any thing among you, save Jesus Christ, and him crucified" (2:2). In this significant epistle you will find that Paul constantly brings his hearers back to the cross. He is convinced that the answer in each controversy and to every failure, as well as all hope for the future, is "the word of the cross."

First, we consider these two conditions which Paul describes for us here: perishing and being saved. To comprehend the meaning

of that dreadful word, "perishing," we need first to fully understand the meaning of the words "being saved."

These days the word "salvation" is rather like a well-worn coin,
which is being passed from hand to hand until it is almost unrecognizable. In many instances it has been reduced to a convenient little
formula, and if you fit the formula you are all right. But in the New
Testament sense, the word "salvation" has both a negative and a
positive implication. Negatively, it means being saved from danger,
being made secure; positively, it is emancipation from sin: sanctification. It is deliverance from guilt and the forgiveness of all our
sins by virtue of the blood of Jesus Christ our Lord shed for us on
Calvary.

Joy abounds in a forgiven sinner as he realizes the blessedness
of his experience. He is very glad to be able to announce to everybody, "I have been saved!" But it is not long before such a man
begins to recognize that the sins from which he has been forgiven
are only the symptoms of a disease that goes far deeper. Soon he
begins to cry out to God, "Is there no deliverance from this fire
still burning in my life, this untamed passion in my soul?" He prays
from the depths of his heart in the words of the psalmist, "Create
in me a clean heart, O God!" (Psalm 51:10).

Can his prayer remain unanswered? Is the man forgiven from his
past sins to continue to live unsatisfied, defeated, impure? Let me
remind you that the pardoned man does not change his circumstances, neither his home conditions nor his job. He does not run
away from his past situation in life—if he attempts to do so, he
cuts the very nerve of the refining process that would make him a
saint. But in his life he begins to discover that the demands upon
him as a Christian are absolutely overwhelming; they are impossible
for him to meet by himself. There comes from his heart a deep
cry, "O God, give me power—power over myself, power over my
sin, power over what I am by nature." He is a forgiven sinner, but
he is a defeated man.

Am I exposing a basic need in your life? Are you conscious of
feeling that you are only half delivered? You know you have forgiveness from sins, but there is a cry in your heart, "Is there no
answer to the problem of what I am?"

In the New Testament sense of the word, "salvation" is not merely a negative thing, the forgiveness of sins. That which leaves a man stumbling and defeated, impure and unholy, is an incomplete and imperfect redemption. Praise God, salvation is more than this! When the Lord saves a man He does not bar the gate through which sins enter and attack him, but He opens the gate through which Holy Spirit power can come in to make him holy. When God saves a soul, He does not simply blot out the memory of past sin—it is that, thank God. Nor does He simply see that man with a righteousness that Christ imputes to him—it is that, thank God, but it is not only that! Salvation is positive: taking a man who has been twisted and bent by the disease of which sins are the symptoms and causing him to glory in complete deliverance.

Now let us look at the second word, "perishing." It means entire failure to be what God intends a man to be: the disease of sin running its course unchecked. It indicates an increasing distance from God, a gradual sinking into depravity, a withdrawal of the only source of real happiness and power. It is the drift downward in spite of all the efforts made to pull oneself up.

Each one of us is in one or the other of these categories: either we are being delivered from the disease of self and sin, or we are becoming more sinful and more selfish and more depraved in spite of all our self-effort.

But notice, in the second place, that both "being saved," and "perishing" describe a continuing process. Life is pictured for us here as something that is moving and active. In the New Testament we have the great idea of salvation considered from at least three different points of view. Sometimes it is spoken of as having been accomplished in the past, "Ye have been saved." That describes the initial act of faith in the blood of Jesus Christ as Saviour. Again it is spoken of as in the present, "Ye are being saved," as in verse 18. Sometimes it is relegated to the future, "Now is our salvation nearer than when we believed" (Romans 13:11). But there are many passages which describe salvation as a continuous experience, running through life, such as "By one offering he has perfected forever them that are being sanctified" (Hebrews 10:14).

One thing that will characterize the life of every genuine believer in the Lord Jesus, truly born of the Spirit of God, is growth, development. He will not talk about having arrived; he does not say he has had a tremendous second experience of sanctification; he would not boast in his holiness, nor exalt his own experience, but there are evidences of his growth in his behavior. As he is more and more filled with the Spirit, he grows more gracious, more gentle, more Christlike, and as we stand back and watch his life, we see God working a miracle. As the clay in the hand of the potter, so the man's life is being molded, shaped and conformed to the image of the Lord Jesus.

May I say kindly, yet firmly, that unfortunately many professing Christians show no evidence of such growth at all. In fact, do I exaggerate if I dare to say that it is the majority of them? They may have been saved, perhaps, for twenty years, but they are still as mean, hot-tempered, selfish, jealous, unkind, impure, and worldly as ever. There are no marks of maturity, no evidences of becoming more like the Lord Jesus.

The moment we accept forgiveness through the blood of the Lord Jesus we are obligated by bearing His name to stand for righteousness, purity, and holiness. Our business in life is to seek to win somebody else for Jesus; the redemptive ministry of the love of God should be expressed through our lives in service to others. That is the mark of the real thing. How desperately we all need power to stand for the right, power to speak for the Lord Jesus, power to live for Him day by day.

Just as "being saved" is a constant process, so is "perishing." It is becoming more and more interested in worldly things, accepting defeat and compromise without blushing. How many who have professed to be Christians for a long time find it so much easier now to submit to things that are selfish, mean and worldly!

Paul describes salvation as a process that is going on constantly. Therefore, it is not only registering a decision for Jesus that evidences your destiny; it is the direction of your character. Perhaps that decision has even brought you into Christian training or some form of ministry, but if it is not accompanied by direction of character, there is room to question whether or not it is authentic. The Bible tells you to examine yourself, whether you be in the faith (II Corinthians 13:5).

May the Holy Spirit challenge your heart with this New Testament description of real salvation! What has been the trend of your character in the past twelve months? Your body comes to church, maybe to teach a Sunday school class. You listen to sermon after sermon, but deep down in your own soul, is there progress into the Lord or regress into sin? Do you have increased hunger for truth, for holiness, for righteousness, for the Lord Himself? Or is there carelessness and worldliness and superficiality, an easy slipping into habits that you never dreamed you would allow a year ago?

We make constant progress along one road or the other, but what is the determining factor? What guides our direction and governs our destiny? It is the "preaching of the cross." Now let us be careful that we understand what that phrase means. It does not mean the act of preaching, itself. We have here the Greek word *logos*, the same word that is in the first chapter of the Gospel of John: "In the beginning was the Word, and the Word was with God, and the Word was God . . . And the Word was made flesh . . ." (John 1:1, 14). It is "the *word* of the cross."

When we speak, so often we express just a dream, a wish, a desire. When God speaks, He speaks with authority and conviction; "the word of the cross," which God proclaims, is power and action on a divine scale.

I heard an eminent professor of theology say to students in his seminary class, "Gentlemen, I ask you to remember that you are called upon to know something of the foolishness of preaching, not the preaching of foolishness." In my heart I retorted, "He is wrong! The word of the cross is absolute foolishness." It says so in my text: to those who are perishing, the word of the cross is foolishness. It stands in contradiction to all the philosophy, education, and knowledge of this world, for the preaching of the cross puts the sentence of death upon them all. It is the word of absolute power, but it is also the word of absolute weakness.

With the shoes off our feet, and with heads bowed reverently, let us go up a green hill outside a city wall and hear the word of the cross: "Father, forgive them; for they know not what they do" (Luke 23:34). Here is a cry of unutterable anguish from the heart of our Redeemer, coming through pain and suffering, but the prayer was heard!

"To day shalt thou be with me in paradise" (Luke 23:43). A dying Man, crucified and helpless, turns to a fellow sufferer and speaks the word of victory, and the word was heard!

"Woman, behold thy son. [Son,] Behold thy mother" (John 19:26-27). Heartbreak and loneliness, a sword going into the soul of Mary, but the concern of her Son in the hour of His death introduces her to a new and wonderful relationship.

"My God, why hast thou forsaken me?" (Matthew 27:46). Alone in the darkness, utterly cut off from God, He is introducing a countless multitude to glory; this is victory through isolation.

"I thirst!" (John 19:28). Out of the agony of lips that are parched there flow rivers of living water to men and women like you and me.

"It is finished!" (John 19:30). Obedient unto the very death of the cross, Jesus Christ fully accepted all the will of God. He has been forsaken by friend and foe, but now it is all finished, the price is paid, the last drop of the cup is drunk. The outcome—resurrection!

What is the word of the cross in your life and mine? It is power through weakness, life through death, resurrection through crucifixion. What does that involve in terms of personal experience? How can you make contact with that word of the cross? It is only when you get to the end of every attempt to do anything without Jesus Christ, when you lay aside your ambitions, crucify your prejudices, die to your so-called intellectual approach, and humble your pride that you can look up into His lovely face and say, "Lord Jesus, I live; yet not I . . ." (Galatians 2:20).

It may sound easy to say, but it is mighty hard to face! We have to get to the place where we can say to Him, "O Lord, I yield to Thee. I am willing to be nothing. I recognize that this self in me with all its pride, its haughtiness, its self-righteousness and self-importance is only worthy of crucifixion." At the moment we agree with His knowledge of ourselves, then we come into contact with His throne and begin to touch omnipotence and receive power.

If you need to get rid of impure thoughts, burn the books and pictures that incite such thoughts. If you would break the habit of drink, throw it all out of your house. If you want to touch the power of the cross, cut off every friendship that is leading you into sin; stop every habit that is pulling you down. Look into the Lord's face and say, "Lord, I know this thing is sin. I am going to get rid of it today, and I will never allow it again."

Which direction are you going? Deep down in your heart is the direction downward? You may be a Sunday school teacher or a Christian worker of long standing, and you want desperately to touch the place of omnipotence and stop the drift. Outwardly you are one person, but inwardly you are quite another. Outwardly you are perhaps theologically correct and sound, but inwardly far away from God. Now you want to look up into the face of the Lord Jesus and tell Him that you agree with His verdict upon self, your utter weakness and bankruptcy.

It is time to take action. Are you prepared to break that unworthy friendship? Are you prepared to finish with that habit, leaving no possible line of retreat? Are you prepared to go to your room and clear out those books and trashy magazines that only incite you to sin? "Therefore . . . let us cleanse ourselves from all filthiness of the flesh and spirit, perfecting holiness in the fear of God" (II Corinthians 7:1).

> Cleanse me from my sin, Lord;
> Put Thy power within, Lord;
> Take me as I am, Lord, and make me all Thine own.
> Keep me day by day, Lord;
> Underneath Thy sway, Lord;
> Make my heart Thy palace and Thy royal throne.
> —*R. Hudson Pope*

CHAPTER 3

DOWN PEACOCK'S FEATHERS

I Corinthians 1:19-31

THE HEADING given to this chapter is not original. It is the title of a book written by an Episcopalian minister, a commentary on a prayer in the Church of England prayer book called "The General Confession," which begins, "Almighty and most merciful Father, we have erred and strayed from Thy ways like lost sheep." In the most amazing language, this prayer gives expression to the bankruptcy and helplessness of man's best—all that we can ever be apart from the grace of God and the redemption that is in Jesus Christ our Lord.

Such is the major theme of Paul's message to the church at Corinth: down with pride of intellect, down with self-confidence—"He that glorieth, let him glory in the Lord" (I Corinthians 1:31).

This letter is addressed, as the second verse of this chapter tells us, to "the church *(ecclesia)* of God which is at Corinth." They would have known what he meant by "the *ecclesia* of Corinth," because that was the title given to the civic authority of that day, those called out from among the population of Corinth to administer the affairs of the city. "The *ecclesia* of God," by analogy, is the called-out of God, the church which has been redeemed in Jesus Christ our Lord, in order that through them the will of God may be made known and the authority of heaven be brought to bear upon the world.

Corinth was known for its divisions and party spirit, for its philosophy, and at the same time for its sinfulness. Boasting of its culture, the city was bankrupt in its morality. And the greatest tragedy

27

was that the spirit of Corinth was invading the church. This little group of believers, instead of attacking the city in the name of the Lord, was being infiltrated by the worldliness of Corinth. Instead of representing the authority of Christ there, they were being overwhelmed by the pagan city and their testimony was becoming completely devitalized. Instead of bringing to bear upon that city the transforming power of the gospel, the Christians were succumbing to the sin around them.

Speaking to this church that was being conquered by the spirit of the age in which it lived, Paul emphasizes the dynamic transforming power of the word of the cross. Right through this chapter he contrasts two things: wisdom and foolishness, the wisdom of men and the foolishness of God, then the foolishness of men and the wisdom of God. "The wisdom of words," in verse 17 is set against "the preaching of the cross" or "the word of the cross" in verse 18.

The wisdom of words was the thing that had seduced this church. Earlier in this chapter we noticed how the party spirit had crept into the church, bringing divisions and arguments. Paul turned upon them and asked three piercing questions: "Was Paul crucified for you?" "Is Christ divided?" "Were you baptized in the name of Paul?" He didn't answer them; they were intended only to point out how ridiculous was their spirit of division, which had eaten into the testimony and power of the church.

The remedy for the situation, Paul insists, lies not in philosophy, but in the revelation of the Son of God by the Holy Spirit in their lives. The moment a Christian, or a church, departs from the principle of revelation and goes into higher criticism or intellectual understanding of the Bible, all spiritual authority is lost.

This is very relevant to the days in which we live and to the land in which we live. Instead of attacking a city in the name of the Lord, the very spirit of the city gets into the life of the church. The local church becomes full of party strife and division, and believers become materialistic. The Bible is approached on the basis of "What I cannot understand I will discard." If we submit the Word of God to our own intellect and refuse to believe in the possibility of absolute authoritative revelation, the church loses its power and authority. And if it loses its ability to say, "Thus saith the Lord," it has no answer to the problems of our times.

If the church in our day is to invade a city for God, then it must get back to a place of absolute dependence upon the wisdom of God. But what is the wisdom of God? The translation in the margin of the American Standard Version (the revision of 1901) is, "Christ Jesus, who was made unto us wisdom from God, both righteousness and sanctification and redemption" (1:30). The wisdom of God, therefore, seems to sum up the whole thing; it is given to establish righteousness and to produce sanctification and holiness.

Notice Paul's scornful words in verses 27 and 28: "God hath chosen the foolish things of the world." Yes, the wisdom of God is utter foolishness to the worldly philosopher, the self-opinionated, clever person. "God has chosen the things that are base and despised." Certainly righteousness was despised in a city like Corinth. "God hath chosen the things that are not to bring to nought the things that are"—the things that are not: redemption, deliverance from all that separates us from the presence of God; sanctification, being made into the likeness of Jesus Christ. Against all their cleverness and ability, their philosophy and education, their helplessness to do anything about the sinfulness of the city in which they lived, God puts His wisdom, which is the message of Calvary: His righteousness, His sanctification, His redemption.

For us today there is this tremendous contrast. On the one hand we have the opportunity of seeking to meet the need of the day by human intellect and education. On the other hand, we have access to the wisdom of God, which leaves men with absolutely nothing to glory in, for "he that glorieth, let him glory in the Lord." There faces all of us this choice, these two principles, and the tragedy today is that very largely the church has chosen its own wisdom and lost its power.

We must look a little more closely at what is meant by this definition of God's wisdom: righteousness, sanctification and redemption. What is this word, "righteousness"? Here is the wisdom of God, for it means that somehow God is able to take hold of a life that is twisted and broken, sinful and defeated, immoral and down-and-out, and to make it conform to the standard of His Son. He is able to make a crooked life straight; He is able to make a broken life whole. The life that is marred, sinful, impure, unholy, by the miracle of His grace He can remake into the image of Christ.

The righteousness of God is not just a dry doctrine, but the act that brought a holy God down from the throne of heaven to the manger at Bethlehem and then to the cross of Calvary, in order that He might rescue us and bring us to Himself, cleanse us from sin and make us whole. To use a theological phrase, it means Christ *imputed* to me. That is, the moment I cease from my own effort and trust the living Christ for salvation, from that moment God sees me as in the righteousness of Christ Himself. When I am prepared to come to Calvary as a guilty, sinful man, knowing that there is nothing I can do, and that I am utterly dependent on God's grace for forgiveness—at that moment He makes me right.

However, that is not the last word of Christian experience, but the first. Just as you formed habits that led you to failure and sin until now, when you accept God's righteousness you will begin to form habits that lead you into the holiness of His image and into His purpose for your life. That is Christian living, and it is no easy thing.

There is no short cut, and therefore we have the second word, "sanctification." This is the wisdom of God which means not only that Christ is imputed to me, but that the life of Jesus is *imparted* to me. I recognize that I am separated for God's will and service, and therefore I must be yielded to Him for whatever He may want me to do. This growth into the likeness of the Lord is slow. I know that is true, not because I look at other people, but because I have to live with myself seven days a week.

But perhaps it need not be as slow as it is. Two Christian men were talking together, and the first one said, "I am so glad that God knows our frame, and He remembers that we are but dust."

"Yes," replied his friend, "but do you really think we ought to be as dusty as we sometimes are?"

That was a good answer! That is why our progress in Christ is often so slow. We remain in the dust when we have no business to be there. We allow Satan to keep us down when we ought to be growing in the likeness of the Lord Jesus.

I would interject a thought here. There is nobody in all God's universe who is more orthodox than Satan—he knows all the truth, every bit of it. And you too can know the truth like that, and still not be a believer. The test of genuine faith in Christ is that there is submission to Him and growth into His likeness. The evidence that you are saved is that you begin to look with the eyes of Christ, you begin to love with the heart of Christ, you begin to think with the mind of Christ. Because the living Christ is in you, His character begins to express itself through you.

The third word is "redemption," a word that occurs only eleven times in the New Testament. On each occasion it is used in reference to that tremendous day when we will find ourselves in the very presence of our Lord, when we are fully redeemed. There is a sense in which a man is redeemed the moment he is forgiven, but there is a great deal yet to be done in the man. "Now are we the sons of God," says the Apostle John, "and it doth not yet appear what we shall be: but we know that, when he shall appear, we shall be like him; for we shall see him as he is" (I John 3:2). Redemption is the completion and fulfillment of all the purposes of God. Surely that is the wisdom of God. There is no other answer to the world's need except the wisdom of God that can make a man right and pure, and one day will take him, in the very image of the Lord Jesus, into the presence of the Father, spotless and faultless. What other hope is there than that?

What had all the intellect at Corinth done to meet the situations of human need? What had they accomplished? "Where is the wise," asks Paul. "Where is the scribe? where is the disputer of this world?" (1:20).

It is an amazing and tragic thing that when emphasis on philosophy, intellect, and ability seeps into the life of the Christian church and into our Christian service, we discover ourselves with no authority, no spiritual power, nothing that we can do to bring blessing to a soul. But when the living Christ comes into my life, somehow the desert of my heart begins to blossom. The man who has been paralyzed by sin, helpless and down in the dust, is taken hold of by the Spirit of God, and is made anew. That is the wisdom of God and the power of God.

The righteousness of God puts a man back in the center of God's will. The sanctification that God brings to a man makes him grow day by day in the likeness of the Lord. The redemption of God one day will lift him faultless into the very presence of God. That is the message of the cross.

Perhaps somebody has been thinking, "Now does this mean that

I just scrap my brains altogether? Are we supposed to become robots that never do any thinking for ourselves?" Of course it doesn't! It just means that if you want an enlightened mind upon the Word of God, you have to live a crucified life; that's the principle.

During the last century we have talked about the spread of modernism and neo-orthodoxy as if those things were new. But they are as old as the New Testament. The moment a man begins to put his confidence in his own mind, in his ability to understand the Word of God, in his personal criticism of the Scriptures, he is finished as far as divine revelation is concerned. But if he is prepared to come to the cross, if he is prepared to take the place of death with Christ, if he is prepared to glory in the Lord and not in himself, that man will have an enlightened mind upon the Word of God that can challenge any philosopher. God gives the illumination of His Spirit into the life that is crucified with Christ at Calvary.

Are we supposed to ignore the problems that confront us? No, but half a dozen men on their knees for sixty minutes, waiting upon the Lord with the absolute conviction that they have no answer, that their human ideas and programs are ineffective and bankrupt— they will accomplish more than fifty men around a table discussing their problems for a whole year.

Where God can find a little group of crucified men, upon those men He will give the enlightenment of His Spirit upon every problem that might threaten to overwhelm them. That is not only true in Christian work, it is true in your home life, in bringing up your children—to every practical problem of life, the answer is the wisdom of God. "He that glorieth, let him glory in the Lord," says Paul.

You have two alternatives before you. One is the philosophy of men, depending upon human intellect, human ability, pushing your way through, determined at any cost to get to the goal you set before yourself. Or you can take your achievements, intellect, talents and put them all in one scale—and in the other, the wisdom of God, in which a man glories not in himself but in the Saviour. You must choose the principle on which you will guide your life, on which you will study and work, on which you will serve the Lord. May we each say, "Not I, but Christ."

CHAPTER 4

STANDING IN THE POWER OF GOD

I Corinthians 2:1-10

THE STATEMENT, "I determined not to know any thing among you, save Jesus Christ, and him crucified" (2:2), should be for us all, not a record of achievement but, humbly before God, the desire of our hearts in our ministry for Him. That is the way the course of the ship of the church (or the life) must be set to catch the breeze of the Spirit of God from heaven.

That brings me right to the very heart of the message of this portion of Scripture. Paul is addressing himself to a situation which, humanly speaking, is far too big for him—a situation in which many a preacher has found himself ever since. He sees in Corinth what I would call, in the first place, a mission to be fulfilled: "That your faith should not stand in the wisdom of men, but in the power of God" (2:5).

In a city like Corinth, so full of human pride and sin, Paul knows perfectly well that the little group of Christians cannot face the challenge of presenting Christ if their faith is based only on intellectual assent. Their faith must stand on the rock of revelation rather than on the sands of human philosophy. Nothing but the miracle of the grace of God revealed in lives transformed by the Spirit of God can ever convict a Corinth. If these young Christians lack reality, they will crumble under the pressure and be sucked into the quicksand of sin around them. Corinth is far too clever for them, and far too sinful; therefore their faith must stand in the power of God and not in the wisdom of men.

This is Paul's concern for the young church, the mission that as preacher, servant, and ambassador of the cross, he knows must be fulfilled, or else the outcome will be disaster. Somehow the little band of believers must confront that great city with the reality of their faith, proving that their message is something that God has communicated to them from heaven itself.

That is equally true today. Whether or not we realize it, if you and I are even to survive as Christian people (putting it on the lowest level), let alone live triumphantly in Christ, a theoretical presentation is totally inadequate. The world we live in is too clever and sinful for that, and if we have nothing more, we will be sucked under by the whirlpool of philosophies and "isms," the tides of sin and vice.

"We have this treasure in earthen vessels," says Paul, "that the excellency of the power may be of God, and not of us" (II Corinthians 4:7). These earthen vessels are helpless and weak in themselves, and in the battle of life we must stand "By the word of truth, by the power of God, by the armour of righteousness on the right hand and on the left" (II Corinthians 6:7). In other words, we must recognize our own weakness, even glory in it, that the power of Christ may rest upon us.

Oh, that our world may feel the impact of faith—your faith and mine—that stands in the power of God! So that in whatever circumstances of testing you may live, others will see in you the miracle of standing not only in the power of God, but also in the authority of God. As you live, surrounded by every possible evil influence that would contrive to pull you down in this wicked age, you have a mission that must be fulfilled, to stand in the power of God. It is dependent upon your acceptance of the verdict of Calvary, of the bankruptcy of self and the futility of anything untouched by the power of God the Holy Spirit.

How can our mission be fulfilled, then? By the message we have to proclaim: "I determined not to know any thing among you, save Jesus Christ, and him crucified" (2:2). The emphasis Paul intends is this, I think: "not to know anything among *you* save Jesus Christ, and him crucified." That is his theme for Corinth, and that should be the theme of all preaching today. It must be the message of your life in your circumstances, the principle of your life if you are to stand in the power of God.

I would remind you that Paul had come to Corinth, as he says himself, in weakness, in fear, and in much trembling. He had come to the European continent for the first time and his reception had not been very pleasant. He was imprisoned at Philippi, smuggled out of Thessalonica, driven out of Berea, and when he reached Athens and started to argue with them on the basis of their agnosticism, he accomplished very little. He was pressed in spirit as he came to Corinth, and God Himself had to encourage him: "Be not afraid, but speak, and hold not thy peace: For I am with thee, and no man shall set on thee to hurt thee: for I have much people in this city" (Acts 18:9-10).

Knowing the strength of Corinthian wisdom and the character of that city, the depths of its sin and the tremendous boast of its intellect, he determined that he would not argue or debate with anybody, but present the crucified, risen Lord in the conviction that what Jesus said was absolutely true, "And I, if I be lifted up from the earth, will draw all men unto me" (John 12:32). So the man must get out of the picture, the personality of the preacher become obscured, and the Lord be at the center of all. "For we preach not ourselves, but Christ Jesus the Lord; and ourselves your servants for Jesus' sake" (II Corinthians 4:5). The Lord gets the glory, and the result is absolutely convincing: "My speech and my preaching was not with enticing words of man's wisdom, but in demonstration of the Spirit and of power" (2:4).

The principle here is as true today as it was then. First there must be a life willing to efface itself, to retreat from its imagined cleverness and wisdom, from its own efforts to stand against the pressure. There rests upon such a life the anointing of the Spirit of God, with this tremendous result that faith shall stand, not in the wisdom of man, but in the power of God.

When Paul says, "I am determined not to know any thing among you, save Jesus Christ, and him crucified," quite obviously he is excluding other things. What were they? "The Jews require a sign, and the Greeks seek after wisdom: But we preach Christ crucified" (1:22-23). Slowly but surely today—and I say this with a deep conviction of heart—God is driving the church into a corner from which there is no escape. There are various alternatives which we have tried in place of this message—I am not speaking of the message that Christ died for our sins, but that of our death to sin in Jesus, the message of a crucified life. The poor, cheap, noisy substitutes which the church has tried in place of that message are being exposed for the paltry, futile things they really are. Along with all the so-called progress there is the most alarming spiritual decline. The church has never had better machinery, neither has the church ever been so helplessly ineffective in meeting the problems of the day.

One by one the gadgets are dropping out of our hands when we are recognizing their spiritual ineffectiveness. God is stripping from us every false hope and making us face reality. He is teaching us these days that nothing less than the outpouring of the Holy Spirit in revival can ever meet the need. God is trying to tell us that our currently popular version of Christianity—comfortable, humorous, superficially interesting, worldly-wise—is exposed for the irreverent presentation that it is of the Gospel of Christ.

When revival comes, we shall find our lives revolutionized and our values turned upside down. Do you know why revival tarries? Because God does not take our praying seriously when we behave the way we do in public. When our confidence is in gimmicks, programs, schemes, and planning, and we have not learned to seek first the Lord in the power of God the Holy Spirit, in brokenness at Calvary, we inevitably go on being defeated and losing the battle. May the Lord drive us into that corner, so that we will fall before Him and say, "Lord, I would know nothing except Christ and Him crucified."

One might equally well say, "I am determined to know *everything* in Christ and Him crucified." This is not excluding something, but including everything that really counts, for the message of the cross includes everything to meet the need of the human heart. Of course, it does not meet the demands of an entertainment-crazy generation that is seeking for a sign, but a preacher is commissioned to give people, not what they want, but what they need. No man has any business to be in a pulpit to entertain; he is there to present Calvary in all its fulness of hope and glory.

When Jesus Christ was asked for a sign to prove His authority, He replied by saying, "An evil and adulterous generation seeketh after a sign; and there shall no sign be given to it, but the sign of the prophet Jonas" (Matthew 12:39). As Jonah was three days in the fish, so the Son of Man would be three days in the heart of the earth.

Dare we say the message of Calvary is not good enough today? It goes straight to the bottom of your need and mine. It brushes aside the superficial; it exposes sin for what it really is. And when a man or woman, fellow or girl, is prepared to accept the verdict of Calvary upon pride, self-sufficiency, and intellect, and to come trusting and resting entirely upon the cross, there falls upon his or her life the anointing of the Spirit of God. Their testimony then is not in their own faith and wisdom; they do not have to meet men on the basis of human philosophy, but stand in the power of God and with the anointing of the Spirit.

When you are prepared to meet Jesus at Calvary He will drive you into a tight corner. Has He put you on the spot? Has He put you into some desperate experience? You try to wriggle and squirm to get out of it, but the Lord is relentlessly holding you there until you learn that your wisdom is useless and your philosophy has no answer, and that you are helpless to stand against the current of temptation until you learn to cling to Him.

Once you are determined to know nothing in this particular situation (whatever it may be) but Christ and Him crucified, then you are also saying, "By the grace of God, in Christ and Him crucified I have everything."

"That's all very well," you may be saying to me, "but I'm afraid of putting it into practice. Suppose I let go and let God, what then?"

Then there is a mystery to be revealed. "Eye hath not seen, nor ear heard, neither have entered into the heart of man, the things which God hath prepared for them that love him," says Paul. "But God hath revealed them unto us by his Spirit" (2:9-10).

The preaching of the cross, the living out of this Christian life day by day, is not unintelligent: "we speak wisdom among them that are perfect [i.e., full-grown or enlightened]: yet not the wisdom of this world . . . but . . . the wisdom of God in a mystery" (2:6-7). The Christian is not a fool, although the world may frequently think he is. He has an enlightened mind, and he is speaking wisdom to those who can understand, "speaking the wisdom of God in a mystery."

What is a mystery? Is it something you cannot understand? No, in Scripture a mystery is something that once was hidden but now is revealed: "God hath revealed them unto us by his Spirit" (2:10). When the Lord Jesus comes to dwell in your life, your eyes are opened, your ears are unstopped, and you begin to understand some of the things that God has prepared for you. What are they? Jesus said, "I go to prepare a place for you . . . I will come again, and receive you unto myself; that where I am, there ye may be also" (John 14:2-3). Hope of heaven, and the resources of heaven down here, also: "The mystery which hath been hid from ages and from generations, but now is made manifest to his saints: To whom God would make known what is the riches of the glory of this mystery among the Gentiles; which is Christ in you, the hope of glory" (Colossians 1:26-27).

Persecuted, harassed, distressed Christian, God has not left you to fight the battle alone. "I will not leave you comfortless [orphans]," said the Lord. ". . . the Holy Ghost, whom the Father will send in my name, he shall teach you all things. . . . Peace I leave with you, my peace I give unto you" (John 14:18, 26-27). Peace, hope, heaven —these are some of the things that God has prepared for them that love Him, things He has revealed unto us by the Spirit that "searcheth all things, yea, the deep things of God."

Wonderful truth—the Christian has the life of God in him! He has access to the One in whom, says the Word, "dwelleth all the fulness of the Godhead" (Colossians 2:9); the One "in whom are hid all the treasures of wisdom and knowledge" (Colossians 2:3), for all that is in Jesus, and He is in you. That is the mystery which the Holy Spirit reveals to the life that has confessed its bankruptcy and is shut up to the mercy of God.

In the light of what has been said, which course are you going to follow? Are you so operating in your sphere of Christian service that you may expect revival? With your confidence in Him, are you living your life, conducting your program, and thinking about your problems in such a way that you may expect the Holy Spirit to come in power at any moment? Or, secretly, is your confidence in the flesh and in the machinery of human effort? In what do you glory? Where do you place your trust?

Let us be realistic. Are you prepared to change gears? Do you recognize your bankruptcy? Are you willing to place no confidence in the flesh, to step out of the place of frustration and despair, anxiety and futility, into the place where the Holy Spirit can come with anointing and with power? Then look up to Him and say, "Now, Lord, it's up to You."

There must be no false gods, no misplaced confidence in something or someone, no secret boast that says, "I can pull it off; I can see it through." No compromise, no unconfessed sin, no theoretical faith, no unsurrendered life, no critical spirit, no unbroken heart, no worldliness, no self can be allowed—*nothing!* For "I determined not to know any thing among you, save Jesus Christ, and him crucified."

CHAPTER 5

WHICH CLASS ARE YOU TRAVELING?

I Corinthians 2:11—3:6

THERE IS a unique factor in the Christian gospel which makes all talk about comparative religions utterly beside the point, in my opinion. The life of the Founder of our faith inhabits the personality of every person who trusts Him for salvation; every child of God has living within him God the Holy Spirit—not an influence, but the Third Person of the Trinity.

"If any man have not the Spirit of Christ, he is none of his," said Paul in Romans 8:9. And in I Corinthians 6:19, "Know ye not that your body is the temple of the Holy Spirit?" Therefore every Christian—no matter how weak and feeble, how poor and helpless, perhaps with a sense of utter inability and frustration—whatever his own personal feeling may be, is indwelt by the Third Person of the Trinity. The Holy Spirit has come into our lives so that we might develop character; the "fruit of the Spirit" in Galatians 5:22 is character-fruit, the reproduction of the character of Jesus Christ.

We ought to hang our heads in shame as we ask ourselves, "Why is it that so little of His life is produced in us and so much of ourselves still remains?" The answer to that question is in the verses we are to study here.

Paul introduces us to two different kinds of Christian life. He says in 3:1, "I, brethren, could not speak unto you as unto spiritual, but as unto carnal, even as unto babes in Christ." Please notice the word "brethren"; he is writing to those who are born again of the Spirit of God and who are within the Christian church. Here are two different classes of people, both of them Christian, both of them born of the Spirit of God, but one of them is designated "carnal," and the other, "spiritual."

I would remind you that Paul describes yet another kind of person in 2:14, the "natural man." Of him Paul says that he "receiveth not the things of the Spirit of God; for they are foolishness unto him." This, of course, is the unbeliever, perhaps the charming pagan, the intellectual agnostic, or the nice religious sort of well-educated person, but still the "natural man." Because he is "natural," he does not understand the things of the Spirit of God, having never been born into the family of God.

Now the tragedy is that many who profess to be Christians react so often on the level of the "natural man." You have heard Christian people say something like this: "You know, Mrs. X said something utterly untrue about me—it was only natural that I should be angry." "Only natural"—exactly! And unfortunately there are those born of the Spirit of God who, in terms of daily life and reactions, are still living in the natural realm. Though latent within every child of God is the possibility of reproducing the character of Jesus Christ, the fact is that this is not always accomplished. Why? Because too many Christians continue to live on the carnal level.

In the first place, a carnal Christian is living a life of perpetual conflict and repeated defeat: "For ye are yet carnal: for whereas there is among you envying, and strife, and divisions, are ye not carnal, and walk as men?" (3:3). The fellowship of the Corinthian church was split by envy, strife, and divisions—Paul calls it "carnality." But what a group of Christians are in their fellowship is simply the reflection of what they are individually. Therefore, here is a statement of the condition of a Christian life that is lived on a carnal plane.

Remember the language of Paul back in Romans? "What I would, that do I not; but what I hate, that do I" (Romans 7:15), and later on in the same chapter: ". . . when I would do good, evil is present with me. For I delight in the law of God after the inward man: But I see another law in my members, warring against the the law of my mind, and bringing me into captivity to the law of sin which is in my members" (Romans 7:21-23).

That whole chapter is a portrait of the carnal Christian. Within

him there is a constant conflict, a moment by moment battle between
two natures, the one spiritual and the other carnal. He is forgiven, he
is born again, he is living as a child of God within the fellowship of
the Christian church, but he is desperately unhappy. Occasionally
the Spirit of God gets the victory, but the perpetual habit of his life
is downward, away from God into sin and failure. Although indwelt
by the Holy Spirit, he is mastered by the flesh.

Does that describe you today? Is your experience perpetual conflict and repeated defeat? You may be rejoicing in the forgiveness of
sins, but you find no power over the principle of sin in your life.
Therefore you are often torn by envy, strife and division; there is
no song of joy on your lips, no spring in your step, no light in your
eyes, no radiance on your face. The carnal Christian has left the
world he used to live in and entered into a new experience, a new
area of fellowship, but he cannot enjoy it because he is defeated:
constantly fighting and constantly going down.

Another mark of the carnal Christian is that he is living a life of
protracted infancy and retarded growth. Paul calls these Corinthians
"babes in Christ," saying, "I have fed you with milk, and not with
meat: for hitherto ye were not able to bear it, neither yet now are
ye able" (3:1-2).

It is a very wonderful experience when a baby comes into a home,
but it is a tragedy if the child does not grow. What are the characteristics of a baby? In the first place, he is absolutely dependent upon
other people. He cannot walk; he has to be held up. He cannot feed
himself; another has to feed him. And he is only happy, really, when
he is the center of interest.

So it is with the carnal Christian. He is always leaning on other
people, always seeking this preacher and that leader for spiritual
counsel. He cannot walk by himself; he always has to be propped
up. You get him going for a little while and you think, "Praise the
Lord, he has got through at last!" But before long he is down again,
because he is dependent upon human friends and Christian fellowship
to see him through.

He cannot feed himself, either. His minister is a kind of spiritual
milk bottle that feeds him on Sunday, but that is all he gets. He has
not learned to feed himself upon the Word of God, and therefore he
does not grow spiritually. Of course, if he is the center of interest,

then he is happy, but he is very sensitive and touchy, quickly angry
if he is criticized. He constantly displays the marks of protracted infancy and retarded growth.

A third mark of the carnal Christian is that he is living a life of ③
fruitlessness and worldliness. "Every branch in me that beareth not
fruit, he taketh away" says the Lord in John 15:2, "and every branch
that beareth fruit, he purgeth it, that it may bring forth more fruit."

I am not speaking of outward success, but of genuine New Testament fruit in terms of character and Christlikeness. The carnal
Christian is one who spends too much time with his television and
neglects his Bible. He is more interested in novels than in the Word
of God. You do not find him very often at a church prayer meeting;
nor is he in the heart of the fellowship of the church. He is not re-
liable; he will sometimes work at a job in the church, but will very
easily quit and someone has to take his place at the last minute. Quite
obviously his heart is still mostly in the world, and there is an atmosphere of worldliness about him. The carnal Christian is a child
of God, born again and on his way to heaven, but he is traveling
third class.

Do you find yourself looking into a mirror? This is not my description, but that of the Word of God. The carnal Christian may
believe what he ought to believe, may even have been trained in
doctrine; he may know his Bible in some measure, theoretically, at
least. But his life is constant conflict and defeat, infancy and retarded
growth, fruitlessness and worldliness. It is possible to live all your life
like that: the Holy Spirit within you grieved, quenched, and powerless to do anything through you because you live on a carnal level.

Then what are the marks of a spiritual Christian? What does Paul
say about him? "He that is spiritual discerneth all things, yet he himself is discerned of no man" (2:15). In other words, you cannot explain him. I would suggest, in the first place, that he is living a life of
perpetual conflict but repeated victory. Did I say conflict? Yes, I
did; there is no place in the Christian life free from inner conflict,
not until we get to heaven.

But there is a sense in which the conflict of a spiritual Christian
is fought on a higher plane than that of the carnal Christian. "For we
wrestle not against flesh and blood, but . . . against spiritual wickedness in high places" (Ephesians 6:12). The spiritual Christian—the

man who is going on with God and who is determined to be as pure
and godly as a man saved by grace can be—that man is the focal
point of the attacks of the devil. He knows never a moment's release
from the heat of the battle. But in the midst of the conflict, the
spiritual Christian knows a deep and absolute peace in his heart, "the
peace of God, which passeth all understanding" (Philippians 4:7).
Throughout the constant temptation and battle, he is trusting, resting and conquering in the Lord Jesus Christ.

It is not that such a man does not commit sin, but that he does
not practice the habit of sin. It is not that he does not slip, but rather
that it is always possible for him not to do so. He is sometimes very
conscious of failure, but the trend of his life is not downward, but
upward; the habit of his life is victory and not defeat. The spiritual
Christian can say with Paul, "In all these things we are more than
conquerors through him that loved us" (Romans 8:37), and "Thanks
be unto God who leadeth us in every place in triumph in Christ
Jesus" (II Corinthians 2:14).

Another mark of the spiritual Christian is a life of progressive
growth and radiant Christlikeness. It would be wrong for me to
suggest that the Christian who is living on a spiritual plane is the kind
of person who goes about saying, "Well, now I have arrived." This
man knows that he can glory in nothing save in the cross of Jesus
Christ our Lord. But as you watch, as you observe him day by day,
you see evidences of growth in holiness and purity, in temperance
and grace, in meekness and gentleness—likeness to the Lord Jesus.
There is the fruit of the Spirit instead of the working of the flesh.

In the midst of the testings of life, deep down in his heart there is
peace; he is drawing upon infinite resources that are sufficient to
strengthen and keep him, to enable him to walk with God. Day by
day, as he reacts to troubles, misunderstandings, and heartaches, his
actions all glorify the Lord Jesus.

A third mark of the spiritual Christian in the Word of God is that
he is bringing forth permanent fruit. "I have chosen you that you
should bring forth fruit, and that your fruit should remain," said the
Lord Jesus in John 15:16. There is something about the spiritual
Christian that is constantly revealing faithfulness. There is character
that is being formed; it is not simply what he says, but that back of
what he says there is a life that is real. Just as the carnal Christian re-

veals worldliness, so the spiritual Christian reveals a life of separation to the Word of God and devotion to the Master.

Are you a believer, knowing you have received forgiveness of sins? Then in which class are you traveling along the road to heaven? Are you a carnal or a spiritual Christian? Is it perpetual conflict and repeated defeat in your life, or is it perpetual conflict and repeated victory? Is it protracted infancy and retarded growth, or is it development in Christlikeness of life and character? Is it a life of pathetic fruitlessness, or is it a life filled with permanent fruit for the glory of God?

If this mirror of God's Word reveals that you are traveling "third class," then how do you move into "first class"? How can you move into the life that is spiritual?

May I give you a simple threefold statement of principle by which, if you are prepared to follow it, you may begin to live your life on another level, you may move from carnality and defeat into spiritual victory and power? This is not something that happens as the years go by, something into which you grow automatically. This crisis is as real and definite as was the moment of your conversion, when you passed out from "condemnation" into "no condemnation," out from guilt into forgiveness, out of alienation from God into adoption as His child.

In the first place, it is the crisis of cleansing: "If we walk in the light, as he is in the light, we have fellowship one with another, and the blood of Jesus Christ his Son keeps on cleansing us from all sin . . . If we confess our sins, he is faithful and just to forgive us our sins, and to cleanse us from all unrighteousness" (I John 1:7, 9).

The trouble with the carnal Christian is that he is unclean. God demands that we face this fact; things that are allowed to continue in our lives which are contrary to the nature of the Spirit of God: worldliness, faithlessness, lack of growth are marks of uncleanness.

He is "the Spirit of truth" (John 14:17). When a Christian continues acting a lie or professing to be something he is not, God demands that such sin be dealt with.

He is "the Spirit of faith" (II Corinthians 4:13). The Christian who is not trusting in God to deliver him from the root principle of sin goes on being a carnal Christian. God demands complete trust and commitment.

He is "the Spirit of grace" (Hebrews 10:29). Do you allow bitterness in your life? Are you harboring resentment against another child of God? Then you are continuing that which is not of Christ, but of the enemy.

He is "the Spirit of holiness" (Romans 1:4). Do you allow in your life that which is unholy? "Know ye not that your body is the temple of the Holy Ghost?" (6:19). What sort of traffic has been going on in the temple of your life?

He is "the Spirit of glory" (I Peter 4:14). Are you allowing worldly affections and desires to go on, unchecked? Are you living for His glory, or are these things, the hangover of unconverted days, still part and parcel of your life? It will take a crisis to deal with them. You cannot deal with them one by one; they are far too many: by the time you deal with one little sin here, one big sin there, another one breaks out somewhere else.

Perhaps the Spirit of God has been speaking to you about these things. Confess them to Him and trust Him for cleansing, for when the Holy Spirit convicts of uncleanness, then the blood of Jesus is applied.

The next condition of moving into "first class" is surrender, the surrender of your body: "I beseech you, therefore, brethren . . . that ye present your bodies a living sacrifice" (Romans 12:1). If you would move by a definite crisis experience out of the wilderness into the land of blessing, there must be confession that leads to cleansing, surrender that brings power upon the life, faith that secures the anointing of the Spirit of God.

Surrender says, "I present my body." Faith says, "Christ now lives in me." Surrender says, "Lord, what wilt Thou have me do?" Faith says, "I can do all things through Christ, which strengthens me." Surrender crowns Christ as Lord of my life. Faith appropriates Jesus to *be* my Life. Therefore surrender is one step, but faith and appropriation is the other.

I ask you again, in which class are you traveling to heaven? The Lord can enable you to take the step of faith that appropriates Jesus Christ to be your life and lifts you from the class of carnality to that of spirituality, in which it is no more you, but Christ in you, the hope of glory.

CHAPTER 6

THE CHRISTIAN'S CHARACTER

I Corinthians 3:7-23

PAUL'S LETTER to the church at Corinth deals with the carnality which revealed itself in many different ways. They had written to him asking certain questions about church government, but not exposing their real need—typical, so often, of people who seek counsel. In the first few chapters of this letter Paul is making them face the reality of the sin in their lives so that he might point them forward to spiritual attainment, that they might grow into fulness of blessing in Christ.

What, then, is his line of emphasis in such a situation? We do not find it to be a word of anger nor denunciation. Rather, he shows these believers what they are in the sight of God, pointing out to them the purpose for which Jesus died, rose again, and ascended into heaven: that they might become a people worthy of His name.

In the midst of all their strife and failure, he reminds them of what they really are: "Ye are God's husbandry; ye are God's building" (3:9); "Ye are the temple of God" (3:16); "Ye are Christ's, and Christ is God's" (3:23). They were God's possession, so why should they live on such a low level? The problem, so often, in the life of a Christian is to achieve his true character, to outgrow "babyhood" and move into the spiritual maturity in which God intended him to live.

One of the marks of carnality in the Corinthian church was their worship of leadership, personified in Paul and Apollos: "I am of Paul," and "I am of Apollos." It was a church divided by loyalty to people. Speaking of himself and of Apollos, and of the others who

47

were subjects of hero worship in this church, Paul says, "We are [but] labourers together with God." In other words, "Why bring us into the situation? We are only God's messenger boys; we simply do what He tells us to do and don't ask any questions. That is what *we* are, but *ye* are God's husbandry."

In the margin we read, "ye are God's tillage"—God's field, if you like. "I have planted, Apollos watered"; says Paul, "but God gave the increase. So then neither is he that planteth any thing, neither he that watereth; but God that giveth the increase" (3:6-7). In that field there must be plowing and sowing and watering before there is a harvest. Paul and Apollos had planted the seed and watered it, but they could not make it grow; only God could do that.

We are reminded, of course, of the parable of the sower in the Gospel of Matthew. A man went out to sow the seed, which was the Word of God, and some fell by the wayside and the fowls came quickly and devoured it. Other seed fell on a stony ground where there was not much soil, so that it sprang up quickly and was scorched. Other seed fell among thorns and thistles, and although it grew for a little while, it soon became choked out. And still other seed fell on good ground and brought forth fruit.

After speaking this parable, the Lord Jesus took His disciples, who alone could understand Him, and explained it to them. He said that the seed which fell by the wayside is like the man who does not understand the Word which has been given to him, so he does not heed it, and the fowls of the air snatch it away—it never comes into his life and character. Then there is seed that has been sown in rocky ground, and it has sprung up quickly because it has no depth of soil. This is the man who receives the Word joyfully for a while, but because he is superficial and shallow, the Word has never taken lodging; it has been scorched by the trials of the day, and the man has never grown. The third category is the seed which was sown among thistles and thorns, the cares of this world and the deceitfulness of riches which choked the Word. But there is yet another, the man who receives the seed into good ground. His heart is prepared and hungry for it; he has taken it all in gladly. It has been planted, watered, and there is fruit: thirtyfold, sixtyfold, and a hundredfold.

Now to bring my illustration back into the context of this chapter: Paul says to the Corinthian church, "Ye are God's husbandry."

All he has done is to plant the Word and water it, but the life-giving principle is not from the one who plants, nor from the one who waters, but in the seed. It will grow according to the way in which it is sown and the way in which you receive it.

The seed may be received carelessly and heedlessly. It may be choked by the pressure of worldly cares, or ambition, or riches. It may be received on dry, hard ground, where it cannot take root, and quickly disappears. Or it can come into a heart that is wide open for all that is of God in Jesus Christ: the seed is fallen into good ground and brings forth fruit abundantly.

Twenty-five per cent of the seed in the parable brought forth fruit; the rest was wasted. I wonder if that is not a fair average. There are some in whose lives the seed has been planted, but it has not been understood; the principle of life in Jesus Christ seems vague and unreal; the Word is snatched away and forgotten. There are others who have received it gladly, with much emotion and many tears; the Word has sprung up quickly, but because there is no root, the plant has been scorched, and they are not growing, for they have not grasped the principle of it.

Others have listened amid the pressure of many cares and responsibilities. How hard it has been to sort it all out, to shake free from the things that pull in many directions! The Word has been received with a hungry heart, but the deceitfulness of this world's goods has choked it. However, there are some who have received the Word with open hearts; they have been like a plant watered by the rain, growing under the sun and bringing forth much fruit.

Whatever our state, we are God's field, and He is looking for the harvest. One day the great Husbandman is coming to take the harvest of our lives. Everything depends upon how we have received the seed—not upon the preacher, nor any man who has planted or watered.

Another mark of carnality in the church was their lack of growth: Paul calls them "babes in Christ. I have fed you with milk, and not with meat . . . For ye are yet carnal." He reminds them, however, that even in that protracted spiritual infancy, "Ye are God's building." All he had done was to lay a foundation. "As a wise masterbuilder, I have laid the foundation, and another buildeth thereon. But let every man take heed how he buildeth thereupon" (3:10).

But what a foundation he laid! It was strong and thorough and deep. We read in Acts 18 where even the chief ruler of the synagogue in Corinth was converted. The foundation is foursquare, "For other foundation can no man lay than that is laid, which is Jesus Christ" (3:11).

"Upon that foundation take heed how you build," he says. You can choose to build upon this foundation gold, silver, and precious stones, or wood, hay, and stubble. Then, one day, "Every man's work shall be made manifest: for the day shall declare it, because it shall be revealed by fire; and the fire shall try every man's work of what sort it is. If any man's work abide which he hath built thereupon, he shall receive a reward. If any man's work shall be burned, he shall suffer loss: but he himself shall be saved; yet so as by fire" (3:13-15).

I would remind you that something more has gone into the building of your life even in the last week; it is inevitable that the building is going up. The Lord Himself has laid the foundation, if we are His children; He is the rock upon which we stand, and upon that solid rock we are building. But what kind of materials are we using? During the days just past, have you put in some bricks? Have you put in the window of prayer? Is there the gold of a pure testimony, the silver of a life that is radiant for the Lord Jesus, the precious stone of victory over temptation? Is there submission to the will of God in the time of suffering? Is there surrender to the cross which we would not have taken of our own choosing? Is there progress along the path of the Master's choice, a forsaking of what seems to us more attractive? If we have chosen His will, in our life the building is going up to the glory of God with gold, silver and precious stones.

But in another life there has been much feverish activity, pressure in business and at home, or even in Christian work, and that life has become prayerless. There has been too much to do, too many things to cope with. There has been futility, irresponsibility, defeat, powerlessness—the building has gone up, but it is just wood, hay, and stubble.

One day every man's work is going to be put through the fire at the judgment seat of Christ. The Lord, who shall judge us in that day, is the One whose eyes, John tells us in the Book of Revelation, are as a flame of fire. The building which we are putting up, the building of our character, is going to pass under His scrutiny, and if any man's work shall abide in that day then, says the record, he shall receive a reward. But if the eyes of our Lord, which are as a flame of fire, shall find only wood, hay, and stubble, it shall all be burned. That man shall suffer loss, although he himself shall be saved, but as by fire. Take heed how you build!

Paul approaches the subject of their carnality from yet another angle: "Know ye not that ye are the temple of God, and that the Spirit of God dwelleth in you? If any man defile the temple of God, him shall God destroy; for the temple of God is holy, which temple ye are" (3:16-17).

Two different Greek words are translated in our New Testament by the English word "temple." One means the building itself, the other means the sanctuary, the Holy of Holies where the glory of God dwells—that is the word here. We are God's sanctuary, the place of His holy, awesome presence.

Paul goes on to say, "If any man defile the temple . . . him shall God destroy." But the word "destroy" does not mean to annihilate, it means to spoil or mar: "If any man spoils (corrupts) the temple, him will God corrupt or defile." If we defile the sanctuary of God, then it is not very long before our whole life becomes corrupt, worldly, indifferent to the things of God. One of the evidences of carnality in the Corinthian church was jealousy—envy, strife, and division. The whole testimony was being spoiled; the holy place, which should have been filled with the glory of the indwelling Christ, was marred by all kinds of carnality. The temple was being defiled, and therefore the church had become corrupt and worldly.

You too are God's sanctuary; your body is the temple of the Holy Spirit. You are not simply the structure in which He lives, you are the dwelling place of the Shekinah glory. God wants to reveal Himself there, controlling and guiding your life, shining through it with His radiance and power.

Remember the Old Testament tabernacle with its outer court where the public walked, the inner court which was the holy place of service, and the Holiest of all, the sanctuary of the presence of Jehovah. We are not to live our lives in the outer court, which is public property. We are not to live only in the busy rush of Christian service that is the inner court, the holy place. We are introduced into the Holiest of all by the blood of the Lord Jesus—we are the sanctuary of God. Therefore we should walk as holy men and women, with dignity and reverence and worship.

Paul has one more thing to say to this church, and this is the most precious of all: "Therefore let no man glory in men. For all things are yours; Whether Paul, or Apollos, or Cephas, [for what they are worth, they are yours] or the world . . ." (3:21-23) that is yours, too.

I love to go out into the country and remember that this is my Father's world, and because it is His, it is mine. I may never own legal title to an inch of it, but it is all mine in the Lord Jesus. "Or life, or death, or things present, or things to come; all are yours," Paul says. Yes, even death is yours, because Jesus Christ has taken the sting out of it; it is now a defeated enemy.

Everything is working together for good to them that love God, and best of all, even though you are still living in carnality, just remember: "ye are Christ's; and Christ is God's" (3:23). You are an heir of God and a joint-heir with Christ; you have an inheritance in Him, and the Lord Jesus has also an inheritance in you: "They shall be mine, in that day when I make up my jewels [i.e., special treasure]" (Malachi 3:17).

Paul counteracts carnality by pointing out the kind of people we are intended to be. Have we received the Word and borne fruit? We are God's husbandry, and He is looking for a harvest. You are God's building, according to Paul, and you are responsible for what you put into the building. Have you been putting in the bricks of prayer and testimony and faithfulness?

You may be thinking, "But you don't know the pressure of my life: how many hours I have to study, how many problems I have to cope with, how many people I have to try to satisfy." But if you say you have no time to see the spiritual building of your life, then I say to you in the name of the Lord, you are just too busy! For you will never have more time than you have right now. There will never be less pressure; indeed, if I may venture to say so, the more you go on with the Lord, the greater the pressure will become.

You are the sanctuary of God; you are intended to reveal the glory of the Lord. Most of all, you belong to Him, every bit of you! How could we ever live on the low level of carnality when we have such a Saviour as He!

CHAPTER 7

THE ROAD TO FAME

I Corinthians 4:1-21

IT WOULD BE well to remind ourselves of the great thrust of Paul's letter to the church at Corinth, lest we get lost and cannot see the wood for the trees. They had written to him about certain matters which affected church administration and policy, in which things they were concerned to be very exact and orthodox. They had not, however, said a word about the real state of affairs, that within their church there was sin that was unmentionable and Christian living that was carnal in the extreme.

Paul knew how they boasted of their learning and philosophy, and that their religion was more a matter of head knowledge than heart understanding. They were concerned about correctness and niceties, but deep down there was desperate need and much sin. To this condition Paul addresses himself in this letter, and the crux of what he had to say to them is in the twentieth verse of chapter 4: "For the kingdom of God is not in word, but in power."

Just before that, he tells them they are living in a kingdom of their own vain imagination. They were so proud, and they imagined that they had all the answers! "Who maketh thee to differ from another?" he asks. "What hast thou that thou didst not receive? now if thou didst receive it, why dost thou glory, as if thou hadst not received it? Now ye are full, now ye are enriched, ye have reigned as kings without us: and I would to God ye did reign, that we also might reign with you" (4:7-8).

The amazing sarcasm of those verses ought not to be missed. "You think you are authoritative; you think you are in the place of kingship and control, but look at the condition you are in! You are all talk and intellect; your religion is just theory without reality. The kingdom of God," Paul declares, "is not in word (it is not just philosophy and dogma), but in power, the one thing you haven't got!"

The whole trouble with them was—and I don't use a modern phrase but the words Paul used—"You are just puffed up gas bags!" (4:18a, 19). "It is reported commonly that there is fornication among you, and such fornication as is not so much as named among the Gentiles," Paul says, "And ye [in the face of that] are puffed up" (5:1-2). What an incredible situation existed in that church! They were so proud of what they thought they had, so sophisticated, and yet in the one important thing they were destitute: Holy Spirit power and authority.

Although we study this situation way back in the New Testament era, is it really very far from us, today? These are times when we are eager for education, talent, wisdom, philosophy—the church today strives after these things. We all seek, rightly, to know all we can about truth—I would not decry the search for knowledge and understanding, the necessity for discipline and training for the ministry. There is a great need for proper preparation, because the Lord should have the best of all we possess. However, I wonder if sometimes competence is a covering for our lack of the transforming power of God the Holy Spirit. If we do not have that, what is the value of all these other things?

Paul builds up his argument by telling them, "in every thing ye are enriched by Christ," and in Him they have "all utterance, and . . . all knowledge" (1:5). The kind of knowledge and understanding that will give authority, wisdom, and power is not to be found simply in education, but in the Lord Himself. For that reason, Paul continues, when I came to you, it was "not with the wisdom of words, lest the cross of Christ should be made of none effect" (1:17).

He came not with excellency of speech, but determined to know nothing among them but Jesus Christ, and Him crucified; therefore his preaching was in demonstration of the Spirit and of power. He turned his back on an intellectual approach to the situation because there is no philosophical argument that can meet the need of a church like that, where sin is permitted to exist unrebuked.

On the other hand, the wisdom of God is not something foolish, outmoded by civilization and education. "We speak the wisdom of God in a mystery" (2:7). The message of the cross, in all its fulness, is the message of God's wisdom and authority. Then Paul went on to remind them that in spite of all their appalling failure, they were intended to be God's husbandry, His field from which He looked for a harvest. They were His building, erected upon the foundation which is Jesus Christ. They were His sanctuary, from which the glory of the Lord should shine.

Most of all, they were God's own purchased possession—that was Paul's answer to their situation, pointing them to the path he, himself, has chosen, the royal route to heaven.

Two roads are clearly offered to each of us in life. One is the road of the self-life that seeks after intellectual entertainment and wins the applause of men, but ends in corruption, failure, and defeat. The other road leads a man by the way of the cross, the path of unpopularity, making him a spectacle to the world, often criticized and derided, even persecuted, certainly thought out-of-date and old-fashioned. That is the road Paul chose. Which path are you and I traveling today?

We find here the principle of all ministry, the background for all Christian living, the thing that distinguishes the man who knows God and walks with Him from the man who is just theorizing about religion and accumulating philosophy, but whose heart is empty and hopeless. Paul says, in effect, "I want you to think of me as no more than a minister of Christ and a steward of the mysteries of God," and "Moreover it is required in stewards, that a man be found faithful" (4:2).

The word "minister" here literally means "an under-rower." It pictures the great ships of Paul's time, which were manned by galley slaves, two rows of men under the lash of their overseer—and those on the lower deck were the most despised of all. They were the "under-rowers," and Paul affirms he is no more than that. It is the same word the Lord Jesus used when He said to Pilate, "If my kingdom were of this world, then would my servants [under-rowers] fight" (John 18:36). It occurs again when Paul and Barnabas set out on their missionary journey and took Mark with them as their "minister," their "under-rower" (Acts 13:5).

Paul was glad to count himself a slave of the Lord Jesus Christ,

completely submitted to His authority, happy in the Master's service.
A one-time leading member of the Sanhedrin, the man who boasted
of his religion and intellect, a proud Pharisee among Pharisees, now
he delights to say, "I am nothing—simply a slave of my Lord Jesus
Christ."

Paul says, moreover, he is also a steward of the mysteries of God.
That is our English word "housekeeper," or "manager," someone
who gets in the supplies to dispense to the family. A happy slave of
Jesus Christ—that is his relationship to the Lord; a steward of the
mysteries of God—that is his responsibility in view of this relationship. What he had received of the Lord Jesus, that he delivered to
the church. He was content to be a channel through whom God's
power and authority and Word could go out in blessing to the world.

The first step along the road to fame, therefore, is for a man to
turn his back deliberately upon all self-ambition and self-confidence,
submitting to the sovereignty of Jesus Christ in his life. When he has
done that, he is entrusted with the flaming message from heaven. Because his relationship with God is that of a bond-slave, his relationship to the people is that of God's messenger speaking in demonstration of the Spirit and of power.

The second step on the road to fame is that we face judgment as
we go through life. It is not something relegated only to the future;
judgment comes daily from three different quarters.

Notice in the text: "But with me it is a very small thing that I
should be judged of you, or of man's judgment: yea, I judge not
mine own self. For I know nothing by myself [and I think I am
correct in saying the translation here would be "I know nothing
against myself"]; yet am I not hereby justified: but he that judgeth
me is the Lord" (4:3-4). Paul had come under the scrutiny of people
who were wondering if he would lead them off into extremes! Isn't it
amazing how people are far more scared of holiness than they are of
sin? But he was not concerned with what they thought about him;
he was not responsible to them. He even declares that he is not judging himself, because he could not find anything in his life of which
he was aware that was against him: there was no known sin that he
was committing. The one thing he says he is concerned about is the
scrutiny of the Lord, who knows all our hearts, our desires, our every
thought and motive.

"Therefore judge nothing before the time, until the Lord come, who both will bring to light the hidden things of darkness, and will make manifest the counsels of the hearts: and then shall every man have praise of God" (4:5). One day God will make manifest "the hidden things of darkness," not necessarily the evil things, but our inner motives: why it was we turned from our own ability and philosophy of life and chose this path of the cross. He knows why, and one day every man shall receive—and mark the next word— not blame or condemnation, but *praise* of God!

The man who has chosen the path of the crucified life, the path of unpopularity, must expect misunderstanding down here. But his concern is not for the judgment of the world, only that day by day the Lord has His eyes upon him. The road to fame and glory is, first of all, submitting to the sovereignty of Christ, and then being a channel through whom the message of the living Word of God burns like a fire.

Paul's experience is a costly one, and perhaps we can follow him thus far, seeking to stand for the same message and preach the same full truth of salvation which can save a man from inbred corruption as well as from the sins of daily life. But do we want to go with him all the way? For in the course of his path he says, "We are made a public spectacle . . . We are fools for Christ's sake" (4:9, 10a). "But you think yourselves wise," he continues, again with a touch of scorn, I think. "We are weak, but you think yourselves strong. You are honorable to other people and are popular along the way you have taken, and it is accounted a good thing to be in that line," he says, in effect; "but we are despised" (4:10b).

"Even unto this present hour we both hunger, and thirst, and are naked, and are buffeted, and have no certain dwellingplace; . . . being reviled, we bless; being persecuted, we suffer it: Being defamed, we entreat: we are made as the filth of the world, and are the offscouring of all things unto this day" (4:11-13). Here Paul and I have parted company. Why? Because, though deep down in my heart I can face you and say that to the best of my knowledge I want this life which glories not in the flesh but only in the Lord— and maybe you could say "Amen" to that—there is something in all of us that wants both.

We want a middle road, a little bit of praise and popularity, a little bit of recognition and thanks, a little bit of the applause of men. At the same time we want the anointing of the Spirit and the authority of God; we want the power without the cost. So Paul has said "Good-bye" to some of us and gone ahead, because for him to tread that path for the Lord Jesus has meant he became a gazing-stock to the world; in short, it meant crucifixion.

The royal route that leads to glory is the route the Master trod. He, being defamed, prayed, "Father, forgive them." Being reviled, He reviled not again; being persecuted, He submitted without a murmur. Everything that Paul faced, Jesus had faced before him. Everything that Paul went through, Christ had gone through, only more. He endured to the very end, down to the last drop of His blood on the cross outside Jerusalem, to redeem man from his boasting and confidence, from his self-importance and human pride.

The road that leads to heaven is the route of faithfulness to God; it is the way of crucifixion with Christ. Therefore, Paul said, "I will come to you shortly . . . and will know, not the speech of them which are puffed up, but the power. For the kingdom of God is not in word, but in power" (4:19). One thing he knew: when he came to that church to speak with them face to face, he would know wherein lay their power.

You may be going out to the mission field soon to blaze a trail for God, or you may teach a Sunday school class week by week, or you may minister the Word of God in a church. Whatever your service for the Lord, you can only meet the needs of the people around you in the power of God the Holy Spirit. It is only as men and women have hearts aflame for Jesus and are channels of the power of God that they are going to meet the needs of the age in which we live.

Up to the limit of the light that God has given us, are we walking the royal route to heaven today? Being approved by Him is really all that matters. If you are crucified with Christ, then when you work in the office before unconverted people, or you visit a home where people are unsaved, or you teach your Bible class, or you stand in a pulpit, you will know the power of the Lord, which can break into the hearts of corrupt men and overcome sin in His name. Have you begun by submitting to the sovereignty of Jesus Christ in your life? If you have, then you are beginning to prove His power in the place of your own ineffectiveness.

CHAPTER 8

WATCH YOUR STEP!

I Corinthians 5:1-13

THE VARIETY of subjects with which Paul deals in this letter makes it very profitable for meditation and study. We come to grips now with the root of the trouble in the church at Corinth, the sin that ruined its testimony and made their pride in worldly wisdom and human philosophy so blatantly out of place. Here we deal with no easy subject, but a very important one, a thing which is all too often the crippling factor in Christian testimony today, yet over which there is deliverance in the Lord Jesus, and in Him alone. It is not just something in Greece many years ago, but in America today. I ask you, therefore, sympathetically and prayerfully, with an open mind, to follow as we seek the profitable lesson in this portion of God's Word.

In the first place, I would like to look with you at this disaster which has to be faced. "It is reported commonly that there is fornication among you, and such fornication as is not so much as named among the Gentiles, that one should have his father's wife. And ye are puffed up, and have not rather mourned, that he that hath done this deed might be taken away from among you" (5:1-2).

The church at Corinth, so obsessed by its wisdom and philosophy, had become completely careless of the moral implications of the gospel. Their pride of human intellect had tragically failed to prevent a moral breakdown; these Christians were paralyzed, absolutely powerless. On the other hand, the wisdom of God, the word of the cross, the message of the full gospel, devastatingly exposed their sin and possessed mighty power to save from it. All through this Corinthian letter these two things are contrasted.

Paul now brings this group of believers face to face with the disaster that has taken place in their fellowship. The message of the cross, with its implications in Christian behavior, was being ignored. Therefore, Paul says, "it is commonly reported," or "it is everywhere noised abroad," that a certain situation exists. This is not the gossip of a few people—it is the talk of the city! I need not dwell on the particular case except to state quite bluntly that it was a matter of the perversion of one of the most sacred things in human personality—the perversion of sex. It was of so serious a nature that no case so flagrant could be found even among the unconverted people in Corinth.

Now the whole point was this: not simply a breakdown in the life of one individual, but the wide influence that sin was having upon the life of the church that tolerated it. This group of people had been separated to Christ through the word of the cross, called into fellowship with the Lord Jesus, and their testimony was the channel by which God could reach the whole city. Yet the purpose for which they existed was in danger of total collapse because of sin in their midst.

"And ye are puffed up," Paul accuses them, "you are haughty and proud, so occupied with your discussions and theological arguments that you are closing your eyes to this terrible thing that is going on right in the very center of your church life." There was no possibility that they were ignorant of it, because it was known everywhere. Maybe they were proud of their tolerance and blind to the fact that their testimony was being ruined, that the church had become a laughingstock to the people outside. Their only real weapon, God the Holy Spirit, was grieved, quenched, withdrawn. So occupied were they with window-dressing, discussions and arguments, that they were insensitive to sin. They did not mourn about it; they did not weep over it; they did not feel the shame and agony of it.

Is this something so remote as a group of Christian people in Corinth nineteen hundred years ago? Who can tell how paralyzed is the witness of the church in these days of moral laxity because of this kind of thing? The alarming horror of juvenile crime has, as one of its biggest factors, sex perversion. This evil stems from the self-indulgent age in which we live; from the kind of thing that people watch on television and hear on the radio; from the kind of printed trash available on almost every corner; from the lack of parental control; and most of all, from the lack of the presence and power of God the Holy Spirit in Christian living.

Occupied so much with our correctness of doctrine, we are in grave danger of failing to recognize that this evil thing is not only outside the camp, but inside. There are people who have decided for Christ and claim to be converted—they have come to Him to seek forgiveness and cleansing from this very thing. Oh, that I might speak with utter tenderness and candor about such a subject as this, and not with an attitude of censorious judgment! There are people who have carried such sin over into Christian life without having victory and deliverance. They are in the Christian church and are taking leadership in Christian activity, and therefore sex perversion is found within the holy fellowship of the church of God.

In the second place, there is a duty to be performed: "I verily, as absent in body, but present in spirit, have judged already, as though I were present, concerning him that hath so done this deed. In the name of our Lord Jesus Christ, when ye are gathered together, and my spirit, with the power of our Lord Jesus Christ, To deliver such an one unto Satan, for the destruction of the flesh" (5:3-5).

Paul made up his mind what must be done. The guilty man, who brought this sin of his own life into the setting of Christian fellowship, must be put outside. It interprets what the Lord Jesus said in Matthew 18:15-17: if your brother sin, you are not to condone it. You are not to say that it has nothing to do with you, because you are a fellow member of the body. Because he is within the Christian group, the whole fellowship is affected by it. Go, therefore, and see this man alone, and if he hears you, you have won him. If he won't hear you, take two or three others; if he won't hear them, take it to the church, which then must act. If he refuses to listen, to repent, to confess, then there is only one course left: he must be dealt with as a heathen and a publican. Thus saith the Lord, and thus saith Paul: "Deliver such an one unto Satan, for the destruction of the flesh."

We must be sure we understand what that means. Some who ex-

pound this verse say that this man had to be put outside, and then
he would suffer some awful physical disease in order that he might
be brought to his senses. I do not think it means that at all.

Paul did not say "the destruction of the body," he said, "the destruction of the flesh." It was the flesh which had mastered this man.
Paul makes a distinction between the Christian who is carnal and
the one who is spiritual. The man who, though indwelt by the Spirit,
is still under the control of the flesh, is utterly carnal, yielding to
all the principles of the old nature, which was supposed to be on
the other side of the cross. Now, this man in the Corinthian church
is to be given over to Satan until that principle of yieldedness to
the flesh is ended, until this principle of the self-life is finished.

Hand him over to Satan, Paul says, before whose authority he
has been surrendering. Cut him off from Christian fellowship; remove him from any false feeling of security within the Christian
church; expose him to the dreadfulness and loneliness and awfulness of the sin of which he is guilty. Let the world see that sin
cannot be tolerated within the holy fellowship of God's people. Put
him out for the destruction of carnality, until he loathes the very
thought of the thing which he is practicing.

This is the duty to be performed, but is this man to be left ex-
communicated and abandoned? No, indeed! This guilty man is a
sinner for whom Jesus died. There is a deliverance to be secured.
Notice the second part of this verse, which I omitted above: "To
deliver such an one . . . for the destruction of the flesh, *that the
spirit may be saved in the day of the Lord Jesus*" (5:5).

When Paul gave these instructions, I am sure he did it with the
love of the Saviour in his heart. Indeed, when he refers to this again
in his second letter, he says it was "out of much affliction and anguish
of heart I wrote unto you with many tears" (II Corinthians 2:4).
The man must sample the awfulness of his sin; be cut off, if you
like, from the imaginary halo of church membership that might enable him to go on in sin and think he was getting away with it. Let
him be satiated with it until, like the prodigal, he begins to be in
want and cries out, "I will arise and go to my Father!"

How far from God can a Christian go? How deep in sin can a
man sink after he is born of the Spirit? Only a backslider who has
tasted the bitter fruit of an experience like this can ever know. But

someone may say, "Is it not a dangerous doctrine to suggest that a man can live like this and yet be saved?" Oh, no!

I remind you that the medicine Paul prescribed for this man and for this church proved effective. Look at the second letter: "Sufficient to such a man is this punishment, which was inflicted of many. So that contrariwise ye ought rather to forgive him, and comfort him, lest perhaps such a one should be swallowed up with overmuch sorrow. Wherefore I beseech you that you would confirm your love toward him" (II Corinthians 2:6-8). And a few chapters later: "For behold this selfsame thing, that you sorrowed after a godly sort, what carefulness it wrought in you, yea, what clearing of yourselves, yea, what indignation, yea, what fear, yea, what vehement desire, yea, what zeal, yea, what revenge! In all things ye have approved yourselves to be clear in this matter" (II Corinthians 7:11). The man was forgiven and restored; the church repented with godly sorrow and was blessed. This is always the outcome of dealing with sin in the life of a genuine Christian.

The only security we have is in the Lord Jesus Himself, and He will not let us go. Even though He has to chastise, perhaps allow a man to drink the fruit of his sin until he is nauseated with it—if that medicine does not succeed in bringing the man back to God, it only proves that he was never saved in the first place. No true Christian can go on sinning and be happy in it. Yet if he is refusing to judge himself, then in order that deliverance might be secured, he has to be given over to the power of Satan until this principle of yieldedness to the flesh is overcome. You see, that action sorts out the genuine from the spurious; it shows the reality of conversion as against a mere profession in the Saviour.

But Paul also points out that there is a distinction to be observed: "I wrote unto you in an epistle not to company with fornicators: Yet not altogether with the fornicators of this world, or with the covetous, or extortioners, or with idolaters; for then must ye needs go out of the world. But now I have written unto you not to keep company, if any man that is called a brother be a fornicator, or covetous, or an idolater, or a railer, or a drunkard, or an extortioner; with such an one no not to eat" (5:9-11). Judgment, says Paul, must begin at the house of God.

The attitude of the Christian toward the unsaved should never be one of judgment because of his sins. There are many who, perhaps by heredity or environment, perhaps by reason of their own passions, are victims of this dreadful business—but we are not to hold up our hands in holy horror. We must go after such people with the flame of Calvary love and with the message of deliverance, never shocked or deterred by the depths of sin that we find revealed. We have only to look within our own hearts to see the potential of it there, but for God's grace. Ours is the privilege of proclaiming deliverance even from a perversion of this character.

Here is an example which I would put simply and bluntly. Consider a man who is homosexual, and the poor fellow is absolutely beaten and defeated. One day the gospel is preached to him, and there is no difficulty persuading him that he is a sinner. He is pointed to the way of the cross, the way of forgiveness and cleansing, and he gladly receives it. Then he is brought into the church, accepted for membership on the basis of his profession of faith in Jesus Christ.

Before long he is given Christian work to do and opportunities for testimony. Everything goes well for a while, until Satan attacks and he is down again, tripped up by the same thing that conquered him before he was saved. In the love of Christ and for the sake of the purity of the fellowship, this man has to be brought to understand that, when he comes to Jesus Christ, he accepts responsibility for the standards of Christian living, and he must live worthy of his high calling. He cannot be allowed to continue in Christian leadership, or even in the fellowship of the church, until the sin has been confessed and repented of, and he is right with God. If he refuses to face that himself, the church must face it for him, for his sake and for theirs.

Why? Because there is a dynamic to be restored: "Purge out therefore the old leaven, that ye may be a new lump, as ye are unleavened. For even Christ our passover is sacrificed for us: Therefore let us keep the feast, not with old leaven, neither with the leaven of malice and wickedness; but with the unleavened bread of sincerity and truth" (5:7-8).

Paul's final answer to every problem is the cross. Look at this wretched sin in the light of the blood that has been shed. See what carnality has done to the church and to the individual, in spite of his profession. It hasn't been altogether his fault: he was given Christian leadership, and perhaps was unwisely put in the limelight. But there has been no judgment of sin in his life, no repentance, no confession. Such a member causes the church to be absolutely paralyzed in its witness, takes away the power, removes the authority of the Holy Spirit. An unholy fellowship is always defeated. To tolerate sin is going to ruin the church, says Paul; the extent to which sin is permitted is the measure in which appetite for the Word will depart. The Christian who is pure is powerful, but the man who is compromising is spiritually impotent.

"But remember," says Paul, "Christ is sacrificed for us. Therefore purge out the old leaven." The passover was eaten with the unleavened bread of purity, the symbol of deliverance. Then he tells how: be what you are, "a new lump, as ye are unleavened." That is the position in which you are placed; that is how God sees you. "If any man be in Christ, he is a new creature; old things are passed away; behold, all things are become new" (II Corinthians 5:17). Take up your position on the resurrection side of the cross and claim your heritage.

The dynamic that has gone out of the church fellowship must be restored. Don't let such things go on a moment longer—the futility of our testimony, the powerlessness of our service must be dealt with. Do you recognize the disaster?

Poor struggling soul, gripped by the bondage of this sort of thing, I beg of you that you would just cling today to your place in Jesus Christ and remember you are on resurrection ground. "Now ye are clean," says the Lord Jesus, "through the word which I have spoken unto you. Abide in me" (John 15:3-4). Do you believe that? Though this bondage of sin has gone on so long in your life, the power of the blood goes further and can cleanse you from all sin. There is no power of Satan to grip this human body, either by temperament or heredity or by your own choice, that can outreach the grace of God which can save you from slavery to sin.

Then feed on Him: "Therefore let us keep the feast, not with old leaven, neither with the leaven of malice and wickedness; but with the unleavened bread of sincerity and truth." If you would seek to be on the royal route to heaven, claim His life by obedience which submits to His control, by surrender which brings His love and His power into your heart and life.

CHAPTER 9

THINGS GOD EXPECTS YOU TO KNOW—I

I Corinthians 6:1-11

As YOU GLANCE at the whole scope of this sixth chapter of First Corinthians, you will see that over and over Paul addresses this church with the challenge, "Know ye not?—Don't you know?" I cannot escape the conclusion that it is almost with a touch of sarcasm that he writes, in effect, "You who profess to be so clever and intellectual, can it be that you are ignorant of these basic facts?"

Paul asks them six questions that fall into two divisions. Notice the first three: "Do ye not know that saints shall judge the world?" (6:2). "Know ye not that we shall judge angels?" (6:3). "Know ye not that the unrighteous shall not inherit the kingdom of God?" (6:9). In other words, "Remember what you are."

Look at the next three: "Know ye not that your bodies are the members of Christ?" (6:15). "Know ye not that he which is joined to an harlot is one body . . . But he that is joined to the Lord is one spirit?" (6:16, 17). "Know ye not that your body is the temple of the Holy Ghost, . . . ye are bought with a price?" (6:19, 20). In other words, "Remember to whom you belong."

All the way through this epistle Paul adopts the principle that the mightiest drawing power to lift a man out of carnality, worldliness and sinfulness is the cross of Christ. We need to remember how we have been redeemed, what we are in the sight of God, and to whom we belong, our Lord Jesus Christ. I believe that to be the most effective weapon in the hands of any preacher. Paul does not condemn this church, though he speaks to it in mighty straight language. He simply reminds them that they are not their own; they have been bought with a price.

The argument of these first eleven verses is rooted in a particular condition that existed in the Corinthian church, but which is to be found potentially in almost every fellowship today. Paul begins with a rebuke for their trivial disputes, then he asks them to see these things in the light of their true dignity as children of God and their great destiny as Christians. In view of that, he issues a recall to triumphant discipleship.

Let us look at the first of these things, the rebuke for trivial disputes within the church: "Dare any of you, having a matter against another, go to law before the unjust, and not before the saints?" (6:1). Here Paul is addressing himself again to the carnality of the church at Corinth. He had said previously, "are ye not carnal, and walk as men? for there is among you envying, and strife, and divisions" (3:3). Now he directs his attention to these divisions among them, and to what was even worse: instead of settling them privately, they had presumed to ask for settlement in a pagan court. "Brother goeth to law with brother, and that before the unbelievers" (6:6).

"Surely there is one man among you who has enough sense to settle the thing privately among yourselves," he implies. "If you cannot find anybody to do it, then instead of parading your dissentions and carnality before an ungodly world, let God vindicate the right, or rather allow yourselves to be defrauded than bring scorn upon your testimony" (6:5, 7).

Of course, that does not mean that a Christian must never go to law. There may be circumstances when it is necessary. But disputes and divisions among brethren should be settled within the church and not outside it. Here is the extent to which strife goes, the damage it causes when we forget who we are, and parade our disputes in front of the world.

These conditions are not confined to New Testament times; I think they may be found in church life today. They are tragically emphasized when envy and strife, bickering about points of creed and dogma, are deliberately publicized to an unbelieving world. One of the greatest tragedies on many mission fields is the way in which sectarianism at home is extended abroad and threatens to ruin Christian witness. Insisting upon agreement on every point of the Bible before we can have mutual fellowship, for instance. In fundamentalism today, such divisions frequently are paraded before the general public, to the confusion of the whole Christian testimony. Of course, it usually begins when one Christian has a quarrel with another, and it is not settled privately, but becomes public. No wonder people are amazed and repulsed by a church which is supposed to be united in Christ but which constantly demonstrates its disunity. These things ought to make us bow our heads in shame. Clearly revealed unity and love have great power to draw the unbeliever. How contrary is internal strife to the command of the Lord Jesus: "By this shall all men know that ye are my disciples, if ye have love one to another" (John 13:35).

Here, then, is the basis upon which Paul is building his argument. This church, which is squabbling publicly about practically nothing, is at the same time ignoring glaring moral breakdown within its fellowship. How does Paul, by the Holy Spirit, address himself to this situation? By a reminder of the true dignity of the child of God: "Do ye not know that the saints shall judge the world? and if the world shall be judged by you, are ye unworthy to judge the smallest matters? Know ye not that we shall judge angels? how much more things that pertain to this life?" (6:2-3).

These Christians had become shortsighted, occupied with their own strife and trouble. Paul asks them now to lift their eyes, to look beyond the present, to think of that day when they will be associated with the Lord Jesus Christ in the judgment of the world and of angels. For one day the tables are going to be turned. The world, which has despised the Christian faith, is going to be judged by those whom it has, in this life, condemned as foolish.

Listen to the words of the Lord Jesus in Matthew 19:28: "I say unto you, That ye which have followed me, in the regeneration when the Son of man shall sit in the throne of his glory, ye also shall sit upon twelve thrones, judging the twelve tribes of Israel." Listen again to the language of Jude 14 and 15: "Behold, the Lord cometh with ten thousands of his saints, To execute judgment upon all, and to convince all that are ungodly among them of all their ungodly deeds which they have ungodly committed, and of all their hard speeches which ungodly sinners have spoken against him." Listen to Paul writing again in II Timothy 2:12, "If we suffer with him, we shall also reign with him."

On that great day of final judgment, far beyond the time when the church will be caught up by the Lord Jesus to be with Him, beyond even the millennial reign of Christ, the church, ransomed and glorified, is going to participate in the overthrow of everything that is ungodly and unrighteous. We are going to be counted worthy of judging the world, and not only the world, but angels! "God spared not the angels that sinned, but cast them down to hell, and delivered them into chains of darkness, to be reserved unto judgment" (II Peter 2:4).

What a day! The world against which we have fought to maintain our stand for Christ, the world that has called us narrow, bigoted, out-of-date, escapists from reality, the world with its ungodliness, its immorality, its sin, its utter rejection of the authority of God— one day the children of God are going to sit in judgment upon that world! And the devil, who has flung temptation at us from every direction, who has done everything in his power to discourage, to deter, to frighten, and to make us doubt, who has flung one fiery dart after another to hinder our progress to glory, to cause us to fail and to sin—one day we are going to share in the judgment of Satan!

"This is to be your ultimate destiny," says Paul in effect. "Why, then, are you spending your time quarreling about inconsequential things? Surely you are capable of settling your petty disputes! If you are not, how do you think you are going to be worthy of the dignity that is yours as a Christian? Remember what you are!"

Then he pulls them back again, as much as to say, "Now you may think that is very much up in the clouds. That overwhelming thought may be too much for you to grasp, for it concerns eternity. But what about this life, here and now? I want to turn you from your carnality to the kind of life that you have been saved to live." He recalled them to triumphant discipleship: "Know ye not that the unrighteous shall not inherit the kingdom of God? Be not deceived: neither fornicators, nor idolaters, nor adulterers, nor effeminate, nor abusers of themselves with mankind, Nor thieves, nor covetous, nor drunkards, nor revilers, nor extortioners, shall inherit the kingdom of God" (6:9-10).

What an awful, ugly list! Some of these things are unfit for public mention. We dealt with them in part in our last study—the collapse of sex relationships, the disintegration of human personality, the descent to bestiality, instead of an ascent to a life that is worthy of a child of God.

As I read again in the presence of God this list of ten unmentionable sins, I had no trouble with nine of them. I could bow before the Lord and say, "Yes, Lord, surely none that is guilty of this could ever enter the Kingdom of God."

There was one word, however, that puzzled me, one right in the middle of the list: "effeminate." Why should such a word as that find its way into this list, among the things that make entrance into the Kingdom of Heaven an impossibility? As I looked into it a little more carefully, I found that it touches the very root of the problem in the church at Corinth. It took the strength out of their discipleship, the tang out of their testimony.

The word means "flabby"; "soft" would be the literal translation of the Greek. It is found only in two other places in the New Testament. When God sent the forerunner of Christ, John the Baptist, He chose a man of the wilderness, whose clothing was rough and whose food was locusts and wild honey—a strange, austere figure. Later, some people asked the Lord if such a man could be authentic. He had not come through the recognized religious channels of his time.

Jesus turned upon them and said, "But what went ye out for to see? A man clothed in soft raiment?" (Luke 7:25). That is the word. What did they expect to find, an indulgent man? Did they expect someone spineless, whose doctrine was but cold, dry bones like the other religious leaders of the time? "What sort of man did you expect? Who else would be able to move a day like that for Me?" asks the Master.

This exposes the whole trouble with the church at Corinth: they were just soft. They were tolerant of sin, squabbling among themselves, bogged down by carnality. There was no vision among them, no Holy Spirit dynamic. They had no conviction of their calling, no sense of discipleship, and Paul sought to recall them to this.

How can we escape saying in our hearts, "This would be me, but for the grace of God"? How does a church lose Holy Spirit power? Why does it become tolerant of sin? How can a Christian excuse himself for his obvious carnality? Simply because we are soft: evangelicals, yes, but frequently with more jelly than evangel!

Our vision gone, our burden for souls lost, the self-indulgent church just settles down comfortably alongside things that ought to be destroyed.

Paul's object is to recall the Corinthian believers to triumphant discipleship: "And such were some of you: but ye are washed, but ye are sanctified, but ye are justified in the name of the Lord Jesus, and by the Spirit of our God" (6:11). Paul is making them look themselves squarely in the face: "such were some of you, but. . . ." I think that is a thrilling verse; there is a sharp distinction in it, a clear line of demarcation. They *were* all this: idolaters, fornicators, soft, and all the rest of the ugliness, "*but* ye are washed, *but* ye are sanctified, *but* ye are justified. . . ."

Altogether, one distinct, tremendous transaction with God: Ye are washed: "Now ye are clean through the word which I have spoken unto you" (John 15:3). Ye are sanctified: "Through sanctification of the Spirit, unto obedience and sprinkling of the blood of Jesus Christ" (I Peter 1:2). Ye are justified: "Being justified freely by his grace through the redemption that is in Christ Jesus" (Romans 3:24). This is what you are, says Paul to these believers who are flabby and tolerant of sin. He reminds them that they have been washed by the Word, set apart by the Holy Spirit, and declared righteous by the blood of Jesus Christ before the God of heaven.

The man who is made righteous in the sight of God has to be made holy by the grace of God. It is impossible to live like the devil's children and hope to go to heaven with God's children. Here they were: defeated, idolatrous, effeminate—and such were some of you. But here they are now: washed, sanctified, justified. How can they walk in their former sins?

With so many professed Christians it is sometimes hard to discover where their Christianity ends and the world begins in their lives. There is no clear line of demarcation; they love being coddled and they do not like being challenged. But the business of the church is not to coddle the saints, but to challenge them to win others for Jesus Christ. "Remember who you are," says Paul.

Oh, the tragedy of carnality: people occupied with petty quarrels that ruin Christian testimony, when they are destined one day to judge the world and angels! We are intended in this life to live in the glory of Christ and by His power in us. This is what we are by the grace of God and in the sight of God. Therefore, in the power of the Spirit, we should be what we are, so that one day we will be fit to take part in the judgment of the world and of angels.

CHAPTER 10

THINGS GOD EXPECTS YOU TO KNOW—II

I Corinthians 6:12-20

THESE CHAPTERS of Paul's letter require very careful and prayerful treatment in public ministry. But I believe they concern matters of importance to the whole Christian church and to each one of our lives today. Paul addresses himself straightforwardly to the sin which lay at the root of the situation in the Corinthian church and gives the supreme answer to it. Victory and deliverance are yet possible. He is always seeking to point people away from their failure, to get them to look up to the Lord; Paul's answer to every situation is Calvary.

He has already dealt with the individual who was personally responsible, telling the church what they must do: deliver him to Satan for the destruction of the flesh and the saving of the soul in the day of our Lord Jesus Christ. Then he goes on to rebuke them for their petty disputes and calls upon them to remember what they are as Christians: washed, sanctified, justified. Now we hear him saying, "Remember to whom you belong," and telling us to bring that relationship between the soul and the Saviour to bear upon every matter of life.

The whole theme of this portion of Scripture is the Christian's attitude toward his body. His moral standards must be recognizably different from others, and he must be able not only to explain why they are necessary but also how they can be maintained.

The Apostle who writes this letter under the inspiration of the Holy Spirit is the one who, perhaps above all others, proclaims salvation in the Lord Jesus Christ by faith alone. "For by grace are ye saved through faith; and that not of yourselves . . . Not of works, lest any man should boast" (Ephesians 2:8, 9). This is Paul's great gospel, that a man comes to know Jesus Christ only on simple faith in the atonement for him at Calvary.

Yet the Apostle Paul also relentlessly declares that no one can claim salvation and go on practicing sin like an unbeliever. If the outer life of a child of God is not made pure, it is evidence that the inward heart has never been renewed. The faith that does not produce holiness is not New Testament faith; it is not saving faith, for "without which [holiness] no man shall see the Lord" (Hebrews 12:14).

With that background in mind, let us turn to what Paul has to say concerning our relationship to our body and think of it carefully, prayerfully, and soberly in the presence of God. First of all, Paul lays down some principles of Christian liberty: "All things are lawful unto me, but all things are not expedient: all things are lawful for me, but I will not be brought under the power of any" (6:12). That was a master stroke on Paul's part, for that was exactly what everyone in Corinth said: "All things are lawful" was their attitude on the matter of sex relationships.

That is also what the twentieth century is saying: "Have your fling! Go to the registrar, if you like, to get a little legal authority to practice what you have already been doing." There are to be no inhibitions, no frustrations because, we are told, these things are not sin. "Express yourself! Away with the prohibitions that come from an outmoded method of life and thinking!" That is what Corinth said, and the spirit of the city had got into the church. Who can say that the spirit of what is practiced today has not penetrated our churches? Has not this very thing eaten into the vital testimony of professing Christianity today?

"All things are lawful unto me," writes Paul, "and there is not a single faculty or appetite of the body which is not for me to use lawfully." But because we are Christians there are two things we must bear in mind as we exercise our liberty.

The first is this: "All things are not expedient." That word means "bearing together," "helping together." Paul is saying, therefore, that he no longer lives to himself; as a Christian he is one of a fellowship, and he can only use the appetites of the body so long as he is not hurting another. He is governed by the effect upon other people, not upon himself.

Not only that, says Paul, but "I will not be brought under the power [authority] of any." If through the unrestrained use of the body he is mastered by these things, then he is denying the right of Jesus Christ to the sovereignty of his life.

Notice his simple illustration here: "Meats for the belly, and the belly for meats: but God shall destroy both it and them. Now the body is not for fornication, but for the Lord; and the Lord for the body. And God hath both raised up the Lord, and will also raise up us by his own power" (6:13-14). We need food for our physical appetite, but a day is coming when God is going to destroy both. That does not mean the body will be destroyed. That will mark the end of its physical desires and physical limitations, the end of its demand for physical satisfaction. Although this thing in which we live may be put in a grave, one day it will be raised and transformed into the likeness of the Lord Jesus Christ. The body is not finished when it is put into a coffin; it is to be brought into the very presence of God. This body is for the Lord, for His use and not for mine.

That gives us a new slant on the problem of sex, an attitude peculiarly Christian, rooted in the fact of the resurrection of Jesus Christ as the "firstfruits of them that sleep." It is based on the reality of eternity; we were not created only to live down here. Our body is God's, and we cannot play fast and loose with it, because it is for His use. We have Christian liberty, but only in consideration of others and in carefulness with regard to the damage we might do. Our liberty is only within the fellowship of God's people and under the authority of the Lord Jesus. The body is not to be played with; it is for Him.

Here, very briefly, is the principle for Christian living. Now, in what sense is the body for the Lord? It is not only that it is going to be transformed into His likeness, but that we will be held responsible before the judgment seat of Christ, as Paul himself tells us, for the deeds done in this body. That will put discipline and restraint into life. It will mean that certain habits must stop because I am a Christian. Certain practices that the world may consider "the thing to do" are going to have no part in my life, because I am a Christian.

When we look further into this chapter, I think we will see why—it is the prevention of license. Notice again one of Paul's great questions: "Know ye not that your bodies are the members of Christ? shall I then take the members of Christ, and make them the members of an harlot? God forbid. What? know ye not that he which is joined to an harlot is one body? for two, saith he, shall be one flesh. But he that is joined unto the Lord is one spirit" (6:15-17).

May I ask you to follow me very carefully here. We who have been redeemed by His precious blood are His body here on earth, the channels through which He works. Our Lord, instead of being subject to the time and space limitations of one physical body, as when He was here on earth, now acts through the bodies of His people in whom He lives. "He that is joined unto the Lord is one spirit," says Paul. Wherever He can find a body surrendered to Him, a man or woman who will receive Him as their Lord and Sovereign, then they become His means of revealing Himself to the world around them. "Ye are members of Christ."

You will always find in Scripture that God works through a human body. That is why it was said of the Lord Jesus, "Lo, I come to do thy will, O God. . . . By the which will we are sanctified through the offering of the body of Jesus Christ once for all" (Hebrews 10:9, 10). It was in a body that man sinned; it is in a body that we sin. It was in a body that Jesus came to earth; it was in a body that He lived triumphantly and overcame where we have been overcome. It was in a body that He died and rose again, and now by His Spirit He comes to live within the body of His people.

Satan always works through a body, also. The only way he can thwart God's purposes is to get a body surrendered to his use, available for his diabolic power and ugly purposes.

This is the question of choice in a Christian's life: shall he take that which is a member of Christ and give it to some unworthy use? Shall he take his body, the means through which God's will is to be done, and yield it to the immoral, sinful purposes of Satan? What will happen if he does? He becomes one body if he is joined to that which is sinful. But if he is joined to the Lord, he is one spirit. That means that in every physical faculty the human frame is under the control of the Lord's Spirit. That Spirit enabled Jesus Christ to live day by day in a human body and never deviate from the will of God, never yield to all the tremendous temptations of the devil.

If we are joined to Christ, we are therefore enabled by His grace to control the body. But if we join ourselves to that which is immoral, we become one flesh with that which we love, and therefore we become part of judgment, condemnation, and punishment, the inevitable result of such action.

Here is the issue from the moment of our birth until the moment when we meet God face to face: either the Spirit of God is to triumph and the life of the flesh die out, or that which is of sin and of the flesh will so control us that the Spirit of God ceases to speak. That tremendously solemn alternative faces everyone. Everything is lawful for the child of God, but only under the authority of the Lord Jesus Christ. What He permits, I will do; what He refuses, I will reject. What His Word tells me is right, I will accept; what His Word tells me is wrong, I will refuse. This is the battle ground where you and I fight every day.

However, lest I seem to place burdens upon you that are impossible to carry, there is something else Paul tells us, the answer to "how?"

I repeat, Paul always brings his hearers back to the cross, back to the place where Jesus died for them. He is never afraid to reveal the ugliness of sin for what it is; he exposes it and drags it to the very foot of Calvary that it may be dealt with there: "What? know ye not that your body is the temple of the Holy Ghost which is in you, which ye have of God, and ye are not your own? For ye are bought with a price: therefore glorify God in your body, and in your spirit, which are God's" (6:19-20).

Here is Paul's plea for loyalty, and it is sufficient to make a man stand when otherwise he would fall. In making his greatest argument for holiness and purity, for power to keep the body in subjection, Paul points back again to the place where "ye were not redeemed with corruptible things, as silver and gold, . . . But with the precious blood of Christ, as of a lamb without blemish and without spot" (I Peter 1:18, 19).

An infinite price, the price of His precious blood, suggests in-

finite pain. I can never enlarge upon the physical pain of our Lord
Jesus, great as that must have been. But I don't believe that was by
any means the depth of the horror of the cross. The pain of Christ
was expressed in His cry, "My God, why hast thou forsaken me?"
It was in being made sin for me: coming all the way down to the
shame and agony of the cross, enduring the judgment of a holy
God on the sin that was mine, paying the price I could never pay.

You who have been playing fast and loose with your body, you
who have been letting the standard down and not caring, you who
have allowed the spirit of the age to catch you: remember you have
been bought with a price. Therefore it follows that you are not your
own. The greatest tyrant in life is self: the demand for freedom
from restraint, a "me first" attitude, touchiness and loneliness. But
the Bible says we are not our own, and what a real comfort that is!

Again I say, if you refuse to acknowledge that, you have no right
to claim salvation. If you refuse the implication of His claim upon
you, then what business have you to hide in the shelter of John
3:16? You cannot have the grace of God without the government
of God. Real deliverance demands real holiness. The price of His
precious blood demands a practical surrender of all your body.
You cannot have free salvation unless, as you accept it gladly from
the risen Saviour, you acknowledge, "I am no longer my own; I
am bought with a price."

Then if that is true, let me say this quietly but firmly: you have
no right to injure God's property. "If any man defile the temple of
God, him will God destroy." You have no right to drunkenness,
immorality, uncleanness. You have no right to indulgence or laziness. You have no right to lack of control in any appetite. Furthermore, you have no right to let yourself lie waste. If you belong to
the Lord, then you should be going to work for Him. You have no
right to any reservations, no right to self-government. When Satan
comes with all his insinuations, you must tell him that you are not
your own. Every power and faculty, all the time, is altogether God's.

Paul concludes his argument by saying, "Therefore glorify God
in your body." How can you? By chastity, discipline, temperance
in the way you eat and drink and sleep: whatever you do, do all
to the glory of God. The feet that led you into sin should now
take you to the house of God and to the place of prayer. The eyes

that once looked upon things that aroused lust should now be turned upon your wonderful Saviour. The ears that listened to doubtful stories should now be eager to hear the Word of God. The hands that once squandered your money should now labor in the cause of the Lord Jesus Christ. The tongue that talked so loosely and glibly should now be singing His praises and telling others of His love.

Your body is the sanctuary of the Holy Spirit. Is everything in the temple singing "Glory to God!" today? I could not conclude more appropriately than to remind you of the great words of Paul in the conclusion of his letter to the church at Rome: "I beseech you therefore, brethren, by the mercies of God, that ye present your bodies a living sacrifice, holy, acceptable unto God, which is your reasonable service" (Romans 12:1).

PART II

Dangers on the Journey

THE SECRET OF A HAPPY MARRIAGE

I Corinthians 7:1-22

HERE PAUL begins to answer the questions the people at Corinth had written to him. He has devoted six chapters to dealing with the carnal conditions of the church there. He has laid down principles of action by which to settle these things, and in every instance he has pointed them back again to the cross of Calvary.

They asked him four specific questions. Certain problems of marriage are dealt with in this chapter, and the following three chapters concern the meat sacrificed to idols. Then Paul has something to say about the place of women in the church, and finally, in chapter 11, he discusses the observance of the Lord's Supper. At the conclusion of that he says (I imagine with a sense of relief), "Now concerning spiritual things . . ." as if to deal with these matters had been a troublesome necessity. All the time he had been anxious to get to spiritual things.

In this passage on marriage are some things that have a local background, and apply particularly to the situation at Corinth. But there are also some principles given here which are desperately needed in days like these.

There is language here which is found nowhere else in all the New Testament. For instance, Paul says, "I speak this by permission and not of commandment" (7:6); "And unto the married I command, yet not I, but the Lord" (7:10); "But to the rest speak I, not the Lord" (7:12); "Now concerning virgins I have no commandment of the Lord: yet I give my judgment" (7:25); "She is happier if she so abide, after my judgment: and I think also that I have the Spirit of God" (7:40).

He is clearly drawing a distinction between specific instructions which he has received from the Lord by the Holy Spirit and his own judgment in cases where he has received no such instructions. In other words, he is using his own judgment supported by what he believes to be the authority of the Holy Spirit. That does not invalidate this teaching in any way. It does, however, recognize that in matters concerning marriage there is no law so inclusive as to apply to every situation. Each case will call for the careful exercise of human judgment under the direction and authority of the Holy Spirit.

As a matter of fact, Paul is using here the office of a scribe, who interpreted and applied the law. The Lord Jesus said concerning such men: "Every scribe which is instructed unto the kingdom of heaven is like unto a man which is an householder, which bringeth forth out of his treasure things new and old" (Matthew 13:52).

That is exactly what Paul is doing in this chapter. Remember, please, that he is doing it in the context of the situation at Corinth. For instance, the Gentiles of that time saw no evil whatever in multiplied wives; polygamy was the practice. And the Jews saw no evil in putting away their wives in certain circumstances. After they had returned from captivity in Babylon, many of them took wives of the people of the land, and Ezra commanded that they should put away their foreign wives. Some of the Jews who were converted to the Christian faith thought perhaps they should follow the same principle. Should they put away their unbelieving partner in marriage?

There is much local background, but there are also tremendous principles laid down here for the most sacred relationship in life. Let me ask you to notice, therefore, that Paul speaks first of marriage in its purity. He makes no attempt here to state the Christian doctrine of marriage in all its wonderful fulness; he does that in Ephesians and Colossians, comparing marriage to the relationship between the Lord Jesus Christ and His church.

At first sight, you would almost think Paul is advocating celibacy and undervaluing marriage. But in the context of the Corinthian church he is saying no such thing: their question was, in essence:

"In view of all the immorality, impurity and unhappiness that is rampant in these days, isn't it safer to stay outside the marriage relationship altogether?"

Paul replies that it is good for a man not to be married, but he does not say it is better. In other words, celibacy is proper and good so long as such a person who is unmarried keeps himself pure: "But if they cannot contain, let them marry: for it is better to marry than to burn" (7:9). For the sake of the Kingdom of Heaven and for the cause of the Christian faith, celibacy may be the high and holy calling of God to a man or to a woman.

The Lord Jesus had something very wonderful to say about this: "His disciples say unto him, If the case of the man be so with his wife, it is not good to marry. But he said unto them, All men cannot receive this saying, save they to whom it is given. For there are some eunuchs, which were so born from their mother's womb: and there are some eunuchs, which were made eunuchs of men: and there be eunuchs, which have made themselves eunuchs for the kingdom of heaven's sake. He that is able to receive it, let him receive it" (Matthew 19:10-12). Then in the very next verse the Lord said, "Suffer little children, and forbid them not, to come unto me: for of such is the kingdom of heaven." How wonderfully the Lord links together the glory of men or women who, for the sake of the kingdom, have kept themselves single, and in the next moment He honors marriage and children.

As to marriage itself, Paul insists on monogamy: "Let every man have his own wife, and let every woman have her own husband" (7:2). That is basic to the Christian faith. In that relationship, Paul tells us, there are sacred responsibilities where the conjugal rights of husband and wife are to be respected and honored. Christian marriage is not to be used as an excuse for lust and license, the satisfying of the flesh. He recognizes the intimacy of such a precious partnership when it is centered in the Lord Jesus Christ.

At the heart of these verses we find that in this relationship of Christian marriage there should be love, discipline, and mutual respect, the one for the other. There is a recognized admission of the rights of the wife and husband in the sexual relationship. Deep down at the bottom of it all, there are two lives united together in the

Lord. This is what Paul has to say about the purity of the marriage tie.

In concluding his argument, Paul says that a man should abide in the calling to which God has called him (7:20). If a man, for the sake of the Kingdom of Heaven, determines that he will stand alone, and he believes that to be the calling of God, the evidence that he is not being peculiar or sanctimonious is that he will be given power from God to keep himself pure. But if he cannot do that, let him marry; let him not take a pious position and say, "For the gospel's sake, I am remaining single," and then live in sin. But marriage is not for license or self-indulgence. It is a holy, sacred relationship between man and woman which has to be kept disciplined in love, with mutual honor and respect, in the power of Christ.

Let me ask you again to consider with me, not only marriage in its purity but—oh, how important—marriage in its permanency: "And unto the married I command, yet not I, but the Lord, Let not the wife depart from her husband: But and if she depart, let her remain unmarried or be reconciled to her husband: and let not the husband put away his wife" (7:10-11). In other words, Paul says there is to be no separation; or if there must be a separation, then there must be no remarriage.

Now this, of course, confirms the teaching of our Lord. When the Pharisees came to Him about this, they quoted the law of Moses as the basis of their authority: Moses suffered a bill of divorcement to be written in certain cases. The Lord replied that Moses did that because of their weakness and unbelief, but in the beginning it was not so. "God made them male and female, and for this cause shall a man leave his father and mother, and shall cleave to his wife: and they twain shall be one flesh . . . What therefore God hath joined together, let no man put asunder" (Matthew 19:4-8).

This relationship, which antedates both Christianity and the law of Moses, goes right back to the very beginning of creation as God's purpose for a man and a woman. There was to be only one exception to its permanency, infidelity within the marriage itself. The Lord Himself tells us that the very act of adultery breaks the sanctity of the tie (Matthew 5:32). Therefore there is only one ground for divorce.

I want to have respect for others who may think differently, but, in my judgment, the Bible teaches that the guilty party can never be remarried. Some of my brethren in the ministry (whose convictions I respect deeply, as I trust they will respect mine) will not remarry either party. They say there is no such thing as divorce under any circumstances whatsoever. In the light of the teaching of the Lord and also of Paul, and in the light of the circumstances of each case, I am happy to grant Christian marriage to the innocent party when a marriage has broken down through the adultery of the other party—and concerning which I am satisfied that he or she *is* the innocent party.

There may be circumstances, as verse 11 indicates, when the behavior of one party makes living together an impossibility. So often people come to my study and talk to me about these things, saying, for instance: "I just cannot go on any longer! My husband comes home drunk and beats me up . . . How much longer must I live with that man?" Then I reply, "I think it would be well if you left him today."

Does that shock you? I have authority for it: "If she depart, let her remain unmarried, or be reconciled to her husband: and let not the husband put away his wife" (7:11). There is no reason I can see why a woman should continue to live with a man who has become a drunken sot and whose behavior is making the home a hell on earth; but that is not divorce. Let the innocent person depart, but let her remain unmarried. And let her motive in leaving (as we have already studied in I Corinthians 5:5) be to deliver him to the devil for the destruction of the principle of the flesh and the saving of the soul.

God knows it will be with many a tear and heartache, if she has to take up her roots and leave the man who has treated her so badly. But her whole desire should be for the deliverance of her husband and for his salvation, that the home might yet be restored in the love of Christ. Just think of the confusion were such a person, having left her husband, to remarry, if perhaps years later the man is saved on skid row. He has the right to come back to the woman who has left him and ask her to take him back again. Although in certain circumstances it may be right for one party of a marriage to leave the other, that does not alter the great truth of the Word of God concerning the permanence of the marriage tie.

May I point out just one more thing in the latter part of the chapter: marriage in its power. What comfort these words bring to some who are suffering the awful heartbreak of an unequal yoke! And that is the issue here.

It is possible for a Christian so to forget his responsibilities to God and the commands of His Word that in a moment of excitement he or she is carried away and becomes linked to an unsaved person. That is, however, no ground for divorce. His part, rather, is to do everything he can to win his partner for the Lord Jesus, that, in spite of his sin and disobedience, God may have mercy upon him and extend that mercy to the person to whom he is married. Again, if one party to the marriage is converted after the wedding, both of them being unbelievers when they were married, what mutual understanding and love is necessary! "The woman which hath an husband that believeth not, and if he be pleased to dwell with her, let her not leave him" (7:13).

Perhaps you have just been saved, and you are the first one in your family to become a Christian, your partner being still unconverted. Be careful how you treat him (or her), won't you? Don't nag at him; don't drive religion down his throat and give him a miserable time because you are saved and he isn't. Be patient and tolerant, although the change in your life may make him absolutely furious with you. If you long to see your loved one converted, then be grateful to God for His mercy in your own soul, and pray with all your heart that you may so live in patient love with your husband (or wife) that the very difference in your life may attract him or her to the Lord Jesus.

A colleague of mine in the ministry had just that experience. When his wife was converted, he thought that was just one more burden to an already energy-consuming business career. His wife had gone off her head religiously! Then he discovered within a matter of a few months that she had become so much more patient and gentle, kind and loving. He said to himself, "She has something that I must have," and he found the Saviour too.

That's the way! Thank God for His mercy, and pray that your life-partner may share it. Be infinitely patient and forbearing, but raise the Christian standard high, even though in so doing it makes your husband or wife angrier than ever. If since your conversion God has spoken to you about drinking, gambling, dancing, shows, or other things, and you feel that you cannot now go to these places, your unsaved mate may say in disgust, "If you don't come with me, I'll go out with another woman (or man)." Then you know the sword in your own soul, but the only way to see him saved is to be true to the Lord, no matter what it costs.

Stay together, says Paul in verse 14, because by your conversion the whole family has been brought onto praying ground: "For the unbelieving husband is sanctified by the wife, and the unbelieving wife is sanctified by the husband: else were your children unclean; but now they are holy." As a child of God, you are His vantage point to reach them, and it is not God's will that one of them should perish. I believe that if one party is saved after marriage, that person has every right to claim the salvation of the whole household, even though it takes years.

But if, in spite of everything, the unbeliever goes, then you must let him go. If he does depart, you have no right to be remarried, unless in his departure he himself commits adultery. But if the unbelieving partner of a marriage leaves because he or she cannot stand the testimony of the other, then let him (or her) go, even though it breaks your heart. But you have no right to be remarried; yours is the right to pray that even in his departure he might be brought to know the Lord Jesus, "For what knowest thou, O wife, whether thou shalt save thy husband? or how knowest thou, O man, whether thou shalt save thy wife?" (7:16). If you hold on and pray and believe, you may see God answer prayer exceedingly abundantly above all you can ask or think!

What is the principle behind the power in marriage? It is summed up in the last little phrase in verse 24, "Let every man, wherein he is called, therein abide with God." This reinforces what is said in verse 20: "Let every man abide in the same calling wherein he was called." If God calls a man or woman to remain single, He will give grace for it. If God calls to the married life, and that involves hardship, or maybe a divided home, or even suffering, He will give grace for that too.

The one whose family life is an example to others is to be respected. The one who remains single for the Kingdom's sake is to be respected. The one who suffers the cruel misunderstanding of an unbelieving partner is to be respected, also. In every instance we are to abide in our calling: submitting to the will of God, depending upon the grace of God, making every effort to bring glory to God, striving to be approved by Him, always bearing in mind that one day we shall all stand before the judgment seat of Christ.

CHAPTER 12

HAPPY, THOUGH UNMARRIED

I Corinthians 7:23-40

SOME VERY delicate and difficult problems had been submitted to Paul for his decision and judgment by the church at Corinth. Among them was the whole subject of marriage from the Christian standpoint. Several related questions were treated in the earlier part of this seventh chapter, and now we come to the problems of those who are not married. Paul looks at this from two different aspects: first those who are daughters of Christian parents, and then those who have lost a partner and are left in a state of widowhood.

The Apostle puts a boundary line around what he has to say about this topic: "Now concerning virgins I have no commandment of the Lord" (7:25). We can search the four Gospels thoroughly without finding any teaching from the Lord Jesus concerning the unmarried state except, of course, by implication.

"The wife is bound by the law as long as her husband liveth; but if her husband be dead, she is at liberty to be married to whom she will; only in the Lord. But she is happier if she so abide, after my judgment." Will you please notice that Paul does not say "as long as the man liveth?" He may have died as a husband, although the man is still alive, when he has been unfaithful in the marriage relationship and leaves his partner. If the marriage is broken by the tragedy of adultery, then the one who is left is entitled to Christian marriage. Our Lord taught that perfectly clearly in Matthew 19. Paul concludes the above advice by saying, "I think also that I have the Spirit of God" (7:39-40).

I want to underline something very significant: here Paul distinguishes carefully between "thus saith the Lord," and that which comes by the exercise of his own judgment. However, that qualification does not render what he has to say any less authoritative. He speaks "as one that hath obtained mercy of the Lord to be faithful" (7:25). He gives his judgment from a mind that has been enlightened by the Holy Spirit and taught from the Word of God.

In both instances, in the case of the virgin (the unmarried daughter), and of the widow or the widower bereft of a life-partner, he comes to the same conclusion: "He that giveth her in marriage doeth well; but he that giveth her not in marriage doeth better" (7:38). "She is happier if she so abide, after my judgment" (7:40).

That is quite startling, especially in these days when apparently the unmarried condition is to be avoided at any cost. Some people most inadvisedly put some kind of slight upon those who are single. How could a man speaking under the direction of the Spirit of God come to the conclusion that under certain circumstances it would be better to remain single? That is our question: how to be happy, though unmarried.

As I studied this chapter, it seemed to me that Paul presents a plan to be adopted: "Art thou bound unto a wife? seek not to be loosed. Art thou loosed from a wife? seek not a wife" (7:27). Two words that stand out here are these: "seek not." For instance, consider how dangerous it would be to fall in love with someone whose idea of loyalty to Christ is certainly not the same as your own. Here is the carefully conceived plan of a man who knows how to maintain the situation under the control of the Spirit of God: Paul says, "seek not a wife."

That stands in refreshing contrast to the frenzied search for a life-partner which is conducted by many people today. When one witnesses the frantic efforts made by some to find a mate, one can only trust that the person who is victim of such an assault has retained enough emotional stability to be able to conduct a strategic withdrawal immediately, before he or she becomes deeply involved in the situation. Much wreckage has been caused by the tactics of a person who seeks a life-partner at any price.

Paul has already given us this principle when he says, "All things are lawful unto me, but all things are not expedient: all things are lawful for me, but I will not be brought under the power of any"

(6:12). Here is a man who is really living in victory; he has control over himself by the power of the Spirit of God. In some instances, as in the thirty-sixth and thirty-seventh verses of this chapter, he recognizes that marriage may be necessary: "Nevertheless he that standeth stedfast in his heart, having no necessity, but hath power over his own will, and hath so decreed in his heart that he will keep his virgin, doeth well." Marriage is perfectly lawful; marriage, in some instances, may be necessary; but, Paul says, that is not the issue.

He is able to disassociate himself from the situation and keep a cool head: the real point is, "Is it expedient?" Is it right for the individual in the light of what Paul describes as "the present distress" (7:26)? Now I take that statement to mean not simply the local conditions that existed in Corinth; I rather think Paul meant the tremendous pressures that were being brought to bear upon this little group of believers by the spiritual forces of wickedness. If that was true then, certainly it is equally true today.

Here is the plan that a fellow or a girl who is unmarried should adopt: *seek not*. You do not come for training at a Bible Institute or a Seminary in order to find a wife or a husband. You do not live in order that somehow or other, at any price, you may be married. You must ask yourself if this is something that is going to be expedient in the light of the pressures that are going to come, and in the light of what you believe to be God's will for your life. Know what it means to stand in control of your affections and emotions. This is no easy thing; it requires intense spiritual discipline. If it is difficult, you may ask, why should this plan be adopted?

Paul goes on to show us that there is a purpose to be achieved: "I would have you without carefulness. He that is unmarried careth for the things that belong to the Lord, how he may please the Lord: But he that is married careth for the things that are of the world, how he may please his wife" (7:32-33).

"I would have you without carefulness . . ." he says, "that ye may attend upon the Lord without distraction" (7:32, 35b). Here are two great purposes to be achieved in a man's life. They are possible whether you are married or unmarried, but, in Paul's judgment, easier to achieve if you are single. If a man or a woman enters into the relationship of matrimony, this may result in the interests of each other crowding out the interests of the Lord.

I have known a man called to the mission field, for instance, who

married a girl with no call, and years afterward have seen him sinking into the quicksands of life. The blessing of God had departed
long since; he had missed God's best. I have seen a girl, too, dedicated
to the Lord, but afraid of going through life alone. She entered into
matrimony out of God's will, and it was not very long before her
home and family and immediate circumstances crowded out loyalty
to the Lord Jesus Christ.

Don't tell me such a person is happy! He has to look back upon
the day he made a choice from which there is no escape, and knows
he is living in God's second best. By involving himself in a relationship out of the will of God, he has become full of carefulness; his
interests are in the things of the world and not in the things of the
Lord.

However, that need not always be the case. There is no question,
obviously, but that marriage in the Lord can be a tremendous blessing, a great and wonderful experience. "But and if thou marry," says
Paul, "thou hast not sinned" (7:28). There is no necessity for marriage to put the Lord Jesus in second place. But if it is marriage out
of God's will, and it is going to lead to distracting care, then it is
better, as Paul says, to remain single.

"Without carefulness . . . without distraction." I would lovingly
put those two words into the thinking and conscience of those who
are single. There is a tremendous potential of blessing in serving the
Lord with freedom and concentration. In any event, Paul says, if you
are going to marry, you are going to have trouble (7:28). No matter
how saintly people are and how far they are on together in the
Christian life, when they begin to live together, problems are bound
to come. It is not on the great sorrows or trials that marriage floun-
ders, but rather upon the irritations of everyday difficulties: a crying
child, a late breakfast, a short temper, an unsympathetic mother-in-
law—this kind of thing can cause a marriage to become shaky, unless
right at the very heart of it is the Lord Jesus Himself.

As we think about attending upon the Lord "without carefulness,"
our minds go immediately to that familiar story where the Lord Jesus
spoke to two sisters and said to one of them, "Martha, thou art careful
and troubled about many things," and to the other, "Mary hath
chosen that good part, which shall not be taken away from her."
(Luke 10:41-42).

It is possible, both in the married and in the unmarried state to live without carefulness and without distraction. It is that which makes married life so wonderful and the unmarried state so full of potential blessing.

One other thing I would get out of this passage, perhaps the most important of all: there is a principle to be accepted. You will notice how Paul brings in eternity here: "This I say, brethren, the time is short: it remaineth, that both they that have wives be as though they had none; And they that weep, as though they wept not; and they that rejoice, as though they rejoiced not; and they that buy, as though they possessed not; And they that use this world, as not abusing it: for the fashion of this world passeth away" (7:29-31).

As Paul gives his judgment on this question of being married or unmarried, he shows us the principle upon which a man or woman may make their decision: the times are troubled; the Lord is coming soon; the opportunity for service is brief. Life is short, at best, and it can end quickly and unexpectedly. Therefore these relationships of life should be treated as though they did not exist, in the light of the urgency of these days. He speaks of marriage, of sorrow and joy, of business life, of the world itself, how to use it and how not to use it. Because of the pressures upon us and the spiritual evil confronting us, these things must take second place—almost be regarded as non-existent.

Now Paul is not implying that we should be callous or unkind; that would be totally contrary to all the teaching of the New Testament concerning our relationship with one another. But he does bring the reality of eternity right into everyday life, so that we may live in the ordinary realm with the recognized presence of the Lord Jesus and in the light of heaven.

What does that involve? It means that on the question of being married, everything is to be governed by our relationship to the Lord Himself. For those who are married, there will often be times when the comfort of the home and joy of each other's presence has to be denied, has to take second place for the sake of the Lord, His work and His service.

Sometimes sorrow threatens to take us away from our duty, our loyalty to the King of kings, our service for the Lord. It must not be allowed to do that; if in the time of heartbreak and sorrow we are tempted to give in, these things have to be regarded as though they did not exist. We must press on in the love of God and for the sake of the Lord Jesus.

Sometimes thrilling circumstances make us full of happiness, but if joy conflicts with our duty to the Master, then it has to be swept to one side. Nothing must be allowed to make us neglect or delay, or to be anything less than our best in His service. If business threatens to interfere with the Christian life, says the Apostle, you cannot help going on buying—but be sure that you hold the things you buy very loosely, and that your interest and affections are not centered on them, but on the things of God.

The principle to be observed, as you seek to apply these things to your own life and come to a decision on important matters, is in the two words we have considered already: "seek not," linked with another command of the Lord Jesus: "Seek ye first the kingdom of God, and his righteousness; and all these things shall be added unto you" (Matthew 6:33).

In other words, if in your life you put God first, and His call, even if it seems at the moment it would tear your heart in pieces, if it means denying some human love, turning your back upon some fascinating possibility, then everything that is in the good and acceptable and perfect will of God for you will be added to you.

If only people today, young and old alike, facing these tremendously intimate and personal problems, would follow that principle, seeking first His Kingdom, how wonderful it would be to watch how the Lord, as He is put first, frequently brings into their lives the partner of His choice. He gives to them the persons He has waiting for them as He sees that they are determined above everything else to serve Him without carefulness and without distraction.

Finally, a word of loving concern and warning. You have seen what the Apostle has to say concerning this situation of marriage or singleness, and I have sought to show you that all this should lie within the sphere of the sovereignty of the Lord Jesus. My word of warning is this: to step into any relationship outside the government of the Lord, that is to say, outside His permissive will, is not only to involve yourself in tragedy, but perhaps to bring sorrow into the lives of a generation yet to be born. For a person who enters into marriage out of the will of God and brings children into the world may cause their whole lives to know the blight of unhappiness and misery, because their parents were married out of the will of God.

What a tremendous thing it is to be able, by the grace of God and by the power of His Spirit, to do what Paul did, to stand in victory, in control of his emotions, making the decision he knows to be God's will, that which is expedient in the light of all the pressures upon him. Then whether you are to go through life single or married, you are going to live without carefulness and attend upon the Lord without distraction. May that be your happy portion and mine until our Lord Jesus comes!

CHAPTER 13

SETTING AN EXAMPLE

I Corinthians 8:1-13

ONE OF THE loveliest things about being a Christian, I think, is the fellowship into which we are introduced with others who know and love the same Saviour. It crosses over boundaries of race, class, and background, and draws us together in the precious recognition that we are one in Christ. There is a fellowship about which the unbelieving world knows nothing, a relationship based upon our spiritual union in the body of Jesus Christ, into which all who love Him are placed at the moment of their new birth.

What a tragedy it is when we reveal our low level of Christian experience by allowing divergence of opinion to break fellowship, or by our example cause another Christian to stumble! But it is a wonderful thing when our fellowship in Christ is experienced and expressed so that the desire of our Lord is fulfilled: "By this shall all men know that ye are my disciples, if ye have love one to another" (John 13:35).

I believe that the greatest soul-winning help in the whole world is unity among believers. Likewise the greatest hindrance to soul-winning is division in the Christian church. Therefore our fellowship in the Lord carries with it a tremendous responsibility. A very important yet most neglected aspect of Christian teaching today is the duty we owe our brother and sister in Christ. This is the theme of the chapter now under consideration, in which Paul answers the second question with which the Corinthian church has confronted him.

Let us be clear about the meaning of the question they are raising: he begins, "Now as touching things offered unto idols" (8:1). This subject may seem to have no possible connection with our lives today. However, as we see this in its true light, we begin to realize that it has immense significance for us. Paul devotes no less than three chapters to his answer, applying it to different aspects of Christian living. It brings into clearer view the whole question of the influence of this young church on the great city of Corinth. Indeed, what should be the influence of any Christian group in a pagan community?

From the context, we find that certain portions of the animals that were offered as sacrifices to idols were put on public sale in the market place. Even in Old Testament times, some parts of the animals sacrificed were retained as food for the priests, and the rest consumed by fire as an offering to God. In Corinth, this kind of meat was very common—the parts of the carcasses not offered in the heathen temples were put on sale at cut-rate prices, and human nature, being the same then as now, was always out for a bargain. Therefore the question arising in the minds of these Christians was this: Does the purchase and use of this meat, part of which has been offered to idols, involve us in compromise with idol worship? The fact that they ask the question of Paul certainly shows that they are uncertain and divided about it.

The immediate situation is purely local, but it is not as local as Corinth, nor as ancient as Paul's day, in its application to your life and mine. Each of us faces the same sort of situation six days a week, in one way or another.

Take, for instance, the Christian and his relationship to movies. Some of them, of course, are obviously rotten and filthy, even in the way they are advertised, so that they are no place for the child of God at all. But not all are like that: some are excellent, others are educational, and some have other kinds of value. Therefore, some will argue, is it not all right for a Christian to practice discrimination, to attend only the ones he knows will do no harm? Or if you have television in your home, you know that some things that are shown are bad from beginning to end, but other things are quite good and of educational value. Therefore, surely you can choose what you will watch—that won't do any harm, will it? This is the argument we often hear in favor of the policy of selectivity.

What about the matter of social drinking? Of course it is wrong to drink too much; nobody is going to argue about that. But just one drink in business circumstances, at a luncheon with executives: "Well, you know, it will help in putting over the deal. And it doesn't do me any harm, I know when to stop." So say some Christians. If we set definite limits and know where to draw the line, why isn't an occasional drink permissible for a believer?

Looking at this truth from the opposite angle, the Christian may say, "I believe certain things about my Bible. I have been brought up in a particular school of doctrine and theology, and I accept certain kinds of interpretation. Therefore I must have no fellowship at all with anyone who does not think exactly as I do."

One could quote many things that would portray the same principle: meat offered to idols. The immediate situation has no connection at all, but the principle is relevant to our lives today. This is the question raised.

Then what is the issue involved? Let us look in the first verse: "We know that we all have knowledge." Here is Paul's immediate answer to the question; he says that because we are Christians we all have knowledge. Now he does not suggest that because we are believers in Christ we know everything. He means that, since we have entered into that relationship to Jesus Christ our Lord when we were born again, the Spirit of God within us has shone a floodlight of revelation upon questions like this.

"Concerning therefore the eating of those things that are offered in sacrifice unto idols, we know that an idol is nothing . . . to us there is but one God, the Father, of whom are all things, and we in him; one Lord Jesus Christ, by whom are all things, and we by him" (8:4, 6). Because we are Christians, our eyes have been opened by the Holy Spirit and we know that an idol is not real. There is only one God, our Father, and Jesus Christ our Lord. There cannot be contamination from something that does not exist. In that respect, there can be no harm in eating this meat—we are perfectly free to do it. Of course we are, if that is the only factor involved.

But wait a minute! To make a decision about what is right in these cases based upon what you know because you are a Christian and the Holy Spirit has revealed to you the Word of truth—to make a decision on that alone is dangerous. As a Christian you do not live to yourself, nor do you live only for the Lord. There are others involved in the situation.

"Knowledge puffeth up," says Paul in verse 1, and he goes on to say, "if any man think that he knoweth any thing, he knoweth nothing yet as he ought to know" (8:2). The key that originally opened the door for us to the Holy Spirit's teaching was a broken and contrite heart, when we came to the Lord in repentance and faith. And that is the only kind of life upon which any truth has shone from heaven about anything. A man may think he knows the truth because his intellect has been taught, but he really knows about the things of God only when the Holy Spirit reveals them to his heart. Things he could never have known by study or research become clear, for the Scripture says that God has revealed them to babes and hid them from the wise and prudent.

In other words, the danger is that when God has shown us truth, even through the experience of a broken heart, we might become spiritually proud and conceited. We can say, "Whereas once I was blind, now I see." We can become humble, yet proud of being humble. That kind of pride can lead to spiritual conceit and dogmatism, which is usually accompanied by contempt for anyone who thinks differently.

If I make a decision, therefore, about what I can or cannot do, based merely upon what I know, I shall go wrong, because there is someone else involved. What about my Christian friend? What about the example I set before the unbeliever? What about my fellowship with other Christians?

The unpleasant side of a movie may not affect a Christian; it has no appeal because he is dead to it all in Christ. He has victory over it and is "free from the law, O happy condition!" The Holy Spirit has shown him this, therefore that which used to attract him has no further claim. He very carefully selects and enjoys the film that is instructional or educational. In the light of his relationship to Christ and on that basis alone, he decides. He knows how to discriminate in the use of his television set. When something comes on that he knows he should not see, he turns it off. He quickly recognizes something that his conscience rejects because he has been instructed by the Lord and enlightened by the Spirit.

Similarly, in the matter of social drinking, he says he can take a drink occasionally because he knows when to stop. In Christ, he has victory over it and power over his own will. He can take a drink and it does not affect him. This type of Christian is saying that because

God has met and saved him, and has filled him with His Spirit and
given him victory in Christ, these things make no appeal now, and
therefore he is perfectly free. But he has never begun to think about
other people.

Let us look at the principle at stake here: "Howbeit there is not
in every man that knowledge: for some with conscience of the idol
unto this hour eat it as a thing offered unto an idol; and their conscience being weak is defiled . . . But take heed lest by any means
this liberty of yours become a stumblingblock to them that are
weak" (8:7, 9).

Paul says that knowledge puffs a man up, making him spiritually
conceited and proud. Eventually he comes to the bursting-point, for
anything that is constantly inflated explodes in the end. "But love
edifies [builds up]" (8:1). If a man has knowledge only, then he is in-
capable of judging aright. But if in his life the knowledge of what
God has taught him is mastered by his love for his fellow Christian
and a deep concern for those who do not know the Lord, then that
love leads him to think of others.

The unbelievers watching these Christians at Corinth do not know
that an idol is nothing to them at all. They worship idols, and do not
understand that the Christian is indifferent to them, that they make
no appeal, that to him the idols are not real. To the pagan they are
very real, an important part of his life. If he watches Christians buying food offered to idols, in his eyes they are acknowledging the
reality of that sacrifice and of the gods to whom the meat has been
offered.

The believers, therefore, have to act not only on the basis of the
knowledge that they have, but upon the basis of the love of God
shed abroad in their hearts by the Holy Spirit. The Christian must
recognize that by his example he may be putting a stumblingblock
in the way of a weaker brother, or keeping some person from Christ,
and that is a sin against the Lord Himself: "But when ye sin so
against the brethren, and wound their weak conscience, ye sin against
Christ" (8:12).

In other words, knowledge and spiritual understanding alone may
lead us astray, so that we become smug and sanctimonious and
spiritually proud. To do things which may not be wrong for us,
which may not be harmful, but which may cause others to stumble

or to be offended, making their path to the Lord Jesus the more difficult, is to sin against the Lord Himself.

You may think you can go to that movie alone or watch that show on television, and it may not hinder you at all. You may think you can take your drink and it does not harm you, but there may be a business associate watching you who is on the verge of confessing Christ. Perhaps he is spiritually troubled and concerned, and in his path to the cross you have put a stumblingblock because you are doing something which is causing him to be offended. Love, therefore, must master the Christian's knowledge, and some of the things he may feel he is perfectly entitled to do he will renounce for the sake of others.

Here then is the principle. It is not that you see no harm in doing this or that, but rather that you cannot afford to do it because of what it might do to someone else. You may say you can go to the movies and it will not affect you at all, but what about your friend to whom it has a base appeal? He does not know that it has no effect upon you, and he is watching your example. You can choose your television programs, but how do you know where to draw the line? How do you make this decision, bearing in mind another who is more easily affected by that kind of thing than you are? Are you a stumblingblock in his way to the Lord?

You know when to stop in the matter of social drinking, but does the colleague who attends the same function with you? As he watches you indulging, even though only in a limited way, does he say, "If he can do it, so can I"? Is he not likely to conclude that a Christian is not so very different from other people after all?

Are you cutting off from your fellowship the man who does not agree theologically with you in everything you say? Are you going to regard him as accursed, or show him the love of God in your heart and through your life? You owe him a ministry that only a Spirit-filled Christian can bring, the love of the Lord Jesus Christ.

Out of this answer of Paul to the Corinthian church on the matter of sacrifice to idols emerges a tremendously significant aspect of the Christian life. What sort of example are you setting as a child of God in your immediate circle of friends? Is the Lord asking you to forego something that you consider perfectly harmless for the sake of someone who is watching your life critically? If you were to face that one thing in your life, it might remove a block in the way of someone. One step to the cross would be made easier for another because the Lord Jesus is revealed in your life the more clearly now that you are taking a stand.

Christian fellowship is a lovely gift, but it carries great responsibilities. Being all one in Christ is precious, but we have to make our every decision not only in regard to our relationship to the Lord Jesus, but also in regard to our relationship to our brother and sister in Christ. Have you thought about that in terms of your entertainment, of what you eat and drink, of where you go and what you watch?

Jesus Christ said, "Greater love hath no man than this, that a man lay down his life for his friends" (John 15:13). He Himself had an even greater love, for He laid down His life for His enemies at Calvary. But that is the principle upon which you are called to live as a child of God in the light of the cross, to lay down your life for your friends, to forfeit things that you may consider to be perfectly legitimate in order that your friends may find the way to Jesus more easily. That is just what will happen. If you lay down your life as a mat for other people to walk on, there will be plenty who will come around and say, "You are too narrow!" There are others who will insist that you are compromising by your fellowship with others who do not agree on some points of doctrine. But the master principle is not what you know by revelation, but how you love by the impartation of the Holy Spirit. It doesn't matter what others think if you can look into the face of your lovely Lord and hear Him say, "Well done!"

As you go out into your daily life, remember others are watching: not only your Lord in heaven, but the person by your desk, in your home, on your street, in the hospital, or at your school. God is asking you to make your decisions about what you do or what you don't do, not only in the light of what He has taught you, but in the light of how it is going to affect the approach of others to Calvary.

Perhaps I should add that as far as I personally am concerned, there is no room in my life at all for movies, television, social drinking or anything else of that character. But my reason for abstention is not based upon a legalistic argument which only serves to create a vacuum in the life of the one submitting to it, but rather upon love to the Lord Jesus Christ which involves total consecration of time, money and everything I am to Him, and also upon my concern for my brethren in Christ, and especially for the young convert, before whom I would ever seek to be an example for His sake.

CHAPTER 14

THE GENUINE ARTICLE

1 Corinthians 9:1-27

IT WOULD seem strange that Paul has to defend his authority at a place like Corinth. As he wrote earlier, "I have planted, Apollos watered; but God gave the increase" (3:6). Here he reminds them again, "Are not ye my work in the Lord?" (9:1). Is it possible that they are the seal of his apostleship and yet they question his authority?

But the evidence of spiritual authority is not success—that is where we go wrong. We judge a Christian by his success, and that is not the basis of heaven's judgment upon any of us; the issue is much deeper than that. It is not enough that Paul had founded the church at Corinth: "You should be adequate evidence; why should I have to say more than that?" He is prepared to face them and give clear reasons for the spiritual unction that rested upon his life and testimony: "My answer to them that do examine me is this" (9:3), he says, and throughout the chapter he proceeds to give his credentials.

"To examine" means to make a searching scrutiny. It is the same word used of Pontius Pilate in his "examination" of Christ. Every Christian must expect the same treatment. We will be examined by people who do not accept the reality of our gospel; we live in the glare of the searchlight. We have no right to expect to be hidden from the world, and that world is going to judge Christianity by those who represent it. The believer will be submitted to a careful scrutiny day and night by his colleagues and friends concerning the quality of his Christian life.

Of course, there are situations in which it is altogether wrong for a Christian to vindicate himself, to stand up for his rights. But that is not the issue here. If a man is to stand the test as a child of God—not merely as a minister, but as a Christian anywhere—he must be able to produce credentials to indicate that he is genuine. I believe the world is tired of religion that is a sham. People want to see in the hearts and lives of those who profess Christ the characteristics of the genuine article. Unless these marks are upon our testimony, others will not desire our Lord. Therefore we must ask ourselves if there is something in our life that gives indisputable answer to those who raise a query concerning this Christian gospel of ours.

We are not to be judged by our success nor by the number of conversions produced by our ministry. We are not to be judged by our creed or doctrine, for people are not primarily interested in what we believe. We are not to be judged by our orthodoxy nor by the particular associations which we may keep in the fellowship of the Christian church. There is one thing by which a Christian is going to stand or fall, and that is his reality with God. Are the marks of Holy Spirit unction about him in his daily walk? Is there a clear and authentic ring to his testimony so that, although people may not agree with what he says or how he lives, they cannot dispute the fact that the man is close to God?

This was Paul's argument, and he produces here three clear statements to defend his apostleship. In considering them we must ask ourselves if there is the same stamp of genuineness about each one of us.

In the first place, every Christian has a right to certain things in life. He has a right to food; he has a right to love, to a family, to a home; he has a right to decent pay; he has a right to recreation and physical activity. He has as much right to these things as anyone else. But Paul is saying that one mark of Christian discipleship is that he has completely renounced his right to these things.

"Have we not power to eat and drink?" (9:4). Of course he had a right to normal rations. "Have we not power to lead about a sister, a wife, as well as other apostles"—especially Peter? (9:5). They all thought very highly of that disciple in Corinth, for some had said, "I am of Peter." He was married; has not Paul the right to be married, also? Has he not the right to romance, to a home and family life?

"Have not we power to forbear working?" (9:6). Of course he

has a right to normal recreation. He has the right to care for his body, to have physical exercise, to take time off and enjoy it. "They which preach the gospel should live of the gospel" (9:14). Had he not the right to expect that as he preached, he was paid for it? Was he not entitled to normal remuneration, just as anybody else?

Then in verse 15 he makes a tremendous statement: "But I have used none of these things." The Lord Jesus was dearer to Paul than anything else, and he could stand before them and say that he had renounced every one of his rights. The test of apostleship is one that many of us will find very difficult to attain.

Many of our missionary family, however, have denied themselves the right to a normal life. Of every one of them it can be said that they have a right to an adequate salary, to a Christian home, to good food, to reasonable recreation. But each of them can say, "I have used none of these things for the sake of the gospel." We could go to any part of the world and find examples of those who come within this test of apostleship today.

Many of us are in the place where we are because we believe we are in the will of God, but are we there at the loss of even one meal for the sake of Jesus? Has your Christian testimony cost you anything? You have a right to good food, of course, but have you ever denied yourself one meal that something extra might be given to the Lord, or that extra time might be spent in prayer and the Word? That is the practical meaning of fasting.

You are entitled to human love, a wife or husband, a home and children. Perhaps there was a time in your life when you knew God was calling you in one direction and you were involved in a legitimate romance with someone who would call you in another, and at the cost of breaking your heart you let your love go for the sake of the gospel. You were perfectly entitled to that romance, because the other person was a Christian, but he or she was not called to do the thing to which you were called, and you renounced that which was your right for Jesus' sake.

You have a right to adequate pay, but as an evidence of the reality of your Christian testimony you are working for about a third of what you could be earning—because you are in Christian work. Thank God in your heart that whenever people raise the question about your Christian life, you bear the mark of authenticity because you have said "no" to things that are normal and right for the sake of your Lord; you have renounced your claims.

"What things were gain to me, those I counted loss for Christ," was the testimony of Paul thirty years after this Corinthian letter, when he was writing to the church at Philippi. He was able to say that the experience was still true of him: "Yea doubtless, and I count all things but loss for the excellency of the knowledge of Christ Jesus my Lord" (Philippians 3:7-8).

Paul vindicates his apostleship by pointing out things that were absolutely legitimate, but to which he has said "no" for the Lord's sake. Within the scope of that test, what counts is not my doctrine or my orthodoxy, or my connections, but that my heart and life bear the brand of the cross: it has cost me something to follow Jesus.

But there is something else, for Paul says, "Though I preach the gospel, I have nothing to glory of: for necessity is laid upon me; yea, woe is unto me, if I preach not the gospel!" (9:16). He is able to face those who question his authority with the fact that he has maintained a testimony. This is an obligation which is laid upon every one of us.

Have we maintained a clear testimony through the years of our life as a Christian? Has it been kept true and clean? Is our ministry being maintained? Is our testimony above question? If that were made a condition of church membership, I wonder how we would fare. It certainly is made a test of fellowship with the Lord Jesus. Woe is me if I testify not to the Saviour of the world! There will be lost communion and fellowship with Christ, lost opportunties, a fruitless life.

Paul had maintained his testimony, and this is how he did it: "Unto the Jews I became a Jew" (9:20-22). He observed their law; he put himself voluntarily under their obligations in order that he might win them for Christ.

To the Gentiles he became as one of them in their freedom, yet he never forgot that he was the Lord's bond-slave and therefore under His authority. Paul did not compromise his position in the sight of heaven, but he went right alongside those men in their need and sin to win them for Jesus.

To the weak he became as one weak. He refused to use his liberty as a Christian in any way that might become a stumblingblock or

lead another astray. "I am made all things to all men, that I might by
all means save some" (9:22). He maintained his ministry by going
anywhere and everywhere, no matter what the situation and surroundings were, to reach people with the message. He crossed over
boundaries of prejudice in race and religion to win men and women
for Jesus Christ.

I do not wish to be uncharitable, but isn't it sad that in so many instances Christian people move in their own little watertight com-
partments and never launch out into somebody else's situation at all?
They are locked in; their circle never touches the circles of unbelievers. They move only in their little circle of Christian fellowship; very seldom do they take the plunge outside in order to win
another for Christ. I believe perhaps the greatest need of all in our
evangelical circles today is that we might have the boldness in Christ
to cross some of the barriers that exist to win others for Him. "Woe
is unto me if I preach not the gospel!" says Paul.

But there is another acid test that Paul applies here. He exposes
something in his life about which we would know nothing unless he
told us. There is an enemy he has been wrestling with: "I therefore
so run, not as uncertainly; so fight I, not as one that beateth the air:
But I keep under my body, and bring it into subjection: lest that by
any means, when I have preached to others, I myself should be a
castaway" (9:26-27).

J. B. Phillips, in his *Letters to Young Churches*, paraphrases it like
this: "I am no shadow-boxer, I really fight! I am my body's sternest
master, for fear that when I have preached to others I should myself
be disqualified."

I do not think for a moment that Paul was concerned that he
should be lost, but he was desperately concerned that God might remove his testimony and take him from his place of opportunity and
witness because deep down in his heart he had been failing to contend
with the enemy. Perhaps this is the greatest battle any child of God
has to face.

In connection with this whole issue of preaching a so-called
"gospel of works," I would say that the only faith that matters is a
faith that is expressed in the action of your body. The faith that has
qualified a man for heaven gets into his feet, his hands, his mind, his
tongue—in other words, it is expressed in the physical. If his faith

in Jesus Christ does not begin to make his whole body move in the will of God, there is no evidence that it is saving faith at all. It is how a Christian uses his body that proclaims his eternal destiny. That is why Paul says these tremendous things, "I buffet my body; I keep it in subjection." Like any athlete daily keeps himself in training behind the scenes to win an earthly crown, he keeps his body down.

Do you qualify for apostleship under this test? In that body of yours that has not yet been redeemed, what is happening? Are you, as the apostle said of himself, keeping your body in subjection? It is possible for a child of God to be indwelt by the Holy Spirit, yet to be mastered by the flesh. It is possible for appetites and indulgence, all the claims of the body, to rule the life of the child of God.

As other people examine our lives, do they see that you, as a Christian, have left behind certain things to which you are entitled for Jesus' sake? Do they see you as one who is maintaining an unblemished testimony? You have not let down the standards, and you are taking the gospel message out to an ungodly world. But do they see above all a man (or woman) who is triumphing in his own personal walk because he is not allowing the flesh with its appetites and intemperance to dominate his life, a man living under the control of the Spirit of God? These are the authentic marks of Christian experience.

But even the Apostle Paul could never have expressed those things in his life were it not that within him was the indwelling life of the risen Lord Jesus which enabled him to do so. It is true that Paul renounced his rights, but what about the Saviour? The Lord Jesus counted it not a thing to be grasped after to be equal with God, but laid aside every right He had and came down all the way to the cross. It is true Paul maintained his ministry, but what about the Lord? He set His face steadfastly toward Jerusalem and refused to be diverted from a ministry that cost Him his life. It is true Paul engaged the enemy at close quarters and kept his body in subjection, but what about the Lord Jesus? In the wilderness and in the garden, on the dusty road and on the cross, in every detail and at every moment, He answered every accusation of the enemy by quoting from the Word of God, and stood against every temptation that would take Him from God's will until He defeated Satan at Calvary, and from the open tomb.

Perhaps you have been saying to yourself, "I don't know whether I can pass the tests—I'm not sure if I've renounced anything for Jesus. I'm not sure about my ministry; I don't know about this battle with the enemy." But the Holy Spirit within you, my friend, will give you power to renounce your life for Jesus' sake. He will give you unction to maintain your ministry and testimony; He will give you courage to combat Satan at close quarters and defeat the enemy of your soul.

CHAPTER 15

OVERCOMING PITFALLS IN THE WAY

1 Corinthians 10:1-14

IN OUR LAST study Paul was defending his apostleship against those who refused to recognize his authority. He had spoken very firmly to the church at Corinth, for his ministry and whole apostolic authority were under question. Above everything, he had told them something that they would never have known otherwise: "I keep under my body, and bring it into subjection: lest that by any means, when I have preached to others, I myself should be a castaway" (9:27).

As Paul said that, he was exposing the soul of a Christian, for it was something that went on in the inner part of his life. Not that he feared to lose his relationship with the Lord, but he was concerned lest he should lose his apostleship. He feared that somehow the sense of unction might in some strange, irrevocable manner be taken from him, the sense of divine authority, the knowledge that God was speaking to him, the consciousness of Holy Spirit power in his testimony. If that went from him, he knew that he would have nothing left, for this was the evidence of his approval before God and his authority before men.

This holy fear ought to possess not only the apostle but every Christian, the fear that somehow we might so live and so grieve the Spirit that we become like Samson, who went out in imagined strength and knew not that the Spirit of the Lord had departed from him. It is possible that the evidence of real power and supernatural authority may be lost.

This is something that every Sunday school teacher ought to

dread, every mother who has the care of little children, every man witnessing for Christ in the business world. It is something that every child of God ought to fear. If we lose our "thus saith the Lord," our unquestionable mark of integrity, our Holy Spirit life and liberty, what have we left?

You may have natural ability, great personal charm and much education, but if as a child of God you lose that thing which Paul dreaded to lose—that sense of heavenly authority about his life—you have nothing left that can bring a soul near to Jesus. We can never lose His presence, for He is near and ever will be until He takes us to heaven; but we may stumble and fall, so slip in our Christian life that we lose His power and unction.

The Sunday school teacher will speak to the same little group of children, but there is no spiritual effectiveness to her teaching. The businessman may witness to others of Christ, but it is all just talk. The mother may lead her little family in prayer, but she has lost the power that grips their hearts to win them for Jesus. To lose that is to become a sounding brass or a tinkling cymbal. This is what Paul meant when he climaxed his whole warning by saying, "let him that thinketh he standeth take heed lest he fall." On this royal route to heaven there is many a pitfall, and the devil's great objective is to cause the child of God to stumble, to be tripped up so that he loses the power of the Holy Spirit in his witness. When he has lost that, Satan knows, if we do not, that he is helpless.

To illustrate this great truth, Paul draws upon an Old Testament story, the experience of his own nation: "All these things happened unto them for ensamples . . . to us upon whom the ends of the world are come" (10:11). These things happened that they might be a warning and example to us who live in an age which is rapidly folding up, the sunset age, when the night will soon be upon us and no man can work. As Paul goes back to the Old Testament illustration, he points out the great privileges of God's people, and yet the tragedy of their failure and collapse on the journey.

Great are our privileges, and therefore great are our responsibilities, and all the more tragic is it indeed when the child of God loses the authority of the Spirit. What peril we are in when we begin to trust in our privileges, in our Christian home, in our Christian fellowship, without recognizing that they bring us tremendous responsibilities which we must accept or become castaways.

Will you notice that as Paul introduces this theme, he underlines the great sweep of God's love for His people. The first four verses show what immense privileges were those of the people of God. Notice the frequent repetition of the word "all": they were all under the cloud; they all passed through the sea; they were all baptized into Moses; they did all eat the same spiritual meat; they did all drink the same spiritual drink. Every one of them, the feeble, the strong, the sick, the weak—every one of them was brought through. They all experienced the wonderful guidance and protection of God under the cloud. They all knew the deliverance of God from Egypt through the Red Sea.

"They were all baptized into Moses," which is a quaint way of saying that God's purpose for His people was that they should be united and disciplined, linked together under the leadership of one man. They were made into an entity, a community, and ultimately into a great nation.

"They did all eat the same food, and they all drank the same drink"; they were all sustained by the same supernatural power which gave them manna every morning and water from the rock. And there was not one casualty; they owed everything to the supernatural power of their God, Jehovah. There was not a thing that they could do for themselves—everything about that journey was humanly impossible—it was all of Him.

What a picture that is of the privileges of the child of God today: no matter how weak and ineffective, how poor and isolated and useless we may feel, all of us are under His guiding hand. We have all been delivered out of the bondage of sin by the blood shed at Calvary. We have all been baptized into our Moses, into the body of Christ. All of us have been sustained by manna from heaven and by the river of life from the throne of God. You notice Paul says in his Old Testament illustration, "that Rock was Christ."

These tremendous ties bind us one to another in Jesus; the deepest things in our lives we share together. We are not left to be an unruly mob of individuals, unguided and unprotected. We have had the cleansing of His blood, the forgiveness of our sins. We have experienced baptism into the fellowship of the body of Christ. We have known what it is to feed upon His Word, and to drink of the living water from heaven. We are all being sustained by the grace of God, and we have done nothing to deserve it at all.

Then the question coming to mind at once is this, "If that is so, how can such a people ever fail?" But the fact is, the greater the height, the greater the fall. Therefore Paul goes on to point out the seriousness of their failure: "But with many of them God was not well pleased" (10:5).

With many of them? How many? I would say that is about the classic understatement of the Bible, if I may dare say such a thing concerning the Word of God. Nearly three million came out of Egypt. With how many of them was God not pleased? With all except two! Only two who came out of Egypt entered into the land of blessing; only two of that generation went right through with the purpose of God—Caleb and Joshua.

The others were "overthrown" in the wilderness. That same word is used in that graphic incident in the life of Jesus Christ when He entered into the Temple and saw the people exchanging money and selling sacrifices. He took a whip and overthrew the tables of the money-changers, scattering them all over the court of the Temple.

That is what happened to the people of God; they were scattered, overthrown. They were to have been a united people, but soon they were scattered and disintegrated. Why shouldn't that privileged people have kept together and gone right through to the Promised Land? Paul leaves us in no doubt: he shows us four things that spell out tragedy, not only to the people in Moses' time, but in the lives of believers today.

The first of them is lust. We must not confine that word to the narrow meaning that is put upon it these days in a moral sense. The full story is in Numbers 11: the desire of those people en route to the land of blessing was for something out of the will of God. He provided for them all the food they needed, but they wanted more—something different, a change of diet. They asked for something which was perfectly legitimate, but which was not provided for them in the plan of God. He knew what was best for them, but they demanded their way, and God gave them what they wanted.

What a tremendous statement that is in the Psalms where David, recounting the history of God's people, says, "He gave them their request; but sent leanness into their soul" (Psalm 106:15).

In the beginning of human history, when Eve saw that the tree was good for food, and a tree to be desired to make one wise, she took, and ate, and gave to her husband. That is always true: the first thing that takes men away from God is a desire for something other than what God has planned for them. And desire leads to participation, because no one ever sins all alone; he tries to involve someone else. That which started the whole trouble in the world is the thing which has disintegrated Christian fellowship ever since.

God always meets a man on the level of his desire. If we hunger and thirst after righteousness, God will fill us with the fruit of it. He satisfies the longing soul and fills the hungry with good things. But if we desire something out of the will of God, He will give us that, too. If we persist in refusing God's plan and demand something that is out of His will, then He gives us what we want but, terrifying truth, He also sends leanness to our souls. The mark of spiritual authority vanishes, the ring of integrity departs; the one thing that distinguishes a Christian, a man of God, from other people, leaves us.

Paul says that Israel disintegrated with idolatry: "Neither be ye idolaters, as were some of them" (10:7a). The story is in Exodus 32. When Moses had been a long time on the mountaintop with God, the people became restless. Aaron, who had been left in charge, eventually received their gold and jewelry, melted it, and fashioned a calf. When Moses came down and questioned him about this, Aaron said, in effect, "All I did was take the people's gold and jewelry— when I flung it all into the furnace, out came this calf!" (Exodus 32:24).

I don't believe it operated like that! Aaron deliberately set up something in the place of God, pretending it was unintentional, that it really happened by accident. But it was idolatry; he knew what was going to come out of the furnace. And the people worshiped it, they "sat down to eat and drink, and rose up to play" (10:7b). In other words, they substituted play time for prayer time, indulgence for reality; they took the sacrifice out of their religion and made it comfortable and easy.

The third word I find here is "fornication": "Neither let us commit fornication, as some of them committed, and fell in one day three and twenty thousand" (10:8). That story is in Numbers 25, where we find wrong relationship, an unequal yoke with ungodly people. Their standards, which had gradually been lowered, ceased to exist altogether, and they made marriages (and worse than marriages)

with ungodly people, the people of Moab. They became guilty of
illicit relationships which are utterly contrary to God's will, but
which are related in God's Word, that it may be faithful in exposing
the human heart as it really is.

The last word is "unbelief": "Neither let us tempt Christ . . .
Neither murmur ye . . ." (10:9, 10). The story is from Numbers 21.
The people had become weary of the journey, they had become sour
on the whole project of going to the Promised Land.

How often we find Christians living in sourness instead of radiance,
without hunger for God's Word, lacking desire for the royal route
to heaven! Let us humble ourselves before Him and be honest. We
have wrestled against the will of God and desired things out of His
plan. All too often we have put something in His place, as well. We
have allowed wrong relationships. We have complained and grum-
bled about the journey, that it was too hard.

Now the result is that the evidences of God's power have departed altogether, and that is why others are not being won for Jesus
Christ. That is why the Sunday school class seems to be so unruly
and unresponsive. That is why our immediate circle seems to be so
unreached by our testimony.

Oh, the privileges we have thrown away! The responsibilities we
have failed to accept! Is that true of your life today? But the downward process can be stopped; the tide can be turned. There can come
again the authority which once you knew, the power which you
once had.

How? Because there is a secret of deliverance in the Lord Jesus:
"There hath no temptation taken you but such as is common to man:
but God is faithful, who will not suffer you to be tempted above
that ye are able; but will with the temptation also make a way to
escape, that ye may be able to bear it. Wherefore, my dearly beloved, flee from idolatry" (10:13-14).

In this journey on which we are all fellow travelers through the
wilderness of this life, we may have fallen into pitfalls; we may have
been tripped up. God does not say He will remove the pitfalls nor
that He will not permit you to fall. But what He does say is that it
need not happen. The man who falls into temptation knows that it
need not have happened. Just a moment's desire for something out
of God's will, and he has slipped; he knows it could have been
stopped, if only . . . if only what?

God will not remove from you the temptation that is common to all. But He tells you that you are not unique; if today you feel beaten and baffled, utterly at the end of your rope, God is still faithful in everything. He has no pets! All the Israelites came out of Egypt under the cloud; they were all protected and sustained.

Temptation will always be graded to the fiber of your life. God will not allow it to go on a moment longer, nor to be more severe than you can take, for He knows your needs. Why did He suffer the manners of His people in the wilderness? So that He might prove them and humble them, that He might show them the sin in their hearts, that they might see their helplessness and learn to depend completely upon Him.

That is why He allows things to happen to you, that He might show you how absolutely corrupt, sinful, and hopeless you are in yourself, that you might know that in your flesh dwells no good thing. Temptation will be sent along the particular line that God knows you need in order that He might draw you to Himself, but the way of escape is guaranteed. "He will with the temptation *also* make a way to escape."

Check it in your own life and experience—every time temptation comes, there has been a way out, hasn't there? Every time Satan has hit, there has been a way through the temptation, if you had chosen it. Not before it or after it, but alongside it, right with the fiery dart that comes into your life, at that very moment there is a way of victory.

Sometimes the only way of escape is to run for your life. "Wherefore . . . flee from idolatry." Where do we run? Into the arms of Jesus, the only place of safety. That is not cowardice; sometimes it is evidence of strength and spiritual maturity, the sign that you are growing in grace. It is in the presence of Christ that authority and unction are restored. When there is renewed power and grace, from your life will flow again the rivers of living water in blessing to others.

CHAPTER 16

RULES FOR THE ROAD

I Corinthians 10:15-33

WE HAVE now traveled many miles on the royal route to heaven, and should have learned many lessons. This journey involves a Christian in many problems. It certainly is not easy; it is narrow and dangerous, and we are prone to slip and stumble. The man who would walk this way is much watched by others, much criticized and misunderstood. But in his heart is a conviction that nothing can ever shake: on this royal route to heaven he is walking with God.

In the course of a life that is lived like this, inevitably there are questions arising as to what to do in this situation or that. I wonder if any of us have gone through one day without having been faced with some kind of problem: a decision when to do this or that, whether to act this way or that way, how to react in a certain situation, what choice to make, what company to keep.

It is not easy to know how we should walk on the royal route to heaven, and therefore God has provided rules of the road. You cannot go along any highway without regulations, and there are rules for Christian living which, if you break them, result in disgrace to your own life, disaster in the lives of others, and dishonor to the name of the Lord.

In our portion for study Paul gives us three rules of the road. The point at issue would seem to be something very remote from our sphere of living today. Paul dealt with it in some measure in chapter 8, and now he brings to the climax what he has to say concerning meat offered to idols.

Here is the case of a believer who has been asked out to dinner with unsaved friends, and he accepts the invitation. I am so glad Paul underlines the fact that we are permitted to do so; it is tragic that so many Christian people just dare not to go into an unbeliever's home in case they get contaminated. Now Paul says, "If any of them that believe not bid you to a feast, and ye be disposed to go" (10:27a), then go and enjoy yourself.

The life of the people of Corinth was so mixed up with idolatry that it was difficult for a Christian to know where to draw the line. Paul maintains that a believer may go and eat and enjoy it, and when meat is put before him he is to "eat, asking no questions for conscience sake" (10:27b). In other words, he is not to ask where it came from, for that would be rude. But if the host intimates that this was meat offered to idols, then he should not touch it. If the host mentions it to his guest, quite clearly he attaches some importance to it. Therefore the Christian must not be identified with him in idol-worship, and must abstain from eating the meat. If nothing is said about it, and the guest knows nothing about the origin of the meat, then he is not to start trouble by asking; he is free from any possible compromise. That is the point at issue.

Isn't that far removed from us? Not so far as you think! This introduces us at once to the first rule of the road: "Let no man seek his own, but every man another's wealth" (10:24). In other words, live sacrificially for other people. You are saved not only that you might serve the Lord but that you might live before other people so that nothing you do, in your actions or reactions, will cause offense.

You will be able to go into the homes of non-Christian people and eat with them, converse with them; you will move among them in a natural manner, but never for one moment will you lower your standard of Christian living. You will do nothing that will put any kind of hindrance in the way of another, nothing that will be a stumblingblock to him. Your first concern is the spiritual wealth of that person. It may be a social date or it may be a formal occasion, but deep down in your heart your one purpose is that you might enrich that man spiritually. You are on the King's business, and He grants no vacations. This is the first rule of the road.

I would pause a moment to underline something: it is clear from the teaching of the apostle here that the Christian as an individual, or the Christian fellowship as a group, is not called upon to live in some watertight compartment, innoculated against possible contamination through contact with unconverted people. Rather, we are to move among them, talk with them, live with them—but always maintain the standard of Christian living. Principles must never be lowered; stumblingblocks must never be put in the way of an unbeliever. The one objective on every occasion is not a social contact; rather, the great concern of the child of God is the spiritual enrichment of his friend. The Christian's mission in this world is not primarily seeking smugly to make himself more holy, but through contact with an unbelieving world to do everything in his power to win others to Jesus Christ.

Now, of course, if we accept this as the rule of the road, it will cause us to break through many barriers, leap over many walls, and enter many different circles. The Christian is called upon to launch out into uncharted areas among ungodly people and never to fear. He is to go there because God is sending him that he might reach others for Christ, and this situation may be fraught with great peril. How is he going to associate with them and not lower his Christian principles and standards? How is he going to mix with unconverted people and yet himself stand true?

The second rule of the road takes us back a few verses: "The cup of blessing which we bless, is it not the communion of the blood of Christ? The bread which we break, is it not the communion of the body of Christ? For we being many are one bread, and one body: for we are all partakers of that one bread" (10:16-17).

If you apply the first rule of the road, and begin to break through into the circles of ungodly people and associate with them, immediately you will face the problem of maintaining your testimony. What is to be the guiding factor in your behavior?

We have seen previously how time and time again Paul takes us back to the cross, and he does it again here: "The communion of the blood of Christ . . . the communion of the body of Christ." To observe the first rule of the road would be disastrous unless we constantly recognize that we start out from Calvary. We must remember that in our new life our fellowship is not with the world and its ungodly people, but with the Lord Jesus in His death and resurrection.

This teaching is particularly important for those in training for the ministry and the mission field, but every Christian needs to understand it. Paul is saying to the Corinthian believers that they have a table, a special fellowship and sustenance: "Behold Israel after the flesh: are not they which eat of the sacrifices partakers of the altar? . . . But I say, that the things which the Gentiles sacrifice, they sacrifice to devils, and not to God: and I would not that ye should have fellowship with devils . . . ye cannot be partakers of the Lord's table, and of the table of devils" (10:18-21).

This may sound as if it contradicts what Paul has already said, but it does not. He draws here an important distinction to which Christian people today have apparently shut their eyes: our fellowship is at Calvary, but our contact must be with the world. Our fellowship is with the Lord Jesus, but our friendship is for those who do not know the Saviour. Our fellowship is in the blood shed on the cross, in the body of Jesus broken for us, but in His name we become all things to all men that by all means we might win some. The love of Christ constrains us and we should be willing to go anywhere, if only in so doing we might win a soul for Jesus.

In other words, Paul distinguishes between our associations and our fellowship, between our contacts and our communion. Some people do not understand that. If a Christian moves in ungodly circles, has a meal with an unsaved person, goes to the house of unbelieving friends, or has social contact with them, immediately the world says (or worse still, his Christian friends say), "He is lowering the standard, he is having fellowship with unbelievers." He is doing nothing of the kind! His fellowship will stay at Calvary and his heart in tune with God while for the sake of the Lord Jesus he moves into contact with ungodly people that he might win them for Him.

The second rule of the road, therefore, is to live in separation to God. This is something that only you and I as individual Christians can discern when we are right before God. If I move in ungodly circles and discover that my heart is going out to the things they enjoy, if I realize that I am faltering in my devotion to the Lord Jesus, if I am beginning to hanker after the things of the world, then this rule of the road comes with shattering authority to tell me that I must stop. It is impossible to belong to Christ and live in the enemy's camp. Absolute separation to God is demanded, but remember that separation is not isolation.

Separation can include an openhearted outreach in the name of a crucified, risen Saviour. As the child of God moves among others, speaks to others, is in contact with others who do not think as he does, deep down in his heart his fellowship is with the Lord, and in that situation he is kept by the power of God, although others may accuse him of compromise if he associates with idolaters and unbelievers. But if someone doesn't go to them, how are such people ever to be won for the Lord?

The second rule of the road is to be applied in both directions. You must watch your behavior as you make contact with the world, the unbelievers, the people who don't think as you do. Be careful all the time that your fellowship and communion with the Lord is being kept. You must be certain that your heart is right with God, that you are clear and transparent in your relationship with Him, then in all your contacts you are conscious of His everlasting arms around you, and you know He is keeping you by His power. But if that is not true, then you must retrace your steps and get back to Calvary; you must break any possibility of *fellowship* with unbelievers. Will you watch that danger?

On the other hand, you must watch the danger of being so wrapped up in contemplation of the Lord Jesus that you never dare venture out of your "reserved compartment" to seek out souls in His name.

The third rule of the road is to be found in the closing part of the chapter, which is really the climax of the whole argument: "Whether therefore ye eat, or drink, or whatsoever ye do, do all to the glory of God" (10:31). We are not to do some things for the glory of ourselves, to make a name or a reputation. We must maintain a singleminded purpose for the glory of the Saviour.

The child of God who is observing these three rules: sacrificial living for others, separation unto God, singlemindedness of purpose for the glory of the Lord, as he faces many questions almost every day of his life, before making a decision, he will ask himself three things.

First, "Is it a stumblingblock to other people?" For if it is, we must cut it out, because of our concern for their welfare. Then, "Can I ask the blessing of the Lord Jesus Christ on this action that I take?" If we cannot expect Him to bless us in it, then we will not do it, for the blessing of the Lord makes us rich and adds no sorrow—we dare not live for a moment without the sense of His fellowship. After that, we ask ourselves, "Can I do this thing for the glory of God?" If not, then we cannot do it at all. In other words, all this talk today about participating in everything, just taking it a little gently, is not for the Christian who seeks to please His Lord. A Christian is to live boldly, but with a life that maintains absolutely clear-cut principles.

These are simple rules, but to break them brings disaster to yourself, disgrace to your testimony, and dishonor to the Lord. Keep them, and you will experience the liberty of the child of God, free from the condemnation of the law, but, as Paul says in the last chapter (9:21), under the law to Christ. Oh, the blessedness of submission to His sovereignty! May that be your portion now and forever.

CHAPTER 17

GUIDANCE FOR THE HOME

1 Corinthians 11:1-16

WE COME to another very interesting subject which the Corinthian church has raised with Paul, because of the conditions of their time, concerning the behavior and attitude of women in the church fellowship. Once again Paul exposes the fact that their question is not touching the root of the issue, and he takes the opportunity of answering them by lifting the question up from the detail to the principle: the beauty and glory of a Christian home.

There are women who have so misunderstood this portion of the Scriptures that they will not even bow before a meal at home without wearing some sort of head covering. But that is neither the real meaning nor the significance of this passage, which brings us to a consideration of the ideal balance in the Christian home.

One thing that places this nation in great peril is the breakdown of its homes, even Christian homes, and the collapse of the sanctity of marriage. Paul has some things to say about this as he reveals the principle, and against that background he explains the detail about which they had written to him.

He begins by saying, "Be ye followers of me, even as I also am of Christ" (11:1). This is a tremendous claim for a preacher to make, but Paul states that the Lord Jesus Christ is now his standard. Everything that he has to say he first received from the Lord; therefore he can safely say, "Be ye followers of me." He goes on to put in a word of praise: "I praise you, brethren, that ye remember me in all things, and keep the ordinances" (11:2). Whenever Paul could find opportunity to be grateful to others in spite of their imperfections, he was careful to give that word of thanks.

After that very tactful opening of what is, of course, a delicate subject, he draws them away from the question of a woman's behavior to a great principle he wants to bring to their attention: "But I would have you know, that the head of every man is Christ; and the head of the woman is the man; and the head of Christ is God" (11:3). Many people love the middle part of that verse and others dislike it, but no one can understand what it really means unless we see it as the jewel in the lovely setting of the other two relationships. The fact brought to our attention is that the head of the woman is the man in the Christian home. But how do you explain, and how do you carry out the relationship? You do so only when you understand the other two.

"The head of Christ is God," says Paul. Here we enter on holy ground, into a realm of mystery which we cannot fully understand. Yet we can know this much from the lips of our Lord Himself: "I and my Father are one" (John 10:30). Christ is equal with God in character and in deity. He also said, "I am not alone, because the Father is with me" (John 16:32). Christ and the Father were one in cooperation, in service, in ministry. The Lord Jesus said again, "My Father is greater than I" (John 14:28b). Here is the submission which He voluntarily took upon Himself when He humbled Himself and stooped to the death of the cross for us.

Jesus Christ claimed equality with God but offered submission to God. He was claiming to be one with God, and yet delighting in the fact that He was submitting to God. Here submission is in the context of absolute fellowship, complete equality, utter understanding. Here is oneness of character, oneness of service, oneness of purpose, oneness of life. Yet He was subject to His Father for the purpose of redemption.

The second relationship in this verse is that Christ is the head of man. This is true in what I would call the generic sense of the word. That is to say, when God made the human race it was His intention that there should be the same principle of headship as there is between Christ and God. There was to be an equality of life and a communion of nature, for God made man in His own image. There was to be unity of life, identity of character, complete cooperation, but at the same time there was to be a voluntary submission that the purpose of God might be fulfilled and that the glory of God might be revealed.

That voluntary submission was not given by man, however. Instead, there was an act of rebellion, and the identity was lost, the likeness ruined, the purpose spoiled. But the whole message of God's grace is that His likeness is recovered through Jesus Christ: His shed blood, His empty tomb, and the outpouring of the Holy Spirit. That which was lost in the fall of creation has been restored in redemption.

If we are born of the Spirit of God and are members of the body of Christ, there is identity of character, for we are partakers of His nature. There is to be unity of cooperation in His service and submission to the authority of Jesus Christ. Here is the relationship between Christ and man. It is a glorious thing to be the child of God, to share the character of the Lord through His redemptive purpose, and to have the experience of voluntary submission to His authority.

Against that background is set forth the glory of the relationship between man and woman that makes marriage so wonderful and the Christian home so precious. It is in the light of the relationship between God and Christ and between Christ and man that Paul puts into the forefront the relationship between man and women. It is to be exactly the same in God's purpose as the other two relationships.

When God made woman, He took her from the man, but not from the head in case she should dominate him, nor from the feet in case he should trample upon her. God took her from his side, close to his heart, that she might be his companion, his comfort, his love. That is how God made woman, and He said to her, "Thy desire shall be to thy husband, and he shall rule over thee" (Genesis 3:16).

Pául, writing to the Ephesians, insists upon this authority, also: "Husbands, love your wives, even as Christ also loved the church, and gave himself for it . . . Wives, submit yourselves unto your own husbands, as unto the Lord" (Ephesians 5:22, 25). The rule of the family is that, just as Jesus Christ voluntarily submitted Himself to the Father, so the husband is to submit himself to Christ. As the woman is to be man's companion, so she is to submit to an authority which is exercised in love as expressed at the cross. And I do not know a woman in all the world who will not give glad submission to an authority like that.

The marriage relationship is something sacramental. When you think of authority in the home you should think of the cross, where Jesus has brought us into submission to Himself. That is where we learn how much He cares for us, and where we are brought in humility before His feet. That is how He secures our love and our surrender—"even as Christ loved the church and gave himself for it." A man who cannot exercise authority like that had better remain unmarried. A man who can rule only by stamping his foot had better remain single. But a man who knows how to govern his house by the love of the Lord, through sacrificial submission to the Lord, is the man who is going to make a perfect husband. The woman who cannot submit to an authority like that had better remain single.

Dr. Campbell Morgan tells how he asked a friend of his, a lady who was a spinster, "Why do you remain single?" She replied, "Because I have never met a man who can master me." You smile at that, but she knew something of the principle of marriage. Such a person had better remain single, for she is much happier working things out for herself.

Even Christian homes are many times unhappy and broken because authority, if it is exercised at all, is not exercised in submission the one to the other in the light of the cross. Some homes, though fundamental in terminology, are desperately lacking in Christian love and discipline. Marriage has been kept going for appearances' sake, but there is no real love or discipline, no acceptance of authority. In some homes, the wife dare not accept the authority of her husband, because he has never met God in Jesus Christ at Calvary. When a husband exercises his authority away from the will of God, without submission to the Lord in his own life, the result can be tragedy for all.

Here is the basis of the loveliness of a Christian home. God is the head of Christ: He is equal in fellowship, in character, in service, but submitted to the will of God. And Christ is the head of man: we are one in character and in purpose, but submitted to the will of God in Christ. Man is the head of woman, and yet one,

because the woman is taken from the man: one in life, in companion-
ship, in character, for God's purpose to be fulfilled, submissive in
the will of God. Here then is the permanent principle, the lesson
of the Christian home.

But in the light of those relationships, Paul now brings to the
foreground a detail following the principle: "Every man praying
or prophesying, having his head covered, dishonoureth his head.
But every woman that prayeth or prophesieth with her head uncovered dishonoureth her head: for that is even all one as if she were
shaven" (11:4-5).

Notice that the man who prays and prophesies covered dishonors
his head—not the twelve inches above his neck, but God. Christ is
dishonored, for He is the head of man. On the other hand, the
woman who prays and prophesies uncovered dishonors her head,
not the inches above her neck, but the man, for the man is the
head of the woman.

Praying, a man is speaking to God on behalf of others. Prophesying, he is speaking to others on behalf of God. Paul says if he does
that uncovered, he is dishonoring God. If I preached with my hat
on, you would think me very irreverent. But why is it irreverent?

Paul, himself a Jew, is writing to many that are Jews, and what
he says here cuts completely across the understanding of the Jews.
Why does the Jew keep his hat on when he worships God? Because of a misconception of his own history. "Not as Moses, which
put a veil over his face, that the children of Israel could not sted-
fastly look to the end of that which is abolished: but their minds
were blinded: for until this day remaineth the same veil untaken
away in the reading of the old testament; which veil is done away
in Christ . . . Nevertheless when it shall turn to the Lord, the
veil shall be taken away. Now the Lord is that Spirit: and where
the Spirit of the Lord is, there is liberty. But we all with open
face beholding as in a glass the glory of the Lord, are changed into
the same image from glory to glory, even as by the Spirit of the
Lord" (II Corinthians 3:13-18).

The Jews say that Moses veiled his face when he came down
from the mountain because the people would not be able to gaze
upon the glory. But Paul says Moses did it because he knew the
glory was fading, and he did not want the people to see that. But

the veil is done away in Christ; in Him is no fading glory, because He is the same yesterday, today, and forever.

Made in the image of God, but losing that image, man is re-created in Jesus Christ and shines with something of His glory that shall never fail, and therefore the veil is unnecessary. The Christian man worships uncovered in the house of God that he might reflect something of the glory of the Head. Brethren, this means to say that others should see on your face that glory which never fades. The fact that you can worship Him uncovered is a reminder that you have been recreated in Jesus Christ after His own likeness, and the glory that will never fade is yours. It is wonderful to see a man grow old with the glory on his face, one who has been through the battles of life with his Lord along the royal route to heaven. He is not able now to serve actively in the church as once he did, but the glory is on him! There is no fading glory for the Christian.

But if that is true of the man, what about the woman? When she prays and prophesies (and I dare mention that Paul assumes that she does—remember the prophet Joel said, "your sons and your daughters shall prophesy"), if she does it uncovered, says Paul, she dishonors her head, the man. Why?

The women in Corinth who went through the street unveiled were the prostitutes. Now Christian women were saying, "We are all one in Christ; all things are lawful, so we do not need to bother about this covering." Paul says, "Yes, you do! For if you go through Corinth uncovered you will be identified with that kind of woman, and therefore you are dishonoring your husband." We need not quarrel about the detail here: "But if any man seem to be contentious," Paul says, "we have no such custom, neither the churches of God" (11:16).

If you would live day by day in submission to the Word of God, particularly in these days when anyone talking of holiness may be laughed at, I want to suggest to you that true reverence will affect your clothes, and the church will cease to be a sort of dress parade. We meet in the presence of the living Christ, whose glory can never fade, and we behold Him with open face. Paul goes on to say that a woman's hair is a glory to her, and therefore when she meets in the presence of the Lord and the fellowship of believers, there should be no competition with the glory of the Lord.

"For this cause ought the woman to have power on her head because of the angels" (11:10). That word "power" means a covering, authority. This is a reminder that even the angels cover their faces as they worship Jehovah, and they want to look down and see a Christian woman worshiping God also in reverence. It is for you individually to apply the details, but this passage suggests that we should worship the Lord in such a way that the glory is all His.

"Neither is the man without the woman, neither the woman without the man, in the Lord" (11:11). We are nothing without Him, and yet as the woman is from the man by creation, even so is the man also from the woman by human birth, but all things are of God, and in Jesus Christ the man and the woman are together in a love that is submissive for the glory of the Lord Jesus.

CHAPTER 18

PAUSE FOR FELLOWSHIP

I Corinthians 11:17-34

Up to this point Paul's ministry has been very largely corrective. He has exposed the sins and failures of the church and has sought to answer their problems: some delicate, some difficult, some very personal. Now he takes us a step further, because on the royal route to heaven there are moments when we need to get away from the difficulties and conflicts in order that we might be refreshed in green pastures and beside still waters, and might have time for reflection.

It is significant that at this particular point in the letter Paul introduces what he has to say about the Lord's Supper. It is as if to say we are to forget for a while the things that test us and draw aside together to meditate upon our Lord. This is our purpose here, a time of fellowship with Jesus, a pause for reflection upon the cross, upon His resurrection, upon the meaning of the table of communion.

It was the practice in the early church to meet together for what they called "love feasts" in their homes. This was simply a time of social fellowship which they followed with the breaking of bread.

There is the suggestion of this custom almost immediately after the resurrection. Walking on the road to Emmaus were two of His disciples, and the Lord drew near and walked with them. They invited Him to stay for a while in their home and He went in with them. They entertained Him as their guest at the table, but at the end of the meal He became Host, and He was known to them in the breaking of bread (Luke 24:13-32). We find a similar thing in Acts 2:46, where we are told that the early disciples continued steadfastly every day in the breaking of bread and in feasting with gladness and singleness of heart. Such was the practice of the early church.

The trouble was that in Corinth it had gone too far, and the Lord's table had become abused because of the surfeit of eating and drinking. The remembrance of the Lord's death had become a travesty on its solemn significance, and Paul has a word of rebuke concerning their behavior. "When ye come together therefore into one place, this is not to eat the Lord's supper . . . What? have ye not houses to eat and to drink in? or despise ye the church of God, and shame them that have not? What shall I say to you? shall I praise you in this? I praise you not" (11:20-22). "And if any man hunger, let him eat at home; that ye come not together unto condemnation" (11:34). This abuse of the Lord's table could not enter our observance today, yet it does remind us that when we break bread together, we must be careful how we come to His table, how we ought to worship Him.

Paul begins to talk about the first observance of the Lord's Supper: "I have received of the Lord that which also I have delivered unto you: That the Lord Jesus the same night in which he was betrayed took bread" (11:23).

May I pause here to point out a great principle for every preacher: this was not something that Paul got secondhand; it came to him straight from the heart of God. I picture a man meeting the risen Lord on the road to Damascus, going into the desert in Arabia, spending three years in Tarsus before Barnabas brought him to Antioch and into missionary work. It was in those years of solitude and preparation he received of the Lord that which henceforth he was to preach in public. Nothing that you say in the name of the Lord will ever be effective in the life of another unless it comes direct from His heart to yours.

What, therefore, has Paul to tell us in this chapter about the sacred feast of the Lord's table? In the first place, he introduces it to us as a remembrance of the past: "And when he had given thanks, he brake it, and said, Take, eat: this is my body, which is broken for you: this do in remembrance of me" (11:24).

In the margin of many Bibles you will find, "This do *for the* remembrance of me." When we meet around the Lord's table in the company of His people, we are doing not only what the Lord commanded us to do, but what He has asked us to do in case we forget Him. As a Friend He asks for the fellowship of His friends, as a lover asks for the communion of the one who loves him. It is the One who has given something for us at Calvary asking each of us to remember His death, to put that at the very center of our Christian experience. It is He who loved us even unto death calling us out from the busyness, and often the barrenness, of all our pressure and work, that we might wait upon Him in the stillness of our hearts, and worship Him. He points us back, not to His life or example, but to that which is at the very heart of the Christian gospel: the atonement of the cross, the finished work of Calvary and the open tomb.

Perhaps the thing that Paul is asking us to think about most of all is that when Jesus took bread, the symbol of His broken body, and gave it to His disciples, He did not murmur or complain, He did not just endure it, but He gave thanks. At that moment when all the powers of hell were being arrayed against the Lord Jesus, and He was going out into Gethsemane and up the hill to Calvary, He gave thanks, because from the very beginning it was said of Him, "I delight to do thy will, O God!"

The communion table is a memorial of the past, a reminder of the cross and of the centrality of its message, a recognition that there the Lord Jesus was thankful for the tremendous privilege that was His in dying for sinners like you and me. Amazing grace! Therefore our central thought should be worship to Him.

This takes away from the Lord's table any magic, any suggestion that when we break the bread and drink the wine we are partaking of the body and blood of the Lord. The Lord Jesus was in a human body when He took the bread, and He gave it as the symbol of His body. The removal of everything that could be superstitious about this act of worship emphasizes the glorious truth that we meet around His table to remember the One who loved us and gave Himself for us.

But Paul tells us it is to be not only a remembrance, but it is to be an expression of love for the living Christ: "As often as ye eat this bread, and drink this cup, ye do proclaim the Lord's death till he come" (11:26). The word is really "preach," here: "Ye do preach the Lord's death." There is one moment of your life above all others when you are preaching a sermon—that is when you meet around the Lord's table. You are preaching to the powers of darkness, "proclaiming the Lord's death" which has vanquished them. Also, to the Lord in heaven who looks down and sees your heart, you are witnessing your trust in His atoning work. When we meet around His table, we are feasting upon Him as He is received into our hearts by faith; as our heads are bowed in worship around His table we are sharing in fellowship with the living Lord, and are telling Him what He means to us.

The true life-giving principle in a Christian is that every faculty we possess is feasting upon Jesus Christ. My soul is feeding upon Him with thanksgiving that He loved me and died for me, that He protects and guides me, and that one day He will take me safely home. As I meditate upon these things my soul is refreshed, my heart begins to take comfort and courage, and my mind accepts the Word of God and begins to meditate upon it and to rejoice in it.

My heart feeds upon His love, His care, His thoughtfulness, His faithfulness, and responds with thanksgiving and adoration. My will feeds on His commands, and I begin to recognize that His Word is to be obeyed; I bow before the sovereign will of God. My soul hopes in the fulfillment of His promises that have never yet failed throughout history.

Therefore, as we break bread together, every part of our lives—our hearts, our minds, our souls, our wills—are all feasting upon the Lord, and He is at the very center of all.

I wonder how much of all that the Lord has seen in your life as you feast upon Him? "He that eateth me . . ." said Jesus, "shall live by me." Where is the hunger of your heart satisfied, its thirst quenched? Is it in the loveliness of your dear Saviour? As you break bread and bow your heart before Him, what sort of sermon are you preaching? What does the Lord see? What does Satan see? Here is an expression of our love that demands far more than the busyness of our lives; it takes the devotion and surrender and worship of our hearts.

Paul has something else to say to us about the Lord's table, that it is a place of tremendous hope: "ye do proclaim the Lord's death

. . . till he come." I think it is very significant that reference to the Lord's table is to be found in only four books in the New Testament, whereas the coming again of the Lord Jesus is in twenty-three books out of twenty-seven. Of the four in which there is no reference to His second coming, three of them have only one chapter, and the other is the Epistle to the Galatians.

With great emphasis the Word of God sets forth the hope of the Christian church: any moment, any day, the clouds may part and Jesus, our Saviour, may come again. As we break bread together and remember the Lord's death, we are doing it "until he come." Isn't it wonderful to remember that there will be a day when there will be no more need to do that any more? We meet around the Lord's table only "until he come," until the day when there will be no more sin, or regret, or sorrow, or struggle. There will be no more weakness, no more discouragement, no more ignorance, no empty places at our family table—we will all be together with Jesus.

The Lord Jesus went out from the Last Supper with His disciples to die for them. The disciples went out, one to betray Him, others to be prayerless and forgetful, all to desert Him. Often we have broken bread together around the Lord's table, and then we have gone out to do just what those disciples did—we have denied Him.

Paul adds a warning: "Wherefore whosoever shall eat this bread, and drink this cup of the Lord, unworthily, shall be guilty of the body and blood of the Lord" (11:27). He does not say "if we are unworthy," for we could never be worthy; our worthiness is in Christ. Has that statement ever puzzled you? I wonder if perhaps it has even kept you away from the Lord's table. Notice the next verse: "But let a man examine himself, and so let him eat of that bread, and drink of that cup. For he that eateth and drinketh unworthily, eateth and drinketh damnation to himself, not discerning the Lord's body" (11:28-29).

First, when I meet around the Lord's table I am to remember the Lord's body. I believe in this sense the word suggests to us not simply His body that hung on the cross, but the body of Jesus Christ in the world today, His church. I am to discern that I am part of this, and if in my life I am in any way sinning against the body of Jesus Christ, I am grieving the Lord, and am therefore eating unworthily.

Secondly, I eat and drink unworthily, and am guilty of the body and blood of the Lord, if I come to His table without examining myself. "For this cause many are weak and sickly among you, and many sleep" (11:30). That is, of course, many have even died. "For if we would judge ourselves, we should not be judged. But when we are judged, we are chastened of the Lord, that we should not be condemned with the world" (11:31-32).

I believe in faith healing, though I prefer to call it divine healing, but I do not believe that at any moment I may demand physical healing for a person, and these verses substantiate my position. I do not believe that you can go to any sick person, pray over him, and demand that he should immediately be restored. It may be that he is laid aside in the chastening of God because he has failed to examine himself. To demand healing may be to resist the very discipline of God upon the man's soul. Now I would be careful to add that all sickness is not the judgment of God in that sense. But in this instance, it is the chastening of God, because whom the Lord loves He corrects, and it is through the means of illness so often that a man is brought out into strength and renewed testimony for the glory of the Lord Jesus.

Paul is insistently warning us that if we keep coming to the Lord's table without self-examination and heart-searching regarding our sins, there will come a day when God will judge us and chasten us. He does not put a barrier around the Lord's table to keep us from it, but a warning that would drive us to the Lord in confession, in repentance, in meltedness of heart. "Let a man examine himself, and [not 'let him stay away'] so let him *eat*."

Are you a member of the body of Christ? When you break bread, what does it mean to you? The only thing that properly keeps you from the Lord's table is that you have never come as a sinner to the cross and received His forgiving mercy. Today you may come to Jesus, and as you begin to feast upon the living Lord you will find strength for every day's need and all the problems of life. You will rekindle the hope that burns so brightly in our hearts that one day we shall see Him face to face. It is a wonderful thing to be a member of His body!

CHAPTER 19

EQUIPMENT FOR THE ROAD

1 Corinthians 12:1-12

IN THE COURSE of any journey that takes thought and preparation, it is good from time to time to stop and take stock of our position. As we look back over the distance we have come on our royal route to heaven, we see some of the pitfalls from which we have been delivered. Then we look at what lies ahead, and ask ourselves whether or not we really have the equipment that will see us through to the end of the road.

As we look back over the ground we have covered, one thing impresses itself upon my mind above every other: there is no situation in life, no part of the journey, but that the answer is to be found at Calvary. Every problem of a church fellowship, every departure from personal morality, every difficulty of the journey is settled there. Paul takes us back to the cross of Christ constantly in this letter.

As we turn to survey the route we have yet to follow, Paul begins to speak about spiritual gifts. The thing that matters now is whether or not we have the needed equipment for the rest of the journey. Are we quite confident that we are fitted out for the royal route to heaven, and that our equipment is adequate to take us through until we meet Jesus face to face? These two things are vitally connected. The difficulties and burdens of the past and the ruggedness of the road ahead are not separate.

The problem of the Corinthian church was a threefold one. What is the remedy for their divisions and carnality? The unifying life of the Spirit of God: that is Paul's answer in chapters 12 and 14.

What is the cure for their basic immorality and sin? The unfailing love of God that knows no limit to its endurance and will stand when everything else is falling: Paul gives that answer in chapter 13. What is the solution for their difficulties: problems of church administration and of life in general? The ultimate answer to that is the resurrection day when "this corruptible shall put on incorruption." One day their problems will all be ended, their burdens lifted, and they will be ushered into the presence of the King. Paul reminds them of that hope in chapter 15. The pattern of the letter is unified and complete.

As we turn to the portion for our study, notice that Paul speaks here about spiritual gifts, not spiritual graces. There is a big difference between the two. The graces of the Spirit of God are found in Galatians 5:22-23: "The fruit of the Spirit is love, joy, peace, longsuffering, gentleness, goodness, faith, meekness, temperance." These are for myself, that my character may be formed into the likeness of Jesus Christ. Paul isn't talking about them here, he is talking about gifts, which are for my service and for the benefit, not of myself, but of other people. Let us be clear about this point: you can have all the graces, but you cannot have all the gifts. Paul concludes chapter 12 by saying, "Covet earnestly the best gifts." The great thing is to recognize the gifts that have been given to us and to use them for the glory of God, finding out day by day how better to develop and strengthen them for the Saviour's honor.

We are each different in temperament and personality; the members of the church of Jesus Christ are so varied in type, race, social background and much else, but each of us goes to the same source for our gifts: "Now there are diversities of gifts, but the same Spirit. And there are differences of administrations, but the same Lord. And there are diversities of operations, but it is the same God which worketh all in all" (12:4-6).

The same God our heavenly Father, who knows what is best for each one of His children, is in charge, as it were, of all the gifts that He would give to the church. The same Lord Jesus our Saviour, the Head of the church which is His body, desires that all His children should be so endowed that they might be not only equipped individually for the journey but that they might be a mutual blessing, profit and help the one to the other. He knows how to distribute the gifts, and He "divides to every man according as he will" (12:11). In other words, it is His sovereign right to withhold or bestow them. The same Holy Spirit, the great Executive of the Godhead, the Third Person of the Trinity, who lives in your heart and mine, knows how to take the gift that has been received from the Lord and make it useful for His service.

We have absolutely nothing for the road except we receive it from Father, Son, and Holy Spirit. In other words, we are saved by grace, and by grace alone. It was by God's grace and by the shed blood that we came to know our Saviour, and we are kept and equipped for the rest of the journey by grace alone. It is not man's natural gifts that God uses, but the gifts of the Spirit which He imparts. Until we have received the gift of His Spirit for service, we have nothing to offer which can be a help or a blessing to anyone.

Do we really recognize that we have absolutely nothing at all unless we receive it from Him? That is what the Lord Jesus said: "I am the vine, ye are the branches: He that abideth in me, and I in him, the same bringeth forth much fruit: for without me ye can do nothing" (John 15:5). What a wonderful sense of unity and dependence that gives us! What a very precious thing it makes of Christian fellowship when we recognize that whatever we contribute to the service of the King of kings, we must all get from the same source! We are not alone on the road; there are many other travelers—in fact, all who have been washed in His precious blood, and all who are sharing the gift of life in Jesus Christ.

In the second place, Paul speaks about the diversities of ministry, and he brings to our attention several different gifts of the Spirit. He says there are differences of gifts, of administration, and of operation. Now in this particular portion of the chapter we will think only of the first of these; he expands the discussion in the second part of the chapter and returns to it again in chapter 14.

I cannot help being impressed by the significance of the order in which Paul lists some of these gifts of the Spirit. The one that comes first is wisdom, and the last is the gift of tongues.

First, the gift of wisdom. You may begin to say, "I have some of that, for it is something I can attain." No, it isn't! For this letter began by saying, "God hath chosen the foolish things of the world to confound the wise," so you haven't any wisdom at all. When you come to know Jesus Christ as Saviour and Lord, you have only the foolishness of sin and worldliness and you know nothing in God's realm. One of the gifts of the Holy Spirit that God gives to His children is wisdom: understanding and discernment.

Next is the gift of knowledge, of understanding the Book—not cleverness, but the gift of conviction, of that absolute assurance which comes from having enlightenment from God. Then he speaks of the gift of faith. Even faith is not something acquired naturally. To believe God is a gift, to trust in Him even though you do not fully understand Him. It is a gift that will take you through all kinds of emergencies and problems.

Healing is a gift, and I believe without any shadow of doubt God has given it to some—the ability to command disease to be removed from a human body in the name of the Lord. But I believe that for every ten who practice the gift, probably only one has it in the sovereignty of God. There is no gift so trafficked with and commercialized today as this one. It is something nobody can demand in every situation, for sickness is sometimes in God's will, and may be His discipline or His chastening. Nevertheless, healing is a divine gift. There are those also, I believe, who have the gift of healing a broken heart. Do you have that gift of comfort, that ministry of refreshment that brings restoration to a heart that is broken, to a life that is at the end of its rope? What a precious healing ministry that is!

"To another the working of miracles"—that is the ability to do something supernatural. The Lord Jesus said to His disciples, "He that believeth on me, the works that I do shall he do also; and greater works than these shall he do; because I go unto my Father" (John 14:12). This is also the gift of being able to overcome where once you were beaten, to triumph where once you only knew failure.

Then Paul speaks of the gift of prophecy. If I understand that word correctly in its Biblical usage, it is not so much foretelling the future as forthtelling the present: seeing the world in which we live in the light of the Word of God, and bringing the Scriptures to bear upon any generation with absolute, heavenly authority, as "thus saith the Lord." It is the gift of the man who, in the name of the Lord and in the power of the Spirit, is able to speak with authority from the Book to the day in which he lives.

"To another discerning of spirits"—that is detecting between the false and the true. The spirit of discernment enables you to know what is wrong and what is right, which is the spirit of error and which the spirit of truth.

"To another divers kinds of tongues; to another the interpretation of tongues" (12:10b). This, the last in order of the gifts, although perhaps least in importance, nevertheless is a gift of the Spirit. Unquestionably it is to be used for the purpose of praise and adoration of the Lord Jesus, but always by interpretation.

No one, I repeat, has all the gifts. Because you have one of them, you are not entitled to become a spiritual aristocrat because somebody else does not have your gift. Don't demand that, in order for another person to be spiritual, he must heal, or he must speak in an unknown tongue. Be careful when you criticize those who may not have your gift—he has his own, which you may not have, because nobody has all of them. However, God gives to each of His children one or more, not that we may have spiritual pride, not to make us think we are clever, or good, or favored, but for the benefit of others.

There are certain things that you cannot do, but other Christians can, certain gifts of the Spirit that your brother has that you may need in order to get through life to the gates of heaven. All together the church, as it marches along the royal route to heaven in the fellowship of the Holy Spirit, is equipped as a body in victory. Observe closely that victory is in the group and not in isolation. One of the most damaging things that is done today in the name of fundamentalism is to grieve the Holy Spirit and divide the body. For victory, the body must work together in harmony and fellowship and love, under the authority of the Holy Spirit. I need your gift to see me through and you need mine: all of us need each of us, for we have mutual dependence as a body. God forbid that any of us should do one thing, or say one thing, that would harm the Lord's body, the church, by ruining another's gift or destroying the fellowship.

You may ask me, "How do I get these gifts of the Spirit?" That is an important question, because some people masquerade with

gifts that are simply pretense. Many profess to have the gift of healing or of tongues, this gift or that, and the public is exploited by
it. How can you know the sign of reality? How do you know what
gifts you possess? What are the evidences of them?

Paul gives the answer to us very clearly: "Wherefore I give you
to understand, that no man speaking by the Spirit of God calleth
Jesus accursed: and that no man can say that Jesus is the Lord, but
by the Holy Ghost" (12:3). The first part of that verse could be
paraphrased, "No man speaking by the Spirit of God is indifferent
to the Lord Jesus Christ." The man who speaks by the Spirit will
put the Lord Jesus in His rightful place, on the throne. I can speak
the words, "Jesus is Lord," and so can you. Anybody can say it,
because no one can check our vocabulary. But no man can say with
authority and absolute certainty that Jesus Christ is Lord, and back
it up by the evidence of his life, but by the Holy Spirit.

To understand this, let us review our picture once again. The
company of the redeemed is on the road to heaven; every day brings
us nearer the end of the journey, when we will see our Lord face
to face. We have been washed in His blood, and we share together
the indwelling Holy Spirit. We have the same Father in heaven who
knows what is best for His children. Our Lord Jesus Christ is at
God's right hand; He is our Head and we His body. Each of us
is necessary to Him and to each other as the Holy Spirit He has
given to us, on His behalf administers the gifts He bestows.

Therefore, how do I know if I have them in reality? By the submission of my heart to Jesus Christ as Lord. When He is sovereign
in my life, I am not going to ask for the gift of another out of envy.
God bless him if it is real and make him a giant! I am glad of his
fellowship, but don't let him start calling me carnal because I do
not have his gift. The only gifts I would ask for are the gift of
speaking with a tongue controlled from heaven and the gift of
healing and comforting a broken heart.

If I am submitted to the dictatorship of the Holy Spirit, then it
is for Him in His sovereignty to give me a gift: I gladly accept the
wisdom, the knowledge, the understanding, the miracles, the discernment—whatever the gift may be. I will thank Him for it and
for the friends who have gifts that I do not have. I will rejoice that
God has caused my path to cross theirs, that in the church alongside

me there are folks who know the Lord in a different way from myself, some who have the wonderful gift of refreshing those who are discouraged, and who help me along the way.

What a precious thing is Christian fellowship in the body of Christ! If you are walking today in the company of God's people, you find strength and comfort from gifts they have that you do not possess. The secret of reality is a blessed submission all along the road to the authority of the Holy Spirit, who will give you all you need to be a blessing to others.

CHAPTER 20

TEAMWORK ALONG THE WAY

1 Corinthians 12:13-31

THE PASSAGE under consideration is one of the most significant in the Bible dealing with the great theme of the Christian church. It speaks to us about the character of the church, which is its form; the purpose of the church, which is its function; and the relationship of the church, which is its fellowship.

The sad plight of the church today is obvious evidence that the true character of the church is misunderstood, or some of us would not behave as we do. We would treasure it instead of tearing it apart; we would love all men with the love of Christ, and our testimony would ring with a new note of passionate concern. If we are ever to see the answer to our prayers for heaven-sent revival, the dead church must begin to live, the wounded church must be made whole, the indifferent church must be rekindled with the flame of Calvary-love.

This means, first of all, recognition of our real unity: "Now ye are the body of Christ, and members in particular" (12:27). Paul uses the human body as an illustration of our mutual relationship: "For as the body is one, and hath many members, and all the members of that one body, being many, are one body: so also is Christ" (12:12). Paul is pointing out here some obvious lessons: the fact of our unity, our fellowship in diversity, and the fallacy of expecting identity.

To understand the significance of these things we need to go beneath the surface. "The body of Christ"—what does that suggest? Surely not, in the first place, the spiritual union between believers, but the human, physical body in which Jesus Christ lived, walked, talked, worked, and died, in which there was incarnate expression of the whole purpose of God in saving mankind from sin. His physical body was an essential preparation for the fact and function of the spiritual body which is His church. Indeed, the church would never have existed if it had not been redeemed first of all through the sacrifice of the physical body of our Lord Jesus.

When God came down to this earth in human form, miraculously conceived in the womb of the Virgin Mary, He came to reveal to us the whole principle upon which we should live our lives. The physical body of Jesus Christ expressed perfectly what God intends should be perpetuated through the spiritual body of Christ, the church of which you and I are part.

That physical body involved Jesus Christ in three things. First, complete identification: this was seen in His delight to do the Father's will, His submission to the limitations of His human form, His obedience unto death, even the death of the cross. It was seen also in His oneness with us: "the children are partakers of flesh and blood, he also himself likewise took part of the same" (Hebrews 2:14), because He was "in all points tempted like as we are, yet without sin" (Hebrews 4:15).

In the second place, we see His identification with the need and condition of the human race; He prayed for our identification with Him, "as thou, Father, art in me, and I in thee, that they also may be one in us: that the world may believe that thou hast sent me" (John 17:21).

His identification was with a view to total penetration. His coming was an attack on all fronts; it was total warfare, a full-scale invasion from heaven upon every aspect and expression of sin. It penetrated every level of life: social, political, ecclesiastical, moral. He healed the sick, raised the dead, cleansed the leper, restored the sinner, comforted the sorrowing and the weak, scorned the Pharisee, scorched the hypocrite. Crucified in weakness, He was raised by the power of God, and He left behind Him in this poor, prodigal world an indelible impact. There was no part of human life that escaped the penetration of the redemptive purpose of God in Jesus Christ.

But total penetration of this sinful world involved Him in no assimilation of sin itself. He was so close to us, but He was so separate from us. None came so close, but none was ever so different. Holy, harmless, undefiled, yet separate from sinners; touching sin at every point, yet never being contaminated. Healing, blessing, restoring, comforting—touching sin at every point, yet never catching the infection. As He moved in every circle of life, He never assimilated any of the sin, but imparted to everything He touched the very breath of heaven, the very life of eternity itself.

One day His physical body was laid in a tomb. The world crucified Him, rejecting the whole principle of life for which He stood. "We will not have this man to reign over us," was their cry. They were not willing to have this complete identification—they wouldn't stand for total penetration with no assimilation. This kind of thing was too costly for them. But God raised Him from the dead, and He ascended into heaven; by His own blood and His outpoured love He won for all of us the right of access to God's throne.

At Pentecost, the resurrected body of the Lord Jesus in heaven was united, as the Head, to the spiritual body being formed on earth, in order that the principles that involved Him might involve us, and what He had begun in His physical body might be perpetuated in us until He comes again to complete our redemption. I know that we can never add a word, nor a thought, nor a deed, to the finished work of Calvary. That which purchased our redemption was indeed a finished work, but the Lord Jesus in that human body was not ending something, He was beginning a great campaign which He Himself, in the limitations of a human body, could never complete, the task of world redemption.

These principles He made clear as He lived them out, and He gave them back, together with the Holy Spirit power to fulfill them, to a little group of disciples, that they themselves might live in complete identification with God, in total penetration of the world, but with no assimilation of sin.

Therefore, as Paul says, we are the body of Christ, and our bodies are the temples of the Holy Spirit. As the body of Christ on earth, we are here to fulfill in our lives and through our testimony that which Christ, in His physical life, began. We are here that in and through our bodies, by the power of His indwelling life, the redemption He purchased might be brought to complete fruition and total victory. All this lies behind the surface truth here, and throws a flood of light on Paul's teaching concerning the great function and character of the Christian church.

In the light of that background, let us consider the fact of our unity: "By one Spirit are we all baptized into one body . . . and have been all made to drink into one Spirit" (12:13).

Here is the mystery, the glory of the church of Jesus Christ. If we have been saved by God's grace, washed in the blood of Christ, at that moment we were baptized by the Holy Spirit into the body of the Lord Jesus and, therefore, we drink of the same fountain of life, are sustained by the same power, comforted by the same Shepherd, directed by the same Commander-in-chief, kept by the mighty hand of the same wonderful God. This is complete identification.

No matter how great the disparity may be between Christian people—race, gifts, talents, ability, whether a man be a prince on a throne or a beggar in the streets—if anyone is alive in Christ he has been made one by the same quickening Spirit and he is partaker of the same divine nature.

We are very conscious of certain ties that bind us one to another, such as the tie of national origin. Swede meets Swede, Englishman meets Englishman, German meets German, and immediately they discover an affinity. But what about this greater tie, our baptism by the Holy Spirit into the church, the body of Jesus Christ? What does *that* mean to us?

Just as among people there are different complexions, different features, and we are all different, so is the body of Christ. You see that difference in some points of doctrine. Some people are Calvinists, and others are Arminians. There will be differences in points of government and discipline, but there is not one person in the body of Christ today who has not felt himself a lost, guilty soul, and who has not known true repentance toward God and faith in Jesus Christ crucified and risen. This is the church: a company of men and women who have met God as sinners at Calvary, and have been formed into the body of Jesus Christ. No one is a genuine Christian unless he has been through that. We are not a mass of individual units, but a body completely identified with His in His death and resurrection, completely united in our spiritual life, in our ministry of redemption, in the whole purpose for which we are left here.

But, alas, we are unrecognizable—the body of Christ is split from head to foot, torn asunder by this view and that view, because so many of us have accepted only superficially the whole principle of baptism by the Spirit into His body. There has been a refusal to accept the principle of the cross and death to the capital "I." But in the mind of the Lord Jesus Christ we have complete identification—with Him in death and resurrection and with the human race in its need—and are united together by faith and repentance, baptized by the same indwelling Spirit into the same new nature.

There is in this body not only complete identification, but the fellowship of diversity: "When one member suffers, all the members suffer with him. When one member is honored, all the members rejoice" (12:26).

The body of Jesus Christ was for total penetration at every point, into every aspect of life, for the glory of God and for the redemption of men. This is His purpose for His spiritual body, the church. In every relationship of life: religious, ecclesiastical, political, social, moral, there should be felt the impact of a group of people who are so absolutely one that their witness is irresistible. If this is to be accomplished, there must be a recognition of our absolute fellowship in our diversity. Therefore, as Paul points out, there is not one member of the body who can say of another, "Because I am not the eye, I am not of the body" (12:16).

There is a vast difference, of course, between the various members of the body, and yet when one member suffers, all suffer. If you are walking along a country road and a thorn gets into your foot, what happens? Your nerves send out the signal and the whole body becomes active: your back bends and your hands reach out to remove the thorn: your eyes may begin to water and your voice begin to complain—the whole body has felt the impact of that wound.

Fellowship in diversity is caring one for another, illustrated in the covering and protection which we give to the weaker parts of our physical body in order that the life of the whole body may be preserved. When every member of the body is functioning happily in its appointed place, caring each for the other to preserve the life and health of the body as a whole, then the body is prepared for total penetration into every aspect of life.

Alas, the world never feels that penetration at all if we as the body of Christ do not know the meaning of our fellowship in diversity. We become jealous of the gifts of other people, and instead of covering the weaker members for the protection of the whole, we are all too ready to expose them. We criticize, we judge, we condemn, and very often young believers have been disillusioned by the lack of Christian love and care that they have found in the church from which they expected so much.

So often it seems that the flame of love has practically died out within the Christian church! Millions around us go to Christless graves while the church quarrels and bickers, while the body of Christ is torn apart and becomes totally ineffective. The church has forgotten the secret of her absolute fellowship in the midst of so much diversity.

On the other hand, there is the fallacy of identity: "The eye cannot say unto the hand, I have no need of thee: nor again the head to the feet, I have no need of you" (12:21). Picture for a moment what a body would look like if it were all ear or all eye. What a monstrosity! Of course, it could not live, as it would not have the other organs necessary for life and breathing. "God hath tempered the body together" (12:24) so that it should function in the will of God by being perfectly healthy. The impossibility of all being alike, and of all doing the same thing, is shown in verse 28, for God has given—and this is an incomplete list, I hope, for there are no pastors or evangelists here—"first apostles, secondarily prophets, thirdly teachers, after that miracles, then gifts of healings, helps, governments, diversities of tongues." But each of us can get in that little word "helps." We can all do that. All these are necessary in order that the body may function as a healthy whole and that there should be no assimilation of evil. You cannot keep disease out of an unhealthy body, but if the body is strong, and each member is functioning as it ought, then there is resistance to disease.

The church is to function as a healthy body, with every member happy in the will of God. There is no self-depreciation (12:15); neither is there to be depreciation of others (12:21). Here is the whole body without disability, functioning according to the plan of God, its members completely loyal the one to the other.

We are living in an evil age, when morals are lax and even many

Christian homes are caught up into the unhappy, sinful state of society. Yet the church of Jesus Christ should be a body which penetrates everywhere and assimilates nothing. Today there is little penetration but plenty of assimilation in the body of Christ.

A scientist lectured recently to the Chicago Medical Association, and said this, "Consider the average 150-pound body of an individual from its chemical aspect. It contains lime enough to whitewash a fair-sized chicken-coop, salt enough to fill a small shaker, iron enough to make a tenpenny nail, plus water. The total value of the ingredients is 98 cents, or about 60 cents per hundred-weight on the hoof."

That is all we are worth to a scientist! But that is not all the truth about the body: we are fearfully and wonderfully made, and we are worth infinitely more than that to God. We were created that we might be taken up into the mystery, to be formed as the body of Christ, members one of another, an agency through which God's whole program of world evangelization will be fulfilled, and one day to be the jewels in His crown. That demands a recognition of the fact of our unity, of our identification with Christ at the cross as well as complete identification with the needs of man. It means that you as a Christian are not here simply to participate in a church program or to enjoy church services. It means that you are here for total penetration for Jesus, at any price, bringing the good news of His love into every area of life in which you move.

This is only possible as we recognize that within the church we have fellowship in our diversity, as we learn to love and to care for our brethren who are different, always recognizing the utter futility of identity. Are we here in the name of the Lord that there may be total penetration without any assimilation, that God may preserve us blameless and one day present us faultless before His throne? Are you living on that principle today?

PART III

Dynamic for the Journey

CHAPTER 21

LOVE IS THE WAY

I Corinthians 13:1-3

AS WE TRAVEL this royal route to heaven, we have already found many difficulties in the church which have been answered by the message of the cross. The conflict will be renewed before we come, so to speak, to the journey's end, but in this chapter everything is fragrant. It is like waking up to a spring morning full of sunshine and warmth after the coldness and darkness of winter. We will not hurry over this chapter, but savor its refreshment to our hearts. I trust you will get a wonderful spiritual suntan as you look into the face of our Lord Jesus Christ and absorb the glow of His love.

Three chapters here have to do with spiritual gifts: chapter 12 tells of God's rich endowment of gifts to His people; chapter 13 tells of God's energy imparted to our lives, which makes it possible for us to use the gifts to His glory; chapter 14 gives God's instructions for the exercise of the gifts. Between the endowment of the gifts and the exercise of the gifts there is this great chapter on love, showing us that the only way to safeguard and rightly use our spiritual gifts is by administering them in the love of God.

When Paul came to this particular point in dictating this letter, I somehow feel his face lit up with glory. Surely the first twelve chapters must have caused him pain as he wrote to this church concerning their low spiritual state. As he himself said, they "came behind in no gift" (1:7), but they were tragically lacking in this quality of love. I think it must have been a precious release to him to put in this wonderful portion. The love of God is the answer to all the problems, not only in Corinth, but in our cities and churches today.

It is significant that it was Paul the theologian who brought to us this great passage, and not John, the disciple of love. Those two men differed widely in their gifts and ministry, but they were united in this one thing, the greatest any Christian can possess, the grace of love. In fact, Paul tells us quite plainly that if we have no love, we have nothing; but if we have love, though we may lack much else, then we have what matters most.

First, we need to understand the significance of this word, which the Authorized (King James) Version translates by our English word "charity." The revised versions change it to "love," and rightly so. The former word suggests something very different today from what it did in 1611, having now the meaning of benevolence or tolerance, and that is a totally inadequate meaning of the Greek word which is used in this chapter.

There are three Greek words translated by the English word "love." One of them is found only in the Septuagint (Greek Version) in Proverbs and the prophecies of Hosea and Ezekiel. It does not occur in the New Testament at all. It is a word that suggests sensual desire, and it has very unpleasant associations. Perhaps that is why the Holy Spirit keeps it out of the New Testament altogether.

From the second word, the Greek noun *philia*, we have derived, for instance, "philosophy" and "Philadelphia." It means friendship, a natural affection for other people, the love you might have for your friends and relatives. This is a word we find occasionally in the New Testament.

The third Greek noun, used throughout this chapter and used most frequently in the New Testament, is *agape*, from which we get our English "agony." It means the actual absorption of every part of our being in one great passion. It is used most often in relation to God: "God so loved [verb form, *agapaō*] the world, that he gave his only begotten Son" (John 3:16). This word has little to do with mere emotion; it indicates love which deliberately, by an act of will, chooses its object, and through thick or thin, regardless of the attractiveness of the object concerned, goes on loving continually, eternally.

It is a word that speaks of complete self-denial. To love in this way means never thinking of ourselves at all; the self-life does not enter into the picture. It is always used when the will is involved rather than the emotions. That is why, in regard to the Christian's attitude to his enemy, this is the word the Lord used: "thou shalt love [not *phileō*, 'like,' but *agapaō*, 'agonize over'] thine enemies."

This word is the only one in the Bible (and what an honor!) that is used to describe God without any qualification or explanation: God is *agape*. When we sing that lovely hymn of George Matheson's : "O Love, that will not let me go!" we are not singing about an abstract thing. Or again, when we sing Charles Wesley's hymn, "O Love Divine, how sweet Thou art!" we are saying that God is Love.

Every description of love in this chapter is applicable to the Lord Jesus Christ. Jesus suffers long, and is kind. Jesus envies not; Jesus vaunts not Himself, is not puffed up, does not behave Himself unseemly. Jesus seeks not His own, is not easily provoked, takes no account of evil, rejoices not in unrighteousness, but rejoices with the truth. Jesus bears all things, believes all things, hopes all things, endures all things. Jesus never fails.

Love is the one thing, therefore, that is completely indestructible; while other things pass away, love lasts. It is not dependent on anything outside of itself; it is not affected by the worthiness or unworthiness of the one it loves. When we become New Testament Christians, that *agape* is born in us, and if these studies are to mean anything, by the time we are through you and I will have to be able to say, "I suffer long and am kind. . . ." If that love really grips your heart, your Christian experience will be utterly revolutionized.

The distinction between the two Greek words is brought out in the conversation between the risen Lord and Peter by the lake shore that morning after His resurrection; it is recorded in John 21.

"Simon, son of Jonas, lovest (*agapaō*) thou me more than these?"

"Yes, Lord, thou knowest that I like you (*phileō*)."

"Simon, son of Jonas, lovest (*agapaō*) thou me?"

"Yes, Lord, thou knowest I have an affection (*phileō*) for thee."

"Simon, son of Jonas, are you sure that you have an affection (*phileō*) for me?"

And Peter was grieved because the Lord asked him a third time—not because of the repetition, but because the third time He came down to the lower word. Peter cried out, "Lord, thou knowest all things; thou knowest I have an affection for thee!" I know what that poor man felt, and so do you. He was so ashamed because of his denial of Christ that he could not even bring himself to use that tremendous word, *agapaō*. Of course he couldn't—not until Pentecost, that day when the Holy Spirit came from heaven and shed abroad the love of God in his heart.

I feel it is almost a desecration to tear this chapter apart by outlining it, but for the sake of those who like some system in Bible study, here are the divisons we will be using. In the first place, in verses 1 through 3, there is what I am calling the pre-eminence of love, that is, its value; in verses 4 through 7 there is the prerogative of love, that is, its virtue. And in the closing part of the chapter, in verses 8 through 13, there is the permanence of love, that is, its victory. In the first three verses we see a life without love, and in the following verses, love as the strength of a man's life and character. In the closing part of the chapter we see a life with love as its goal and ambition.

We find, first, the picture of an individual who is blessed with gifts and talents to an amazing degree, and yet without love his life is empty and worthless. Here the searchlight of heaven is turned upon a man or woman who has strong powers of emotion, tremendous powers of intellect, and the most amazing powers of will, but lacking love (*agape*), he has absolutely nothing. Notice the three-fold repetition of the phrase: "but have not love."

In the first verse I find this principle: love must be sovereign in the heart. "Though I speak with the tongues of men and of angels, and have not love, I am become as sounding brass, or a tinkling cymbal." Paul has been talking about the gift of tongues, the highest expression of emotion, praise and worship. Here he supposes himself to be in possession of this gift to such a degree that he speaks not only with the tongues of men, but with the tongues of angels, as well. Even if he can do this, and has no love, it is all valueless. In other words, the silver-tongued orator who is a loveless man is just a big noise: a clanging cymbal or noisy gong.

The power behind your tongue, your speech, is not determined by the extent of your vocabulary but by the depth of your heart, by how much you love. What use is eloquence without love? The tongue possesses power to do devastating damage. Its hiss can be as full of venom and spite as a poisonous serpent. It is often the last thing that God gets hold of in the Christian's life. But when *agape* comes to a man's life he does not need words, he has a new medium of expression, for love is universal in every language.

As I was preparing this message, outside in the street a police car passed by with its siren screeching. Then downstairs in the church auditorium there was the sound of the organ. What a vivid contrast it was! The siren was a voice without love, while the music was a voice of worship and love.

I have heard preachers whose oratory has left me breathless and made me go away saying, "Wasn't that magnificent! His command of language was absolutely tremendous." Oratory may command admiration, but only love can reach the heart. That is why Jesus said the most important commandment of all is "Thou shalt love (*agapaō*) the lord thy God with all thy heart . . . and thy neighbor as thyself." Here is love sovereign in a man's emotions and revealed in his speech.

Then we find in the second verse that love must be sovereign in our intellect: "And though I have the gift of prophecy, and understand all mysteries, and all knowledge; and though I have all faith, so that I could remove mountains, and have not love, I am nothing."

There are four things here that belong to our intellect as distinct from our emotions or our will. The first is prophecy, the power to declare the things of God, the power to interpret life, the power to bring the word of heaven to bear upon earth, the power to bring eternity into time. Mysteries—I take that to mean the discernment of spiritual things, understanding God's secrets. Knowledge is intelligence in the truth, an understanding of Scripture. And faith means that firmness of belief which will take a man through difficulties and problems and testings, because he trusts God.

You may possess all these, says Paul, but without love you are nothing. There are men in the Bible who illustrate this. For instance, Balaam was a prophet, but he had no love, and therefore he betrayed his prophetic office. Caiaphas, the High Priest, had discernment, for he knew that one must be slain for the nation, but he was without love, and he became a leader among those who crucified the Lord of glory. Judas Iscariot had knowledge, all that he could acquire at the Master's feet in three years, but he had no love, and he betrayed the Lord.

Prophecy, mystery, knowledge, faith—all these are gifts; love is not a gift, but a grace, and it is the primary proof of a genuine new birth. In Galatians 5:22, the first fruit of the Spirit mentioned is love (*agape*). The first thing that happens to a man when he is born again is the melting of his heart in love.

Apart from this divine love, the gifts of the Spirit may be exercised in selfishness. A man with faith but no love can embitter the lives of other people because in him is the possibility of dreadful cruelty. A man with a faith that can move mountains right out of his path, if he has not love, will throw them right into the path of somebody else. People with many gifts and much power may become celebrated theologians, renowned missionaries, great authors or scholars or teachers of the Word. But if something less than the *agape* of God in Jesus Christ is the animating power behind their lives, then the Bible says they are nothing.

There is one other thing here: love must be sovereign in a man's will. "If I bestow all my goods to feed the poor, and if I give my body to be burned, and have not love, it profiteth me nothing" (13:3).

Love is to dominate not only my emotions and my intellect, but my will. These are the three principle faculties of a human being, and they must be kept in harmony. If we are going to be sane and well balanced under the pressure of days like these, the love of God must be in control to keep our intellect, our emotions, and our will in balance.

Paul takes two extreme examples here. If a man distributes everything he has to feed the poor, or even surrenders himself to the flames—in other words, he goes to the limit of absolute sacrifice—yet has no love, it is all worthless. You might say that he would never do that unless he loved. What about the heathen cutting himself to death to make peace with his god? That is not love, but fear. What about almsgiving to the point of penury? That is not done out of love, but from hope of a reward in the hereafter. These are attempts to make an atonement, and in the same way even a Christian may make a supreme sacrifice for the wrong motive.

I would say this carefully, but I believe the trouble with many of us is that although we will fight and die for our faith, we reject altogether the principle of living in the spirit of love. It is pointless to die for a wrong motive. I recall with a sense of fear in my soul the words of the risen Lord to the church at Ephesus: "I know thy works, and thy labour, and thy patience, and how thou canst not bear evil men . . . and for my name's sake hast laboured, and hast not fainted. Nevertheless I have somewhat against thee, because thou hast left thy first love (*agape*)" (Revelation 2:2-4). What a solemn, terrifying picture of busyness, patience, discernment, toil, endurance, but absolutely without the one thing that matters—love!

Notice, finally, the five "ifs" in these verses. You will find it "though" in the Authorized Version, but the meaning is "if," as in the revised versions. "*If* I speak with the tongues of men . . . *if* I have the gift of prophecy . . . *if* I have all faith . . . *if* I bestow all my goods . . . *if* I give my body to be burned. . . ." Notice, also, the four "alls": "and understand *all* mysteries, and *all* knowledge . . . and if I have *all* faith . . . if I bestow *all* my goods. . . ."

If such an individual ever lived on the face of this earth who did all that, I tell you, without *agape*, he is nothing. Of course he isn't! Why? Because God is love, and without love, he is without God.

You may have all these gifts and do all these things, but without the Lord Jesus in your life, what is the use of it? You are not something or somebody, but you are absolutely nobody, worthless for time and for eternity. What have you got that is going to be currency in that day when you pass from this earthly scene and meet God face to face? Your gifts, your abilities, your knowledge, your sacrifice, your faith—but "he that hath not the Son of God hath not life." The one thing that matters is Jesus Christ and His love, His passion, in your heart. Do you possess that now?

CHAPTER 22

THE LOVE LIFE

I Corinthians 13:4-7

ON THE royal route to heaven in I Corinthians, we have come to the love chapter—the greatest thing ever written on that subject. We are pausing here so that the atmosphere and spirit of love may encompass our lives, that the warmth and glow of love may flood our hearts and minds. I am quite certain there is nothing we need more than a refreshing of the love of God in our lives.

In the first of this chapter there are two contrasting pictures. In the opening three verses we see a man who has a lot of gifts, but no love. In the next four verses we see a man who has a lot of love, but apparently no gifts. In some measure the church at Corinth fitted into the first of these, but it found no place in the second at all, for it was completely without love.

In the second picture there is no reference to any gifts, and yet as we read these wonderful words we feel the impact of this life of love, this Christlikeness of character. While gifts without love are absolutely worthless, yet love, apparently without any gifts, is a quality which will stand the test of time and eternity.

This picture of love is a photograph of the Lord Jesus Christ in His inner character. And in His church, His body, He wants to have many reprints. We are looking at the Original, Himself; He looks at us, for what He is in this world so are we to be. He is looking for the perfect reproduction of His life of love in us. To love like this is to be like the Lord, and our unlikeness to Christ is proportionate to our failure to love. Christians are those born again by the Holy

Spirit, in whom the Saviour has become incarnate again, for we are partakers of a new nature—His Character, which is love.

This description of love shows it in sharp contrast to everything the Corinthian church was, and also of what we have ever been.

Love is very patient, but we are impatient. Love is very kind, but we are discontented and unkind. Love knows no jealousy, but we are always envious of others who have more than we do, or we think they do. Love makes no parade, but we are so proud. Love gives itself no airs and is never rude, but we are ill-mannered. Love is never selfish, but we are self-centered. Love is never irritated, but we become short-tempered so easily. Love is never resentful, but we look for slights and cherish wrongs. Love is never glad when others go wrong, but we take a secret delight in the failures of other people. Love is gladdened by goodness, always slow to expose and eager to believe the best, but we are so censorious.

Sin and Satan have robbed us of all likeness to God's character, but here is an outline of what the grace of God and the power of the indwelling Holy Spirit has come to do in our lives. In verses 4 to 6 are listed the qualities of character with which love has nothing to do, the things about which it is passive and negative. The power of love holds a life in restraint, that it may not do evil. In verse 7, love is active and positive: believing, bearing, hoping, enduring. Here is love sending out, constraining. Love holds us back from what we would be by ourselves; love forces us on to that which, humanly speaking, we are helpless to accomplish.

There are fourteen descriptions of what I might call "the ingredients of love" in these few verses. In each we see Jesus Christ and recognize His purpose that each one of us should be like Him in His character of love.

1. *Love suffers long.* That is the first quality love displays. In other words, having been wronged, love is patient and silent. It refuses to give way to anger, though it could rightfully be resentful when it has been unjustly treated. Though love suffers wounds and injury, it does not strike back. The Lord Jesus, when He was reviled, reviled not again. How about you?

2. *Love is kind.* To endure wrong could be just a triumph of obstinacy, but to be kind to the person who has done the wrong is a triumph of grace. The love of God is not only patient but kind. The

Lord Jesus showed the greatest kindness to Judas Iscariot, who betrayed Him. Even to our friends, how loveless and how unkind we have been. The greatest thing that you can ever do this side of heaven—and perhaps we have not much longer to do it—is to be kind to God's children. Love not only takes the injury, but shows positive grace and kindness to the person responsible for it. Are we like that?

3. *Love envies not*. It does not begrudge the greater privileges and gifts of others, or seek out gain for itself. Only love can see all the inequalities of life and remain content with its own place. Where there is no love, there will inevitably be envy. This was the seed of the first murder in human history, and it has been a seed of murder ever since. Envy appears even in the hearts of Christians, and is a vice so unlovely, so grievous to the Lord, so hard to overcome. But love is perfectly content with the will of God. The Lord Jesus went about doing good and never desired good to be done to Himself. Are you eaten up with envy, jealous of other's gifts, opportunities, abilities, possessions, position in life?

4. *Love vaunteth not itself*. As Moffatt puts it, "Love makes no parade." It does not show off or boast or brag; it is not proud or conceited. Love never seeks to win the praise and applause of others. When a man begins to boast, he is advertising his emptiness and his ignorance. There is no swagger about love, it is too big for that. The Lord Jesus never "showed off." His greatness was revealed not merely in what He displayed but in the things He suppressed. He laid aside His glory and humbled Himself for the sake of others. How about you? Are you boastful, conceited, proud?

5. *Love is not puffed up*. It is never arrogant, but humble. It is never self-satisfied or contemptuous of others. "Love gives itself no airs," is the way Moffatt translates it. The person who is self-satisfied is always contemptuous of others. The Lord Jesus never showed vanity or conceit or contempt of others. Do you?

6. *Love does not behave itself unseemly*. It is not rude or ill-mannered, but always courteous. This is the love of God shown in the little, everyday things of life: the good manners of a child of God. There is so much blundering goodness, uncouth religion, unlovely testimony, unattractive Christian witness, because of lack of love. The Lord Jesus always said and did the right thing in the right way

at the right time. Yet there is such a lack of real Christian goodness and courtesy in our everyday lives. How about you?

7. *Love seeks not her own.* That is to say, love is not selfish, but self-forgetful. Love does not grasp for its own rights, but finds its joy in serving others. How often we seek our own advancements and interests, sometimes at the expense of other people, entirely unconcerned for their welfare, their blessing and growth.

8. *Love is not easily provoked.* That is a shattering statement! It simply means that love is not bad-tempered. Actually, there is no sin that so disrupts a home, so spoils a Christian family, so ruins children in their upbringing, as sheer bad temper. It is often excused as something that people cannot help, but it demonstrates a lack of love. Of course, love can be angry with sin, but love is never irritable or touchy. The Lord Jesus hated sin, but He was never angry at wrong done to Himself. He was never vindictive, and never did He retaliate. Do you find yourself temperamental, thin-skinned, easily offended, quick to be resentful? Love is not easily provoked.

9. *Love thinks no evil.* Love will always keep a record of the many kindnesses it receives, and be thankful for them, but love will not keep a record of wrongs it has suffered with a view to getting even. It does not cherish in its memory a list of injustices; love has an amazing power to forget. The Lord Jesus Christ came to blot out our transgressions and to remember them against us no more forever. For when the blood of Jesus Christ was shed for the remission of my sins, and God sees the blood and my faith in my Lord's atoning sacrifice, He not only forgives, but He forgets. Has that ability been imparted to your life? Or do you build up a list of wrongs done to you and bide your time for retaliation? It is said of Abraham Lincoln that he never forgot a kindness, but he had no room in his mind for the memory of a wrong. How about you?

10. *Love rejoices not in iniquity, but rejoices in the truth.* I like Moffatt's paraphrase, "Love is never glad when others go wrong; love is gladdened by goodness." In other words, love does not delight in exposing the weaknesses of other people. It will weep over sin and be brokenhearted over failure; it will condemn the sin, but love will always yearn to cover and protect the man who has fallen.

How the Lord Jesus yearned over sinners! He often sought to protect them from the injustice of others. For instance, in His interview with the woman taken in adultery, as recorded in John 8, He did not condone her sin, but He protected and forgave her, the sinner. This is a very searching test of character. Are you heart-broken at the misfortune or breakdown of other people? Or do you have a tendency to gloat over them secretly and delight to gossip about them? Love does not do that, for at the cross mercy and truth met; there Jesus condemned sin but pardoned the sinner.

11. *Love bears all things.* Love suffers wrong without retaliation; that is the negative aspect of the statement. But love gets under the load of life and bears it to the limit, and that is positive. Love patiently endures what it has to suffer, and is not shaken by ingratitude; it is proof against hardship and reproach. The Lord Jesus patiently bore all the wrong and injustice, and prayed on the cross, "Father, forgive them, for they know not what they do." At the same time, He put His shoulder under the load of sin and bore the crushing burdens of others. How about you?

12. *Love believes all things.* Not that love is easily deceived—I do not think it means that at all, or that love is blind. Puppy love may be, but not the love of God. Rather, it means that love is not basically suspicious. It takes the kindest view of others in every circumstance, as long as it possibly can. Love will consider the motives and make every allowance for failure. And when a man has fallen, love will think about the battle that he must have fought, and the struggle that he must have had before he went down.

The Lord Jesus never misjudged anybody, because He did not judge by outward appearances. He had an amazing way of looking at an outcast and seeing in him an infinite capacity for regeneration. "Wilt thou be made whole?" He asked the worst case at the pool of Bethesda. He became the Friend of sinners. We are apt to view every action with suspicion and become cynical toward those who are down, but love is not suspicious.

13. *Love hopes all things.* When love is disappointed in the one in whom it trusted, it will yet hope for better things, although others may long since have ceased to do so. Love never despairs of anybody. Of course, it does not try to persuade itself that a thief is honest or that the criminal is innocent, but it knows that God is not willing that one should perish. The Lord Jesus never gives up hope of any-one! When other people have given up hope for us and when we

have become absolutely hopeless about ourselves, the Lord is never discouraged. Christ, because He is love, never gives in to dismay or gives up to despair. I am so glad I have a God like that, for when others give us up it is wonderful to know there is a God in heaven who goes on hoping and planning for our good.

14. *Love endures all things.* This is perhaps the most wonderful thing of all: love cannot be conquered. It bears, believes, hopes, and then endures. In other words, when the person in whom you have trusted has let you down, love never gives in. It holds its ground in the day of defeat and still endures. Such love took Jesus to Calvary. How He endured the contradiction of sinners against Himself! "Hereby perceive we the love of God, because he laid down his life for us: and we ought to lay down our lives for the brethren" (I John 3:16).

This has been a photograph of Jesus Christ, and perhaps you have felt Him looking into your own heart and asking about the reproduction of His love in your life. If you would learn to live like this, first you must receive that love into your heart: you must come to Jesus, take Him as your Lord and yield to Him. How wonderful it is to know that Christ loved you so completely and perfectly! Open your cold, dead heart to welcome Him in, and then go out to love others as He did.

It is not a question of admitting to a truth, but admitting God into your life, and He is the God of all truth. It is not being orthodox, merely, but of becoming dynamic in the power of the love of Jesus. It is not trying to produce these qualities by self-improvement; it is submission to the Holy Spirit, who sheds abroad the love of God in our hearts day by day.

Does this photograph find you out? Does it show your life to be the reverse of everything that Jesus is? If so, I can tell you that grace can triumph, and make you just like this as you yield yourself to Him.

CHAPTER 23

THE PERMANENCE OF LOVE

I Corinthians 13:8

IN OUR two previous meditations upon this wonderful chapter of God's Word, we have seen in the first three verses the supremacy of love, in the next four verses the qualities of love, and now we come to what I have called the permanence of love, or, if you prefer, the power of love.

"Love never faileth." Now "never" is a long time, but love reaches to the uttermost. The greatest thing about love is that it lasts. You ask why? The answer is very simple: God is love. That love of God is shed abroad in our hearts by the Holy Spirit, so that the evidence of genuine Christian experience is not what we say we believe, but how much we love. This love is not only a quality of life but also a responsibility which we owe to fellow believers. The Apostle John reminds us, "Every one that loveth him that begat loveth him also that is begotten of him" (I John 5:1).

The three words, "Love never faileth," are not only the heart of this chapter, they are the heart of the whole message of God to the church at Corinth. We begin, therefore, with a brief consideration of the contrast that love should bring.

Here in the wicked city of Corinth is a church supposedly indwelt by the life of Jesus Christ. It is to be governed by His will and to reveal His love. But the city is mastered by materialism, by antagonism to the things of God, by resistance to the Spirit of God; self-centered, self-willed, and utterly callous to the things of eternity. There should be a great contrast, therefore, which marks out clearly where every inhabitant of that city stands in his relationship to heaven. Even though in everyday life they are rubbing shoulders constantly in business, in social life, in commerce, there is to be one factor which demonstrates unmistakably who is a Christian and who is not.

The church is called into fellowship with Jesus Christ (1:9); all His resources belong to them, and all their resources belong to Him. This is a partnership which, with dual commitment, is intended to be irresistible and completely victorious. It carries responsibility for all others: "I am debtor both to the Greeks and to the barbarians," declares Paul in his letter to the church at Rome. To make Christ known in Corinth is the obligation of this church, and to make Him known by this weapon of love is to insure their victory.

Salvation and obligation have always been inseparable. This contrast is true in the world in which we live today, and you can put the name of your own city or town in the place of Corinth. It is not your belief but your love that distinguishes your relationship to heaven in your particular surroundings.

But the church at Corinth had been failing in its task because its convictions concerning the gospel were shallow and inadequate. Not that there was anything wrong with their doctrine, but there was a great deal wrong with their behavior. A carnal church, a divided church, a worldly church, an indulgent church, a compromising church, can never effectively proclaim a spiritual message.

The trouble, of course, is very simply diagnosed. It is just that the spirit of Corinth—its luxury, indiscipline, cleverness, philosophy, all of these things—had crept into the life of the church. Party spirit, moral laxity, selfishness, and indulgence were sapping the vitality of this little group of believers until they were nearly overcome by the sin of the city around them.

Paul dealt with this, you recall, first by correction (1—11), and then by instructive teaching (12-13). He made it perfectly plain that what happened in Corinth need never have happened at all. It happened because the church was feebly trying to resist the avalanche of corruption by carnal methods: eloquence, wisdom, philosophy. All the time the church was ignoring its only source of victory and power, the law of love imparted by the Holy Spirit. When a church or a Christian begins to function on that higher ground, they live on a plane that puts them beyond all competition.

Once again, all this is manifestly true of the Christian church today. Our convictions concerning the gospel have too often been shallow and inadequate, especially in terms of our responsibility to others. It is not that our beliefs are wrong, but that somehow they do not seem to have affected our behavior. Indulgence breeds selfishness, indiscipline breeds shallowness, worldliness breeds compromise, materialism breeds spiritual laziness. All these things today threaten to engulf the whole Christian church until we lose the reality of our testimony to this generation. The intended contrast between the Christian and the unbeliever is absolutely unrecognized.

Where, therefore, is the conquest of the church? What can put us on a level where no one can compete? The answer to the need of the church today, I believe, is not a new visitation of God from heaven, but that Christians will begin to live in accordance with the principles laid down in the Word of God, especially the love of God imparted by the Holy Spirit when we were born again.

A love that never fails—that is the quality that is to characterize every child of God in every circumstance, seven days a week. The total Christan impact is made by a fellowship of Christian people mastered by the cross of Christ, imbued with the passionate love of the Lord, and therefore impelled by a principle that never fails.

This very remarkable word which we find translated "faileth" in our English New Testament has several significant meanings. Let me give you a few so that you may see the power of the thing that God puts into our lives.

The first meaning would be "love never falls to the ground," like the petals of a flower begin to fall, because there is decay in them. Love never does that, because there is no trace of decay in love. "Love never loses its strength," as does a traveler who sets out on a long, weary journey and grows tired, because love is inexhaustible. "Love never leaves its place," because love is immovable. As you look out on a starlit night, the stars sometimes seem to fall, but love never loses its place. "Love never drops out of line," like a poor, exhausted soldier on the march might do, because love is absolutely tireless. All its comrades may fall on the march, but love doggedly, patiently perseveres, because it can never fail.

As Phillips puts it: love "can outlast anything. It is, in fact, the one thing that still stands when all else has fallen" (13:8). Such love has its origin in heaven and its perfect expression in Jesus Christ our

Lord, who "having loved his own which were in the world, he loved them unto the end" (John 13:1).

This is the love of God from which nothing can separate the Christian, and this is the quality of life by which you and I are to be distinguished from everyone around us. Throughout all time and eternity we will be realizing more fully than ever the breadth, length, depth and height of the love of God which passes knowledge. Disappointments, disillusionments, and defeats can never rob it of its power, for love is of God.

To what extent has this love gripped us? There are some strange substitutes for love which master many people. A colleague of mine in the ministry had a hectic phone call from a young lady who said to him, "Pastor, what shall I do? There is a man who loves me so much he says that if I don't marry him he will shoot himself. What shall I do?"

"Nothing," my friend replied, "let him shoot himself."

Such a threat is not love, it is pure selfishness, desire, lust, whatever ugly word you might like to call it. Real love is self-communication. "God so loved the world that he *gave*. . . ." Love is communication of everything I have, also, for Him.

In 1951, twenty-four leaders of the China Inland Mission Overseas Missionary Fellowship met together in Manila at a moment of great crisis. Their personnel had come out from China intact, but what was to be the next move? One of those who was present told me, "It was a baffling experience. There was no awareness of the presence of God. There was no sense of divine direction; we felt completely at a loss as to what to do."

One day, by invitation, there came into that conference the last surviving daughter of General Booth, the Marechale. As she sat around the table with them, listening to their conversation, she suddenly interrupted: "Gentlemen, how do you spell 'love'?"

There was an embarrassing silence, and someone was on the verge of saying, "Well, l-o-v-e, of course," when the Marechale very gently shook her head and answered their unspoken thoughts. "No, gentlemen. Will you allow me to spell 'love' for you? It is spelled s-a-c-r-i-f-i-c-e."

Into that strategic conference came the melting and moving power of the Spirit of God, and for the past eight years that missionary society, reborn out of the flame of that moment, has undertaken one of the greatest efforts of missionary history in Southeast Asia.

"Though I speak with the tongues of men and of angels, and have not *sacrifice*, I have nothing."

Some people say that in certain churches there is no sense of worship. Maybe they are right, but what do you think can make a sense of worship in a congregation? It is not aesthetic beauty; it is not a building; it is not a psychological atmosphere. It is a congregation who have given themselves to God, and in whose lives there is love and sacrifice to the limit—then that church is just lit up with the glory of the indwelling Christ.

To be very practical, and to bring this right down to earth in our lives—if this is something that we would experience, here are some suggestions.

First, live in simplicity; hold the things of this world lightly.

Second, recover mobility. As a church we must move out today for God, and not be hindered by the machinery of organization or the lethargy of custom.

Third, determine priorities. What comes first in the life of a church, a board of administration or a prayer meeting? What matters most to us, a committee, a service, a bit of work, or travail in prayer?

Fourth, share responsibilities. Not everyone can do the work, but we are each given the measure of grace according to our gifts.

Fifth, limit activities. It is no mark of spirituality to be out at a meeting every night of the week. Busyness can be barrenness.

Sixth, exploit opportunities. Where you are right now, in your job, in your situation—there, attack for Jesus.

What are the consequences of all this? At the Judgment, love is the ultimate test with which we are going to be faced. In Matthew 25 our Lord was speaking about the time when all nations are to be gathered together before Him for judgment, and He Himself separates the sheep and the goats. What is the determining factor? What is the thing that puts them on one side or another for all eternity? It is love!

"I was hungry, and ye gave me meat; I was thirsty, and ye gave me drink: I was a stranger, and ye took me in: naked, and ye clothed me; I was sick and ye visited me: I was in prison, and ye came unto me."

"Lord, when did we do all this?"

"Inasmuch as ye have done it to one of the least of these my brethren, ye have done it unto me."

If I fail right here it is strong evidence that I may not have known Jesus Christ at all. No matter what I have claimed to believe, no matter what doctrine of faith I have supported, no matter what position I may have taken to defend the truth, if I have failed in love, I am not fitted for the presence of God. For it simply means that I have never been near enough to the heart of Jesus to feel His love and compassion.

Not that it does not matter what you believe; it matters a great deal that you should accept the Word of God from beginning to end as basic in your life. But the great test is: How much do you love? Love brings heaven near to others. Love lifts the fallen and comforts the sorrowing. Love challenges corrupt moral standards. Love faces broken homes and leads back to the New Testament standards of life.

How much do you *love?*

CHAPTER 24

THE VICTORY OF LOVE

I Corinthians 13:9-13

THE LAST section of this chapter Paul begins with a great declaration, "Love never faileth." Then he ends with an injunction, because the first three words of chapter 14 really belong to chapter 13: "Follow after love." In between that declaration and that injunction he puts a contrast and a comparison. Love is contrasted with gifts, and love is compared with other virtues. Then his great argument is brought to a triumphant note of victory: "The greatest of these is love."

In the last chapter I did not attempt an exposition of these verses, but that is what I want to do now. Let us look, first, at love contrasted with gifts.

The Corinthian church, you remember, was very proud of its gifts. The word "talents," which is quite popular today in some circles, would certainly have been popular with the church at Corinth. They were a very talented people; they had many gifts and much in which to take pride. But Paul is attempting to deflate their pride and put everything into right perspective.

He takes three of their most cherished gifts, prophecies, tongues, and knowledge, and contrasts them with love. He has already begun this chapter by pointing out that if you have all these gifts, and have not love, you are nothing. Now he considers them again, these things of which we are so ready to boast: "But whether there be prophecies, they shall fail; whether there be tongues, they shall cease; whether there be knowledge, it shall vanish away" (13:8).

In passing, please notice an important distinction: "For we know in part, and we prophesy in part," says Paul, "But when that which is perfect is come, then that which is in part shall be done away" (13:9-10). They will not cease, but they will be transformed. Tongues, on the other hand, will cease altogether. Prophecy and knowledge will be replaced by perfection: "Then shall I know even as also I am known" (13:12).

Tongues are ecstatic utterances, which in some circles are regarded as a mark of spiritual maturity, but which, in fact, are glaring evidence of immaturity. For ecstatic utterances are an indication that the soul has not settled down to abide in God. You find no ecstasy in the life of Jesus, because He always abided in God. Tongues, therefore, shall cease, but knowledge and prophecy shall be perfected.

We need to be very careful before we boast of our knowledge. My father handed down to me an encyclopedia when I was a boy and told me, "This is the last word in everything you ought to know." That was true then, but the encyclopedia is not worth the paper it is written on now as far as its information is concerned.

Knowledge is only in part now, but one day it is going to give way to perfection. Surely when Paul speaks about "when that which is perfect is come," he can mean only "when Jesus is come." The marks of imperfection are upon everything in this life except love. That goes on forever, and has on it the hallmark of eternity. Everything else is passing and transitory.

Paul uses a personal illustration here: "When I was a child, I spake as a child, I understood as a child, I thought as a child: but when I became a man, I put away childish things" (13:11). A person who is a man in years, but a child in mind, is a monstrosity. It is wonderful to listen to the chatter of a little child, but if you hear a man chattering like that, it is tragic! Every man, however, is still in essence a child; he has taken all the elements of childhood into manhood, but they have been developed and transformed; he has put away childish ways of speaking and habits of life and thought. So all spiritual gifts belong to childhood, and no one will go through into glory with them. At best, the greatest of mature Christians is but a child this side of eternity. But when Jesus comes and our maturity is reached, these gifts will become unnecessary.

As childhood is based on growing into manhood, so spiritual life here is based upon spiritual life in eternity. We begin our eternal life now. When I partially know something and I partially attain, I am moving toward the goal of that spiritual life which has its fulness and perfection in glory. Make heaven your goal, make maturity your aim, make Christ your object—but be very careful how you boast of your attainments. As childhood is absorbed into manhood, so one day our incomplete understanding of the things of God will be absorbed into perfect knowledge.

It is going to be wonderful to get to heaven! It will as completely transcend our deepest experience of Jesus Christ in this life as the midday sun transcends dawn. *Now* everything is only a dim reflection. I like that lovely translation of verse 12 by Moffatt, "At present we only see the baffling reflections in a mirror, but then it will be face to face."

We have sometimes been baffled by the reflections we have seen. Nature reflects the glory of God, but we cannot understand the earthquakes and volcanos that destroy so many lives. And history reflects the government of God. As we trace its course, we know that all through the ages God has been ruling in the affairs of men, but we cannot understand war and suffering and the horrors of strife between nations.

The Bible reflects the grace of God. But many circumstances come into our lives which we cannot understand, and we ask God why things happen to us as they do.

These things are just baffling reflections in a mirror, but then there will be no dullness of understanding, no more bewilderment. Then we shall look back upon a hundred and one circumstances that we have fought against, prayed against, complained about, and we will find that all things, after all, have worked together in a pattern for good—though we did not really believe it. Then there will be no sin to cloud our vision; there will be no interruption in our communion with God.

Everything here is imperfect, except love. It is love alone which is going to last, while all the talents, the gifts, the knowledge, the prophecy, the preaching about which we have been so proud, will all be done away. Love never fails; it goes on forever, in contrast with gifts, which pass away.

But I want to hurry on to the lovelier pastures in this chapter, because we find love compared with virtues: "And now abideth faith, hope, love, these three; but the greatest of these is love" (13:13).

How often these three words, "faith," "hope," and "love," are found together in the New Testament. For example, "Being justified by faith . . . we rejoice in hope . . . because the love of God is shed abroad in our hearts" (Romans 5:1-5). Then in the opening verses of Colossians: "we heard of your faith in Christ Jesus, and of the love which ye have to all the saints, For the hope which is laid up for you in heaven" (Colossians 1:4-5). And again in I Thessalonians 1:3, "your work of faith, and labour of love, and patience of hope." These three virtues are put alongside each other and compared; you cannot magnify love by minimizing faith and hope.

What is faith? Faith is trust that rests upon evidence and leads to action. That is the only kind of saving faith I find in the Bible. The whole fabric of life, social, commercial, and political, is based upon this principle. Our civilization could not exist without a measure of faith. But in terms of spiritual things, it is the foundation of our relationship with God. Only by faith do we become His children: "But as many as received him, to them gave he power to become the sons of God" (John 1:12). Unless I have faith, I am not His child, "for he that cometh to God must believe that he is, and that he is a rewarder of them that diligently seek him" (Hebrews 11:6).

What is hope? Hope is confidence in the future. I marvel at the tenacity of some people's hope in themselves and in the world, their attitude of, "Well, somehow it's going to work out all right in the end." From one tragedy and disappointment and heartbreak after another they pick themselves up and go on hoping, because they know if they stop, life will crash and everything become dust and ashes, because their hope does not reach beyond the grave. The child of God has a hope laid up for him in heaven: "But if we hope for that we see not, then do we with patience wait for it" (Romans 8:25). Christian hope is not a vague guess, but an absolute, confident assurance.

Both faith and hope are related to love. You cannot separate them. Faith possesses the past by laying hold upon Calvary and making it real in my life. Hope claims the future, and looks beyond into glory. Love dominates my life right now—this is Christian living. Faith says

Jesus Christ came to save me; hope says He is coming again to take me to be with Him; love says He abides in my heart today.

What is faith without hope and love? Just a cold, intellectual conviction with no saving power at all. What is hope without faith and love? Just a dream, a bubble that will burst one day. What is love without faith and hope? Just passion, just feeling, just emotion, without any principle or any foundation.

These three virtues are linked together, says Paul, and they abide. What is the meaning of the words "Now abideth"? Surely that "now" in this context is not the same "now" as in verse 12, where it relates to time and not to eternity. Some theological commentators say it is; I am no theologian, but I believe the Holy Spirit has spoken to me about this. These Corinthians thought that their gifts abided, but the whole argument of Paul here is that they do not last. The one thing that lasts is love, and along with love these other virtues: "Now abideth faith, hope, and love"—all of them abide. Of course, love is the greatest, but not one of them has the changing, temporary character of the gifts that Paul has been discussing. Here you have to give full force to that word "abideth."

Someone may say, "Surely faith and hope will not abide in heaven, for when I see His lovely face, what do I need with faith then? Will not hope be lost in realization? I will possess everything, then."

> Faith will vanish into sight,
> Hope be emptied in delight,
> Love in heaven will shine more bright. . . .

So says an old hymn—lovely, but you do not find that in the Word of God. The three elements of our relationship with the Lord are faith, hope, and love. When Paul says, "Now abideth faith, hope, and love," he is trying to tell us that just as our relationship with Jesus is forever, so also are faith, hope, and love. They go on as long as our relationship with Him lasts.

That suggests to me that life here and life in heaven are progressive. In other words, faith goes on possessing God more fully, and hope never ceases to catch new glimpses of His glory in the wonder of eternity. It is a mistake to think that eternity is synonymous with finality. In heaven there is perfection, but there are degrees of attainment just as one star differs from another star in glory.

Each of us will have all the blessedness we can contain, but we will have varying capacities and be progressing from stage to stage. "In my Father's house are many mansions," many resting places, the Lord said. These are places for refreshment as we proceed on our journey through the glory-land forever to new and greater discoveries.

Every glimpse of Jesus here prepares us for a greater view in time and eternity ahead. Then we shall see His lovely face—but do you mean to tell me that the first sight I have of Him, five seconds after I have left earth and gone into heaven, is all that I am going to have? Can a mortal being, brought out of the battle and conflict of life into the presence of God, at that moment grasp and comprehend all the glory of God and heaven? No, I believe that in the Bible eternity is presented to us as a continual communication of God whose beauty and glory and majesty are inexhaustible. The resurrected body, united with a redeemed spirit, is brought to live in the very presence of God with a progressive, increasing capacity to receive more and more of His glory. Every new height of glory scaled will reveal more wonderful heights beyond. Faith, hope, love—these three remain.

Our possessions and our gifts we leave behind us—only Christian character abides. At the gates of death we will lay down forever the various weapons which God, in His grace, has put into our hands that we might fight His battles—all our gifts and every other capacity for usefulness. But we will carry through the pearly gates of splendor the moral and spiritual character which the Holy Spirit, through the conflicts and testings of life, has developed within us. The three great elements of Christian character are faith, hope, and love.

Paul says that the greatest of these is love. He does not say it is more durable, or that it lasts longer, but that it is *greater*. It is not only greater than those things which pass, but greater than any of these things which also remain. Why? Because love is the home port —faith and hope are means to the end, but love is the goal. You cannot rest in faith and hope, but you can rest in love, as does God. "He shall rest in his love; he shall rejoice over thee with singing" (Zephaniah 3:17).

Love is greatest, also, because it is sacrificial. Faith and hope develop our own Christian character and strengthen us, but love is what we give to others. Love is greatest of all, because God is love. God does not believe, because He knows everything; God does not hope, because He possesses everything. But God loves, because He *is* love. You will never know the message of God to your own heart until you see, supreme above everything, His love revealed at Calvary.

Love is contrasted with gifts and love is compared with virtues, but most important of all, love is enjoined upon us: "Follow after love" (14:1). That means to practice it in daily life, to take every opportunity to encourage one another in the Lord. When we must say something critical and hard, for instance, or think we must, we should ask ourselves such questions as, "Is it true? Is it necessary? Is it kind? Will it help?" If not, then love is silent.

Then this chapter will read: "I suffer long, and am kind. I envy not; I vaunt not myself, am not puffed up. I do not behave myself unseemly. I seek not my own; I am not easily provoked; I think no evil. I rejoice not in iniquity, but rejoice in the truth. I bear all things, believe all things, hope all things, endure all things."

Therefore, follow after love, for God is love.

> Love of God, eternal love, shed Thy love through me!
> Nothing less than Calvary's love would I ask of Thee.
>   Fill me, flood me, overflow me,
> Love of God, eternal love, shed Thy love through me!
>   —*Amy Carmichael*

CHAPTER 25

THE GIFT OF TONGUES

1 Corinthians 14:1-25

HAVING BASKED for a time in the refreshing sunshine of the great love chapter of the Bible, we come now to thorny territory, for here is the classic portion in God's Word on the subject of tongues and the use of them. It is so easy for a church to become sidetracked from the main issue; it is so easy for one particular doctrine to be stressed beyond all reason until it is twisted from being truth to being error. Constantly it is the task of the ministry, as far as it is able, to ensure that the main responsibilities of church testimony are always in right focus.

Paul clearly states the two major objectives of any Christian fellowship. First, the edifying of the believers: "Even so ye, forasmuch as ye are zealous of spiritual gifts, seek that ye may excel to the edifying of the church" (14:12). Secondly, the conversion of the unsaved, that because of the united testimony of the Christians, those who come into the church might "report that God is in you of a truth" (14:25). This is the twofold purpose of any Christian fellowship, and nothing must hinder it. At Corinth, the question of tongues had received priority consideration, and Paul takes opportunity in this chapter to put things in right balance.

This is a very useful subject for us to consider, because the tongues' movement in this country is quite popular and widespread. We have a constructive job to do, and I don't believe in hitting at people, but I do want to say this very respectfully to those of you who may disagree with me: In most cases the tongues' movement today, at least as I have seen it expressed, is quite sincere, although misguided and mis-instructed. With the practical teaching of this chapter available, I just cannot see how anyone can go wrong on the subject. It is so clear that everyone ought to be able to understand it.

Paul is really applying here the principle of chapter 13, the triumph of love. He has insisted on church unity in chapter 12, and in the midst of that unity, diversity of gifts and operation. Here he refers back to three of these gifts: prophecy, tongues and interpretation of tongues (cp. 12:10). Further in that chapter he questions the Corinthian Christians, "Are all apostles? are all prophets? . . . do all speak with tongues? do all interpret? . . . and yet show I unto you a more excellent way. . . . Follow after love" (12:29, 30; 14:1). It is in that setting that we are to study Paul's instructions on the subject of tongues.

What is the gift of tongues in the New Testament sense of the word? To answer that question, let me ask another. Where do we find it? We find it first on the day of Pentecost (Acts 2). There appeared cloven tongues like as of fire which sat upon each of the disciples, and they were filled with the Holy Spirit and began to speak with other tongues. We find it in Mark 16:17, where the Lord Jesus was saying farewell to His disciples, and He said to them, "These signs shall follow them that believe . . . they shall speak with new tongues." We find it again in Acts 10:45-46, when, following Peter's address in the house of Cornelius, the Holy Spirit fell upon those assembled there and they spoke with tongues. When Paul came to Ephesus he found a few believers who were unrecognizable as Christians. He asked them if they had received the Holy Spirit and they said they had never heard of it. So they did receive the Holy Spirit, and we are told that they spoke with tongues (Acts 19:6). These are the only references in the whole New Testament; I have quoted them all.

Here is a gift bestowed first of all on the *whole* church at Pentecost, then given to *some* of the church on different occasions. The word used for tongues always means "ecstasy," when a man is carried into a realm in which he himself is living completely in mystery. He does not know what he is doing; in worship, he makes ecstatic utterances and speaks in tongues.

Notice this important instruction: "He that speaketh in an unknown tongue speaketh not unto men, but unto God. . . . But if there be no interpreter, let him keep silence in the church; and let him speak to himself, and to God" (14:2, 28). In other words, the gift of tongues (and please mark this carefully) is given for the purpose of speech to God and not to man, for ecstatic utterance in praise of God. If this gift of tongues is to be used publicly, it must be used in the presence of an interpreter, and if there is no interpreter, then let him keep silence in the church. Even the man who exercises the gift and who claims to speak in tongues does not know what he is saying at the time: "For if I pray in an unknown tongue, my spirit prayeth, but my understanding is unfruitful" (14:14). Paul knows what he is talking about, for he also has the gift, "I thank my God, I speak with tongues more than ye all" (14:18). So he is not being jealous. But he says, "Follow after love . . . covet earnestly the best gifts."

As the gift of tongues was given in the first instance on the day of Pentecost to all believers, and then later to other groups of believers, it is possible that some may even receive the gift today. I do not deny that. But if they do, they should remember that it is to be used in addressing God; it is not given for the purpose of witness to other people. It is quite beyond the understanding, not only of the people who listen, but of the person who claims to be using it. If it is used in public, there must be an interpreter present. Otherwise, the clear command of the Word of God is to keep silent.

Surely the instruction and definition in this chapter are beyond any misunderstanding. Yet this is quite different from the practice of the gift as exercised in many places today, where there is hysteria and wild enthusiasm, but no interpretation. Sometimes tongues are even demanded of the young convert as an evidence of the fact that he has been born again, before he is allowed to participate in Christian work. This is totally unscriptural; to demand the gift of tongues as an evidence of the fulness of the Spirit has no basis whatever in the Word of God.

Then what is the use of the gift of tongues at all? In the first instance, when it was given on the day of Pentecost, unquestionably it was used to arouse interest. "Tongues are for a sign, not to them that believe, but to them that believe not" (14:22). And on the day of Pentecost, people heard the disciples speak in their own languages the mighty works of God. They were not preaching; they were expressing worship in ecstasy, in languages by which they had never previously spoken. This led to inquiry which, of course, it was meant to do; in fact, the people thought they were drunk. Then Peter stood up and gave the interpretation, "This is that which was spoken by the prophet Joel . . ." and from that moment, when he had won their interest, he went on to preach the unsearchable riches of Christ.

Will you notice that in the second place there is a distinction to be realized: "For he that speaketh in an unknown tongue speaketh not unto men, but unto God . . . he that prophesieth speaketh unto men to edification, and exhortation, and comfort" (14:2, 3). At once you have the contrast between tongues and prophecy. Please don't put a narrow definition upon that last word. It literally means preaching, testimony, witnessing in our daily life.

In the teaching of this chapter there is a threefold contrast, very simple but very striking. "He that speaketh in an unknown tongue edifieth himself; but he that prophesieth edifieth the church" (14:4).

In relation to the man himself, and his witness, speaking in tongues is not doing anyone else any good, though it may be doing himself good. But the gift of prophecy, or preaching, or testimony, is for the sake of other people. If a man is going to ask from God that which will only please and edify himself, and make him think that spiritually he has gone further than others, is not his motive selfish? Paul says, "Follow after love." The motive of the Christian should not be to put himself on a pedestal; he is to be a channel through whom the Holy Spirit reaches out in blessing to the world. That is why Paul says that to preach or to witness is far better than to speak in tongues. "I would that ye all spake with tongues, but rather that ye prophesied: for greater is he that prophesieth than he that speaketh with tongues" (14:5).

The first point of distinction is in relation to a man's personal witness, the second is in relation to the church as a whole. Verses 5 to 20 deal with this part of the subject, and we cannot study it in detail, only highlight one or two things. If a man speaks with tongues, he does it to strengthen himself. There may be utterance, but, as Paul says in verse 8, if there is no clear piping of the tune, "if the trumpet give an uncertain sound, who shall prepare himself to the battle?" Who is going to prepare himself for the spiritual warfare as a result of confused ecstasy without interpretation? "In the church," Paul says, "I had rather speak five words with my understanding . . . than ten thousand words in an unknown tongue" (14:19). That ought to be enough! Five words: "It is Christ that died"—five words to preach the cross and proclaim a crucified, risen Lord!

Then comes a most important distinction, the thing that tongues cannot do in relation to the unbeliever. In verse 23 is a very interesting statement: "If . . . all speak with tongues . . . will they not say that ye are mad?" Paul had already warned them not to be childish; they are not to boast of their tongues. Their spirit of worship should be such that the unbeliever "will worship God, and report that God is in you of a truth" (14:25). This is what testimony can do that tongues cannot.

I find here also that there is a demonstration that must be recognized through the testimony of a believer. There is a threefold test of the reality of God the Holy Spirit in a Christian's life.

First, the Holy Spirit is primarily concerned with character and not with gifts (cp. Galatians 5:22-23). When the Holy Spirit comes upon a man at the moment of his conversion, He takes hold of him, as clay in the hand of the potter, to make him Christlike—clean, pure, and righteous. That is the work of the Spirit of God. This is why insistence upon the gift of tongues as evidence of spiritual reality is absolutely without authentic backing from the Word of God. The demonstration of reality is Christlikeness in character and in actions.

In the second place, the Holy Spirit comes to a man's life not to glorify Himself, but to glorify the Lord Jesus: "he shall not speak of himself . . . he shall receive of mine and shall shew it unto you" (John 16:13, 14). If you have been seeking for an experience of God the Holy Spirit that has taken you away from the reality of God in Jesus Christ, you are getting off New Testament ground. The work of the Spirit of God is always to make Jesus known. The evidence that a man is really filled with the Spirit is not that he has some extraordinary emotional experience, but that moment by moment he is conscious of the presence of the Lord Jesus Christ.

The third test of reality is that the Holy Spirit has come to equip us for Christian ministry and testimony: "But ye shall receive power, after that the Holy Ghost is come upon you: and ye shall be witnesses unto me" (Acts 1:8). The evidence of Christ within the life is that upon that man there is the anointing, the power, the authority of the Spirit for his witness.

Therefore seek the Holy Spirit in His fulness today! Seek Him with all your heart. Put things out of your life that get in His way, be earnest, be determined. Never let God go until you enter very definitely into a crisis with Jesus Christ, and know all the fulness of His life with you. Then you will blaze out for Him, and from your life will spread the fragrance of the indwelling Christ.

CHAPTER 26

SHARING THE LOAD ON THE ROAD

I Corinthians 14:26-40

I HAVE A conviction that many of us Christians need to have a new experience of the Lord. I am not going to quarrel with anyone about the terminology, but I am concerned about the reality of the experience. One Christian with reality is worth a thousand who are a sort of library of argument. You never win a soul to Jesus at the end of an argument.

Peter came to Christ because his brother Andrew came after him, just filled up with love. Andrew had spent only about twelve hours in the presence of Jesus. Before that he had been with John the Baptist, who had spoken about the Messiah. Andrew followed Jesus Christ to see where He lived, spent the night, and came out from His presence absolutely bubbling over. He went straight to his brother and said, "I have found the Messiah!" It was all so refreshingly simple.

Today we get so tied up in our doctrine and terminology that we lose the simplicity and glory of Christ and His gospel. We are not intended to be Christ's lawyers; we are His witnesses. Far too often today, I think, instead of being apostolic, we are apologetic: we are on the defense instead of on the attack.

How are we going to remedy this? I think it would be by stopping the things that displease the Lord, and starting what pleases Him. This is exactly what we find in this portion of the Word, something which again may prove to be controversial ground. But the simplest way into a new experience with God is through recognizing and rejoicing in our Christian fellowship.

Let us begin with one or two simple, obvious things. First, here is a principle that Paul reveals: "When you come together . . . let all things be done to edify" (14:26). Now I do not think Paul is describing here what I would call a normal evangelistic service in the church, a preaching service, but he is dealing with a fellowship meeting. This is what earlier Christians would call a "sharing" meeting, in which they shared some of the things the Lord had been saying to them; a practice which has, I am afraid, very largely died out these days.

At such a meeting, everyone comes with something to say, and they are all bursting to say it. The problem is to keep them quiet! One has a song he wants to sing. Another has a doctrine, that is to say, an exposition of truth. Another has a tongue, that is, he wants to burst out in ecstasy and praise. Another has a revelation, a simple testimony about some of the things Jesus has been doing for him. Another has an interpretation, that is, he has come to interpret the man who will speak in tongues.

Now that may seem very strange to us. Can you picture it in an average church today? There is no preaching of a sermon in this particular type of meeting. They did not come to church to receive all the time, but they came also to give out. The song comes from a heart that is overflowing, and the testimony comes from a spirit that just cannot contain itself. But nothing could be more powerful or more infectious than that, and it is the kind of thing that cannot be organized.

Notice also that everything is done for the edifying of one another. That is to say, as each believer expresses something either by song, or by tongue, or by testimony, or by word of doctrine, he is contributing to their upbuilding and to the ministry of the whole church.

The principle of this is not difficult to understand. In Ephesians, Paul elaborates on the unity and purpose of the church: "Endeavoring to keep the unity of the Spirit in the bond of peace. There is one body . . . one hope of your calling; One Lord, one faith, one baptism, One God and Father of all, who is above all, and through all, and in you all. But unto every one of us is given grace according to the measure of the gift of Christ" (Ephesians 4:3-7). Then later in the same chapter: "For the perfecting of the saints, for the work of the ministry, for the edifying of the body of Christ: Till we all

come in the unity of the faith, and of the knowledge of the Son
of God, unto a perfect man, unto the measure of the stature of the
fulness of Christ" (Ephesians 4:12-13). Here the principle is twofold. First, there is the unity of the Spirit, then one day we will
come to the unity of the faith.

It is a dangerous thing when Christian people try to reverse those
two things. There is *first* the unity of the Spirit, oneness of life in
Christ. Don't try to demand a unity of faith before you recognize
our fellowship in the Holy Spirit. The basic joy of Christian fellowship is oneness in the Holy Spirit, but that will admit many differences in points of view on some matters of doctrine.

The second principle is that no one individual believer ever comes
to the fulness of the stature of Christ by himself. It takes the whole
Christian church to achieve it in that great day to come. But in that
tremendous goal each of us has a part. As you exercise the gifts
that God has given you, for which He also gives abundant grace,
you are then contributing to the whole of the church, its testimony
and its glory.

What positive contribution are you making to this goal? In the
fellowship meeting, do you express in song, or testimony, or revelation, that which God has spoken in your heart? You say you cannot do very much as a Christian: you have only a song, or a testimony, just a prayer, or a thought from a text, but it is all part
of the display of the glory of the Lord. You can only exercise your
spiritual gifts in the fellowship of the church; you cannot live as a
Christian in isolation.

Such a "sharing" meeting, however, could obviously lead to confusion, and so Paul begins to correct certain practices. First, in verses
27-32, concerning those who in their enthusiasm would break out
into ecstasy all at the same time, Paul says not more than three of
them may speak in tongues at a meeting, and please, one at a time!
If he has no one to interpret, then let him keep silence.

"But I can't," some may protest, "I can't hold myself in." Paul
says you can and must: "the spirits of the prophets are subject to
the prophets" (14:32). In other words, don't let this get out of
hand—anything else is just lack of self-control. Wouldn't it be wonderful to have to quell the enthusiasm of Christian people who are
just longing to express themselves!

He says, moreover, they may all prophesy one by one, that all may learn and be comforted, but "Let the prophets speak two or three, and let the other judge" (14:29). In other words, let not more than three speak in the meeting, and let the others "discern"—that is the word, to discriminate. These limitations should really make us cringe when we think of the silences in our prayer meetings, of the long, painful waiting when nobody says anything! So often the same people pray time after time, and the others never take part.

But here is a little group of Christians just bursting to say something or to sing. Do you know why? Because this chapter is the outcome of the thirteenth chapter. All are cradled in the love of God that has been shed abroad in their hearts. You cannot take this passage out of context; you cannot force it or work it up. This enthusiasm comes because the Holy Spirit has stirred them. What a wonderful thing it would be if such times of sharing together became part of the life of our churches!

Paul now deals with another awkward problem. What are we to say about the ladies? This is another practice he is correcting. "Let your women keep silence in the churches: for it is not permitted unto them to speak; but they are commanded to be under obedience, as also saith the law. And if they will learn any thing, let them ask their husbands at home: for it is a shame for women to speak in the church" (14:34-35). It would seem from these verses to be too bad if she has no husband to ask! In this instance, however, the word means "man": go home and ask a man (for the woman is in subjection to the man). Here Paul is dealing with a situation which could easily get out of hand, and he continues to try to control their enthusiasm: "Don't let everybody speak at once!"

We need to compare this statement with what he has already written: "every woman that prayeth or prophesieth . . ." (11:5). In other words, he assumes that the woman will both pray and prophesy. In verse 23, he appears to contradict that by saying, "Let your women keep silence."

He has stated quite clearly in the first reference the circumstances under which a woman may pray or preach. She must not do it with her head uncovered for the simple reason that in Corinth for a woman to go around like that was an evidence of immorality. She must do nothing which would bring shame upon her head, and the head of the woman is the man. Therefore, let her pray with her head covered, and let her preach like that too, of course. Now this is local, but the principle of it is with us today. Let there be nothing done that might be misunderstood, in dropping a custom, or let there be nothing introduced into church life that might be irreverent.

In the second reference, where Paul says it is not permitted for the woman to speak, it is the common Greek verb *laleō*, translated about three hundred times in the New Testament with a variety of meanings. It means, "talk, question, argue, profess, chatter." It has nothing to do with prophecy or prayer; it is not public speaking, as such. That kind of behavior would disturb any Christian fellowship, of course. Today we admonish our children, "Don't talk in church." Therefore the woman is to keep quiet and ask any questions when they get home, if necessary. We need to understand this, too, that in those times women were in a place of subjection and, in fact, very few were literate. Let her better-educated husband or father explain what she has not understood.

Paul might equally well have said, "Men must keep quiet in the church. Don't chatter, don't talk or gossip, don't argue or question." Elsewhere he says, "I permit not a woman to teach, nor to have dominion over a man." But he might equally well have said, "I suffer not a man to teach by usurping authority," for that is the meaning of the word. Neither the man nor the woman is to teach by usurping authority.

Such statements have been distorted and twisted out of all context until they have brought bondage upon Christian women. I wonder what the mission fields would do without women; I wonder what the Christian church would have done without the ministry of women from the very beginning. What about the woman of Samaria, who preached to a whole city? What about Philip the evangelist's four daughters who prophesied? What about Mary Magdalene, who spread the news of the risen Lord? What about Priscilla, who took the great professor Apollos and put him right on one or two points of doctrine? In the Word of God there is unquestionably a place of ministry for both sexes. What Paul is seeking to say here is that everything must be done decently and in order, without confusion.

In the closing verses of this chapter a plan is outlined for this kind of meeting. Judging by verse 36, people in the Corinthian church were very proud of themselves: "What? came the word of God out from you? or came it unto you only?" In fact, they were so conceited they apparently thought that they had almost originated the Bible! Paul challenges them in verse 37 by saying, in effect, "If you don't agree with me, and think yourself a prophet, or a very spiritual person, then just acknowledge that what I am saying to you is the commandment of the Lord, not my own idea." But the great thing is, "Let all things be done decently and in order" (14:40).

Here is a plan for our lives and all our fellowship. The word "decently" means "with beauty," with comeliness and with honesty. Paul said that our behavior to those that are without God should be sincere; let there be honesty in our testimony. Let there be integrity about all our witness to the outsider, that he may see something of the loveliness of the Christian faith. In the worship of the Christian church, let there be something of comeliness, for this is the same Greek word Paul uses in 12:24 when he speaks about the comeliness of the body. So there should be a beauty, a rightness, a harmony in Christian fellowship and service.

The other word, "order," means "arrangement": let everything be done in beauty and by arrangement. In another connection in the New Testament the writer to the Hebrews speaks of the Lord Jesus being a High Priest after the order or "arrangement" of Melchisedec, with neither beginning nor end. "Perfection" is the full meaning. Let all things be done within the church with sweetness, symmetry and beauty, and with honesty and integrity toward the man outside. Let it be done in perfection, because we have a great High Priest who has an unchanging priesthood, and by whose loveliness and perfection alone we are introduced to our God.

How is this brought about in our lives? The Christian life in the New Testament is portrayed as one of loveliness and integrity. This is only possible when it has been brought into adjustment, into submission to the risen Lord. I wonder if those two words, "decently" and "in order," reveal some glaring failures in our lives today? Have things got out of hand? Is there utter disorder, confusion and chaos? The desire of God is that our lives may have symmetry and beauty, that they may be "in order" after the likeness of our perfect Lord Jesus. There is something very lovely about the prayer life that has orderliness about it. There is something lovely about the private spiritual life of a child of God that has arrangement and discipline. Its perfection is after the order of the Lord Himself.

This is the secret of the fellowship meetings and sharing: you cannot come to such a meeting to pray and sing unless in private you have a heart that is overflowing with love. That only happens when in your life there is the ordered, systematic, personal walk with God. What is your prayer-life like? Is it haphazard? Is your Bible study arranged and disciplined, or is it just hit or miss? It is out of that personal life of sweet communion with God that you can come to a fellowship meeting with a song in your heart and on your lips to give a joyous testimony for the Lord.

CHAPTER 27

YOUR PASSPORT, PLEASE!

1 Corinthians 15:1-11

PAUL IS now approaching the climax of his message to the Corinthian church. From many different angles he has challenged them concerning conditions that existed in their fellowship. He has revealed the emptiness of their supposed brilliance and philosophy. He has preached to them the message of the cross. He has rebuked them for their errors of practice and doctrine. He has proclaimed to them the ultimate triumph of love. In all this, he has presented to them what he calls in the opening verse of this chapter, the gospel: "I declare unto you the gospel" (15:1).

The one thing that matters, as he looks back upon his ministry to this church, is whether they have really received the gospel. How many of them are really following on what I have called the royal route to heaven? In this chapter, he brings heaven very near, and the golden gates seem to come into full view across the horizon.

Now the time has come for him to face these people with a verdict. To bring that about, he demonstrates that this gospel of ours is based upon facts, concerning which there is indisputable evidence, so there is no excuse for failing to believe and accept it. Not merely is the gospel based upon facts, but it has immense personal implications for all of us.

You have listened to the facts of the gospel, he says; if you have received it, therefore, you are standing in the power of the gospel: "By which also ye are saved, if ye keep in memory what I preached unto you, unless ye have believed in vain" (15:2). The awful possibility grips his mind as he thinks that the congregation may after all only have believed in vain. This, of course, all depends upon whether their faith has been resting upon facts based upon evidence, and has led to action. I want to give you some of the evidence of the gospel and point out some of its complications in our lives.

What are some of the facts? "I delivered unto you first of all"—that is, first in order of importance—"that which I also received," says Paul, "how that Christ died for our sins according to the scriptures; And that he was buried, and that he rose again the third day according to the scriptures" (15:3-4). That is the whole gospel in a nutshell. The story is simply that there was a man who lived in the Middle East about two thousand years ago and who was crucified outside Jerusalem. He was buried (He did not just disappear) in a fast-secured tomb, and on the third day He rose again. This is the narrative. But when I recognize that He was none other than Christ, the anointed Son of God, and that He died, as Paul says, for our sin, that He was buried, and that His body was raised from the dead on the third day, then this narrative becomes the gospel.

These facts are inevitably linked together: if you take anything away, you have no gospel. A cross without a resurrection is no gospel. These things: He died, He was buried, He rose again, constitute the basic elements of our Christian faith. Twelve simple men, most of them fishermen, could never have turned the world upside down unless all these facts were true.

What about the evidence for the facts? We have no right to expect that any should believe the gospel unless they have evidence.

One line of evidence is that the death of Jesus Christ must have been related to our sin, "For all have sinned, and come short of the glory of God" (Romans 3:23). The Scriptures say that death is not physical cessation from existence, but separation from God for eternity. If these things be true, then Jesus should never have died. Quite clearly His death was not related to His own sin, because even His worst enemies had to admit that He was without fault. Nevertheless, He died, and for that there is no explanation unless you connect it with the fact of sin.

We go back to the very beginning of the Book, when God spoke with such authority to the one who caused our first fathers to fall, and said to the serpent, "I will put enmity between thee and the woman, and between thy seed and her seed; it shall bruise thy head, and thou shalt bruise his heel" (Genesis 3:15). In other words, Christ was to suffer injury, but the wound inflicted upon the devil at the cross was authoritative and final.

From that very beginning of the redemption story, we can trace all through the Old Testament the fact that "he was wounded for our transgressions, he was bruised for our iniquities: . . . All we like sheep have gone astray; we have turned every one to his own way; and the Lord hath laid on him the iniquity of us all" (Isaiah 53:5, 6). Here is evidence that, as Paul says here, "He died for our sins according to the scriptures."

In that tremendous moment when Jesus cried with a shout of victory, "It is finished!" the hand of God stretched forth from heaven and took hold of the veil of the Temple and ripped it from the top to the bottom. No human hand could have done that: the veil, which kept humanity back from the glory of the presence of God, was torn aside. The veil, through which only one man once a year on the Day of Atonement could pass, in order that he might make sacrifice for his own sin and the sin of the people, was rent so that all might enter the presence of God. Now, because of what happened at the cross, there is a way through to God without any human intermediary: there is "one mediator between God and men, the man Christ Jesus" (I Timothy 2:5). The evidence that He died for our sins is indisputable.

What about the evidence for His resurrection? Without it, you just cannot explain the existence of the church at all; it would not have lasted one week if the truth of the resurrection had not re-vitalized that little group of disciples. Immediately after Calvary they were about to separate, their fellowship was collapsing. The birth and growth of the church is one tremendous evidence that Jesus Christ rose again.

Once again, Paul says that Christ was buried and that He rose again "according to the scriptures." The unfolding of God's plan of redemption in the Old Testament is the story of travail and of triumph. It is the story of suffering and yet of glory. In the same chapter from which I have already quoted, Isaiah 53, we read, "When thou shalt make his soul an offering for sin . . . the pleasure of the Lord shall prosper in his hand. He shall see of the travail of his soul, and shall be satisfied. . . . Therefore will I divide him a portion with the great . . ." (10-12).

There is also the evidence of the disciples themselves. Their incredulity at His resurrection and their unreadiness to believe the message they were going to spread abroad throughout the world reveals the fact that, as the Lord had said, they were "slow of heart to believe." Although they were to be responsible for proclaiming the Christian message, they began by admitting that they did not believe it.

Some have suggested that these early disciples were just being fools, that they knew the story was false. But would they ever have allowed themselves to be martyred for the sake of something they knew was not the truth? If only the Jews or the Romans could have produced the body of Jesus, all the rumors would have been quickly stopped, but they could not produce it.

In the third place, Paul seizes upon personal evidence as the greatest factor of all: "He was seen of Cephas" (15:5a). In an interview about which we know absolutely nothing, Peter met the Master face to face. "Then of the twelve" (15:5b); twice in the Gospels is the record that His disciples meet their risen Lord.

"After that," says Paul, "he was seen of above five hundred brethren at once." Jesus had told them to go into Galilee, where He would go before them. Hundreds of believers, scattered abroad because of their fear after His death, fled to Galilee, and there they met Him as He revealed Himself to them.

"Last of all," Paul says, "he was seen of me also, as of one born out of due time" (15:8). One never-to-be-forgotten day, when he was on his way to Damascus to continue his persecution of the young church, God met him in Jesus Christ and brought him upon his face to the ground.

Paul has marshaled his evidences for the gospel; the facts are completely unshakable. But Paul's concern is to know how far these facts have been effective, and how the Corinthian church has responded to this message of the gospel. That is the vital factor today: how far have you and I responded to the implications of this dynamic message of the gospel of Jesus Christ? We may not dispute these basic facts of the gospel, but what is the result in our lives?

What are the threefold implications of the gospel? First of all, to Paul there was a recognition of his own sinfulness: "Last of all he was seen of me also, as of one born out of due time. For I am the least of the apostles, that am not meet to be called an apostle, because I persecuted the church" (15:8-9). That is different language from what this man once used! In giving his testimony before King Agrippa, he said, "I verily thought with myself, that I ought to do many things contrary to the name of Jesus of Nazareth. Which thing I also did in Jerusalem: and many of the saints did I shut up in prison, having received authority from the chief priests; . . . and being exceedingly mad against them, I persecuted them even unto strange cities" (Acts 26:9-11).

In giving a bit of his own autobiography to the Philippians, Paul said, "If any other man thinketh that he hath whereof he might trust in the flesh, I more: . . . Concerning zeal, persecuting the church; touching the righteousness which is in the law, blameless. But what things were gain to me, those I counted loss for Christ" (Philippians 3:4, 6, 7). Now he is admitting that he did not deserve even to meet the Lord at all. The thing that shook him to the core, as he was confronted with the truth of the resurrection, was a recognition of his own sin—not his immorality, nor his impurity, but the downright arrogance of his proud heart. This was sin at its very root. When he saw that Jesus Christ was alive, he saw what a stubborn, proud, egotistical creature he was, and he fell on his face before the risen Saviour.

Unless this implication has really reached you, you are not a Christian, no matter what you say you believe. It is the crossing out of the capital "I," when you begin to recognize that sin is primarily not immorality or impurity. Of course, that is the fruit of it, but the basis of it all is the wretched, arrogant independence of your own selfishness.

The second implication of the gospel is a revolution of character: "But by the grace of God I am what I am: and his grace which was bestowed upon me was not in vain" (15:10). As Paul continued his own statement in Philippians 3:8, 10, he said, "I count all things but loss for the excellency of the knowledge of Christ Jesus my Lord: . . . That I may know him, and the power of His resurrection, and the fellowship of his sufferings, being made conformable unto his death." It pleased God to reveal His Son in Paul;

in receiving the forgiving grace of God he received the faithfulness and graciousness of the Master.

This man's life was revolutionized in character and personality through the gospel. Is your one concern that you might be conformed to the image of Jesus Christ? A recognition of sin involves revolution of character and habit.

A third implication of the gospel in Paul's life was a redirection of energy. "I laboured more abundantly than they all: yet not I, but the grace of God which was with me" (15:10b). This again is closely connected with Philippians 3:13-14, "I count not myself to have apprehended: but this one thing I do, forgetting those things which are behind, and reaching forth unto those things which are before, I press toward the mark for the prize of the high calling of God in Christ Jesus." Paul does not say he is perfect or that he has attained, but this is his goal, his ambition as he traveled along the royal route to heaven. As if he saw the pearly gates beginning to open, and soon would see the Saviour face to face, this truth of a risen Christ has so gripped him that he labored more abundantly than anyone else. He has given himself supremely to the task, above everything else, of making known his wonderful Lord. But once again he says, "It is . . . the grace of God." Three times in this verse, you notice, he speaks of grace.

Has the gospel got hold of you, or is this thing just theory to you? I tell you, unless in your life there has been a recognition of sin, which has brought you on your face before Jesus Christ, you are not saved! Until there has come a moment in your experience when God has shown you that sin is not only being immoral or impure, but basically it is *self* in all its ugliness, you know nothing of salvation.

If you can say, "Yes, I have come to recognize sin to be what God says it is," then has there been a revolution of character? Has Jesus Christ, your indwelling Lord, begun to form Himself in you? If there has been a revolution of character and manner of life, then has there been a redirection of your energy? If there have not been these three things, then have you believed in vain?

Paul was a Pharisee, fundamental with the best, but until these things happened, there was no new birth, no Christian experience, nothing to take him through the gates of heaven. I trust the Lord will speak to you through the Word and take you from the side-lines of Christian work into that more abundant labor with Paul, that the passion and enthusiasm that was once used in worldliness or rejecting Christ might be poured out for the salvation of others.

CHAPTER 28

IT'S GOOD TO BE ALIVE!

I Corinthians 15:12-34

As we approach the climax of the royal route to heaven and look back over the territory through which God has brought us, and as we are reminded of His faithfulness, His mercy, His patience, His love, surely every one of us can say, "It's good to be alive!" That phrase usually expresses delight in some experience which is here today and gone tomorrow. But here it has a deeper significance, and is far more permanent in this connection. I chose it to imply that our subject is that kind of life which lasts for all eternity.

What does it really mean to be alive in the spiritual sense of the word? Adhering to this context, I want to bring to your attention three suggestions concerning the real significance of life in Christ: what it means to be a Christian and what is involved in living a Christian life.

In the first place, a Christian is one who is implanted in the power of God. "For since by man came death, by man came also the resurrection of the dead. For as in Adam all die, even so in Christ shall all be made alive" (15:21-22). Here are two distinct circles, two spheres of existence: in Adam, in Christ. There is no possibility of a third. Everyone who has ever been born has chosen to live in one or the other of these two circles, and there is no neutral ground.

Implanted by our natural birth into the nature of Adam, we can be implanted by the miracle of the second birth into the nature of Christ. We can be born in Adam's circle, living and dying there.

Or we can be born in that first circle, then by the regeneration of the Holy Spirit be made alive for evermore in Christ's circle.

"As in Adam all die"; that takes us back to the very beginning of history when one man, our first father, the head of the human race, refused to accept the only limitation put on his liberty, namely, the sovereignty of God. He had been warned that rejection of God's authority would mean loss of his freedom, and he would become a slave to death. He had been told that if he wanted to enjoy freedom, it could only be along the path of submission.

But he took the reins in his own hands, defied God's authority, and promptly died. "Oh no," you say, "he didn't die." Yes, he did! The devil said he wouldn't, but he did, for at the moment of his act of rebellion he died spiritually. His relationship with God, the only source of spiritual life and power, was cut off immediately. The marks of death grew upon him, mentally and physically; there came into his life the fear of God, the sense of sin, the futile attempt to justify himself, the flight to escape from his Creator, and then later jealousy and murder.

So began the story, and so has continued the tragic breakdown of human life at every level, out of proper relationship with God. Each of us, by the simple law of heredity, has become involved in the tragedy; as Paul says, "by the disobedience of one the many were made sinners" (Romans 5:15).

It is true that we were not actually there when it happened, but we have all supported it personally by taking sides collectively and individually with that rebellion against God. We have all enthroned the capital "I" where God should be. We have all put self in the center instead of Jesus Christ. Consequently resistance to the will of God becomes natural, and sin in attitude and in action inevitable. The logical conclusion is, of course, that "in Adam all die."

The marks of death are upon each of us today: the stains of sin, of hatred, of all the decaying fruit of the self-life. Unless we move out of the circle in which we were born into the circle in which we are born again by grace, we will go on in rebellion, not only through life but through all eternity in hell.

That is one stream of life, but here is the other: "so in Christ shall all be made alive." Notice in verse 21: "For since by man came death, by man came also the resurrection of the dead." Here is heaven's counterattack, a full-scale offensive, the great invasion into the realm of sin and death. Man, made like God, has chosen the mastery of the devil and become like him. Now God is made like man in order to rescue man from the domain of Satan, and restore again the beauty and loveliness of the character of God which rebellion has obliterated. Because it was a man who rebelled, it is only by a man that the situation can be recovered, the lost ground retrieved. Only thus can the justice of God's throne be maintained.

Of course, it was not necessary for God to do this. Justice would have been completely satisfied if the whole human race had been allowed to perish forever. But God is not only just, He is loving, and love is only satisfied when it reaches out to seek and to save that which is lost. "But God commendeth his love toward us, in that, while we were yet sinners, Christ died for us" (Romans 5:8).

So Jesus came, the seed of the woman, to bruise the head of the serpent, to launch an attack upon the kingdom of darkness because those He loved were helpless slaves to the enemy. There was nothing attractive in the men for whom Christ died, but He took up the fight alone in hostile territory with not a single individual or circumstance to assist Him. He accepted the path of submission to the will of God. It was to be the only path of freedom for Him, as it is always the only path of freedom for any individual. He chose it deliberately, knowing it meant that He would have to be made sin for us that we might be made the righteousness of God in Him.

For the first time, the kingdom of death was invaded by a Man in whose life there was no sin at all. The Lord Jesus stepped down from the throne to the cross, tempted in all points like as we are, yet without guilt, and attacked death itself. He tore the bars away, as Peter said on the Day of Pentecost, "because it was not possible that he should be holden of it" (Acts 2:24). So as by one man's disobedience many were made sinners, "by the obedience of one shall many be made righteous" (Romans 5:19).

The ground has been recovered and the territory restored, and it now becomes possible for the human race to be put back on center, righteously forgiven by a holy God, with sin atoned for in the blood of the Son of God shed on Calvary. As Head of a new race, Jesus Christ won back for us the privilege of freedom and life by accepting the principle of obedience and submission.

In which circle are you living right now? Have you stepped from death in Adam to life in Christ? This is not something that happens by growth as the years pass by, but it is the crisis of a certain moment in your life. Submission to sin means slavery; submission to Christ means deliverance. Upon the man who is not a Christian are the marks of death. Upon the Christian are the marks of life, "For the law of the Spirit of life in Christ Jesus hath made me free from the law of sin and death" (Romans 8:2).

When you see a gigantic jet plane sitting on the runway, you may well stare and think, "How does a thing like that ever get off the ground at all?" Loaded with more than a hundred people and their baggage, sitting like a great dead weight on the ground, how can it ever fly? But presently, as you watch, the engines begin to whistle and whine, and that aircraft roars down the runway, screaming its way off earth into the sky. Has the law of gravity ceased to operate? No, the law of gravity is unable to control that plane because of the mighty power of a new law of aerodynamics, a new authority that lifts it up even against the gravity which would pull it down. The law of sin and death has not ceased to operate, but there is a new law in Christ's death and resurrection which overcomes the power of the old law.

The second implication of being a Christian is that we are involved in the program of God (15:23-28). Brought to life in Christ, the Christian discovers that now he is part of God's plan of redemption. What a great sweep Paul takes here in his theme! He goes back to the beginning of all history: "As in Adam all die, even so in Christ shall all be made alive" (15:22). Then he says, "But every man in his own order: Christ the firstfruits"—and that goes back two thousand years.

All the program of God's salvation for us depends upon that fact. If Jesus did not rise from the dead, then everything else is a fraud. That is the argument in verses 14-19 which Paul is not afraid to face, and I paraphrase it thus: "If Christ is not risen, then our faith is empty, our preaching useless, and he has failed to deal with sin at all. If he has not been raised from the tomb, we are still in our sins and all his promises are absolutely untrue. He is a fraud, an imposter, and his ashes are buried somewhere in Palestine today. There is no hope beyond the grave for anybody, and those who have died professing faith in him are just left there forever." "If in this life only we have hope in Christ, we are of all men most miserable" (15:19). If it is not true that Jesus is alive, you had better be anything rather than a Christian. If you are a professing Christian, and Jesus is not actually living today, you have the worst of everything in life.

"But he is risen!" says Paul. The evidence is indisputable, and Christ is the firstfruits. Then notice that as he sweeps over the centuries, instead of looking back to that day when Christ rose from the dead, he looks ahead and says, "afterward they that are Christ's at his coming." There is going to be another resurrection day when all who through the centuries have submitted their lives to the will of God and lived on the principle of submission to the sovereignty of Christ, will be raised from the dead also.

As if Paul couldn't stop there because his theme is running away with him, he continues, "Then cometh the end, when he shall have delivered up the kingdom to God, even the Father; when he shall have put down all rule and all authority and power. For he must reign, till he hath put all enemies under his feet" (15:24-25). That is the greatest glimpse into the ultimate future that the Bible gives to us. Paul goes further there than any other portion of Scripture. It is thrilling to know that Jesus does reign now! Amid all the storms and upheavals, Christ is on the throne. But on that day, He will deliver up the kingdom to the Father.

There is only one Mediator between God and man, the Man Christ Jesus, our great High Priest who ever lives to make intercession for us, and He will continue until His church is complete, until this new humanity of which He is Head, composed of every individual who has submitted himself to the authority of God in Jesus Christ, is redeemed; then He will deliver up that kingdom to the Father and present us faultless before the throne.

We are involved by grace in that program, stretching through all time and eternity. You and I, if we are saved, are members of a new race, and we live under a new sovereignty, for Jesus must reign until He has put all enemies under His feet. But the price of the enjoyment of freedom from self and sin is still the same: submission to the authority and will of God. Lift your sights high, fellow Christian, and understand the dignity and wonder of your position in Jesus!

But there is one more thing here, perhaps the most important of all, the most significant for us today. What does it mean to be alive in Christ? It also means that a Christian is implicated in the purity of God.

Notice the argument of these closing five verses: Paul says if it is not true that Jesus lives, what is the use of being baptized for the dead? The meaning of that phrase is uncertain, but I feel it can only imply one of two things. First, if Jesus Christ is not alive, why be baptized in the name of a dead Saviour? Secondly, in Corinthian times there was apparently a practice of being baptized on behalf of those who had already died, and who had themselves never submitted to baptism. If Christ is dead, there is no point in it anyway.

Again, "Why stand we in jeopardy every hour?" (15:30). In other words, if Christ is not alive, why suffer for Him? There is no point in that, either: "Let us eat and drink; for tomorrow we die" (15:32b). What is the point of character, morality, or decency? That is the logical outcome if there is no hope after death.

That, however, is answered by a smashing alternative: He is alive! Therefore these things are true, and because they are, "awake to righteousness and sin not" (15:34). "Evil communications corrupt good manners" says Paul in verse 33. Good behavior is essentially based upon sound doctrine; rejecting the truth and believing in absurdity is bound to lead to bad behavior. If that is true, then the reverse is also true: acceptance of Christ means good behavior. There is no margin between those at all, and therefore a Christian is one who is implicated in the purity of God.

The believer has been implanted in the power of God by his second birth, he has received the indwelling Holy Spirit and a new nature able to overcome the old. He is involved, therefore, in the program of God because the life that he has received in Christ has come to inhabit him in order to take him through death into glory. That is eternal life, which death and the grave cannot touch. But he is also implicated in the purity of God.

Do you see that you are involved in this? All who die perish for the sin of Adam. You are involved in that simply by your natural birth. All who live do so by the merit of Jesus Christ, and you have no part in that either; it is all of grace. You are not condemned for what you are by birth; you are condemned if you do not lay hold of Christ that you may not die. You are not judged because you are born with a nature that is sinful, but because you remain the tool of that nature for the rest of your life, when Christ has offered you life and salvation.

You had nothing to do with your first birth, but you are involved in its sin. You have nothing to do with the second birth, but you are involved in its deliverance. By the one you have been made a sinner, and let's acknowledge that you submitted to it time and again and never fought against it. Now by the life of Christ and new birth in Him, you are made righteous, therefore you must submit to that. "Know ye not, that to whom ye yield yourselves servants to obey, his servants ye are to whom ye obey; whether of sin unto death, or of obedience unto righteousness?" (Romans 6:16).

It was by submission to His Father's will that the Lord Jesus won the right for us to step out of slavery into freedom. It cost Him absolute obedience; His total submission from the throne to the cross won us the right to His life, His power, His faith, His purity. Who would ever presume to think that it could be otherwise? Yet there are those who say, "Believe, decide for Christ, and that is all." My Bible also uses the words "submit," "yield," "surrender." You cannot go into the glory except you are under the sovereignty of One who has won the right for you to enter. It cost Him absolute submission to win you. Dare you give Him anything less in return?

Which circle are you in? Are you in Christ, or are you in Adam? Are you alive, or are you dead? Are you the servant of sin, or are you a servant of Jesus Christ?

Here is the ABC of the Christian faith: Acceptance of His sovereignty, the Blessings of His salvation, the Character of His suffering. Have you accepted the sovereignty of Christ? If you have, then you are enjoying the blessings of His salvation, and there is being formed in you the character of God's Son. If not, step out of the sphere of death into the sphere of life, humble yourself to the submission and obedience He knew, and meet Jesus Christ face to face.

CHAPTER 29

WHAT WILL IT BE LIKE WHEN WE GET THERE?

1 Corinthians 15:35-50

WE ARE taking this chapter very slowly to make sure we understand that the royal route by which we have been traveling, in spite of its dangers and trials, but also with its joys and blessings, does indeed lead to heaven.

The chief reason for this fifteenth chapter of First Corinthians having been written is the question in the twelfth verse: "How say some among you that there is no resurrection from the dead?" Paul has answered by stating the evidence and showing the implications of the resurrection of Jesus Christ. Then he went on to show the significance of that in the life of each one of us who follows Him.

There still remain two questions unanswered, and they are in verse 35: "But some man will say, How are the dead raised up? and with what body do they come!"

In spite of all that Paul has said, there are some people who are still not satisfied. This is the question of a skeptic, and he is naturally so. Let us not blame him for being like that; at some time most of us have wondered about it, because we have all witnessed death and decay. There is often a lavish expenditure on funerals to seek to delay the certain inroads of disintegration. What about the body that has been smashed to pieces as the result of an accident in the air or on the highway? What about those who have been drowned in the depths of the ocean? What about those that have been blown into a million bits by bombs? I come from a country in which at least 75 per cent of the burials are cremations, simply because of lack of cemetery space. What about them?

How are the dead raised up? I am reminded of the question that Paul himself asked King Agrippa, "Why should it be thought a thing incredible with you, that God should raise the dead?" (Acts 26:8). Here we face a great question that is on the minds of many people, because they are convinced that it is completely impossible, not being able to understand the process. How could ashes scattered to the elements, bones in the depths of the sea, flesh that has gone back to mere dust, be brought together again?

How does the Holy Spirit answer these very natural questions? How are the dead raised up? With what body do they come? What will we all be like when we get to heaven?

The revised versions are a little more polite in giving Paul's reply to the questioner: "O foolish one!" (15:36a). Paul, with all his brilliance and understanding of the Scriptures, and of the things of eternity, has no problem in his mind about this. In order to answer the questions of those who are skeptical, he approaches the problem of physical death along three lines.

In answer to the first question, "How are the dead raised up?" Paul gives a simple illustration of a death that is an example, in verses 36-38. To answer the second question, "With what body do they come?" he points out a difference that is eternal in verses 39-43. Then he goes on to show us also a distinction that is essential, in verses 44-50.

If it is true beyond all possible doubt that the dead are raised up, it should make a big difference as to how we live our lives down here. If dust and ashes are in fact the end; if the cemetery, the crematorium, the ocean, are indeed the finish, well, as Paul says, "Let us eat and drink; for to morrow we die." But if the dead are raised up, if a man must, in his flesh, see God, if there is an appointment with Him awaiting every one of us, then our preparation for that day is important.

The illustration Paul gives is that of a simple grain of wheat. He invites us to look at it. First take it in your hand, and then plant it in the ground. What happens to it? It dies. But soon you will see a green shoot, and it unmistakably comes alive again, not the same grain you put in, but another plant. Yet by some amazing miracle, that new plant has come out of the grain that you put in the ground. The two are distinctly different, but they are absolutely connected. The grain which is put into the ground dies, but is quickened into life, for there would be no coming again into life except first that grain has died. As Jesus said, "Except a corn of wheat fall into the ground and die, it abideth alone: but if it die, it bringeth forth much fruit" (John 12:24).

The mystery of the resurrection of the body is no greater than that. If you say that because there are mysteries you cannot understand you refuse to believe the resurrection of the body, then logically you have to say, "I don't believe in harvest, because I don't understand the process."

Look at that bare grain you are putting into the ground, and then in a few months look at the harvest. A new life, a new plant, but out of the old grain that has been planted into death. You can only explain the miracle of its growth if you put God behind it, and say in the words of verse 38: "But God giveth it a body as it hath pleased him, and to every seed his own body." All the harvest fields of the world are eternal witness to the work of God who takes hold of death, brings it to life, gives it a new body, and produces the harvest.

We have seen it in the Lord Jesus Himself, "the firstfruits," as He is called in this chapter. Think of Him after His resurrection in a new body, and yet the old body. It was planted into the ground, dead. It was raised a new body, not subject to the laws of the old body, the limitations of conditions of time and space, not touched by exhaustion and pain. Here is the whole principle. As Paul says, it is no more difficult to believe in the resurrection than it is to believe in harvest. It is no more difficult for God to raise the dead than it was to raise Jesus Christ from the tomb.

You cannot explain how God does all that, but you believe in the "resurrection" of the grain because you see it. Because you cannot see it, don't dismiss the fact of the resurrection of the body from the grave, from the ocean, from the crematorium, from anywhere, for God is omnipotent, and with Him all things are possible.

Paul's answer to the second question is given in verses 39 to 43. We know it is true that all flesh on earth is not the same flesh; there is one kind of flesh of men, another of beasts, another of fish, another of birds. But this distinction is not only true on earth, it is true also in heaven. "There are also celestial bodies, and bodies terrestrial: but the glory of the celestial is one, and the glory of the terrestrial is another" (15:40). Then Paul cites again an example from the wonderful panorama of the skies above us: "There is one glory of the sun, and another glory of the moon, and another glory of the stars: for one star differeth from another star in glory. So also is the resurrection of the dead" (15:41-42a). There is a difference that is eternal.

Isn't it breath-taking when you think about it, that there are no two people alike? There are no two stars alike; there are no two fish, or flowers, or even blades of grass alike. There is an amazing distinction in the glory of earthly forms all around us. "So also is the resurrection of the dead," says Paul.

He is teaching that the difference that exists here will exist forever in the glory. A human personality is not wiped out by disaster; it is preserved forever, with all its distinctions and differences. Just as we have differed in appearance here, so we will differ there. That is why we will know one another when we get to heaven.

But as we have stood by the graveside of a loved one with our hearts utterly broken, what have we seen there? Notice three words that Paul uses to describe what every one of us has realized on such an occasion: "It is sown in corruption . . . in dishonour . . . in weakness" (15:42b, 43).

By the grave we have seen the corruption of the human body. No matter how ornate the funeral, and no matter how great an attempt may be made to take away some of the sting by something of fragrance, nevertheless at the graveside we know that there is dishonor. We have witnessed weakness, for as the body is put into the ground the processes of decay are already setting in and the body has to be hurried away.

Paul tells us, however, that there is one thing in which we will all be alike. When the trumpet shall sound, we shall all be lifted out from the grave on that great resurrection day. Something will happen to all of us that will completely counteract everything that took place in that grave. There the body was sown in corruption, but it shall be raised in incorruption, with no disease, no decay, no pain, no suffering, no blemish—perfect.

It has been sown in dishonor, it will be raised in honor, a body to glory in. The bodies of men and women redeemed by the blood of Christ have been indwelt by the Spirit here, but the resurrection body will be the greatest glory in heaven. For there the Lord Jesus is to be admired in all of us who have believed; we are to be the jewels in His crown.

In this body we have sinned; in that body we shall be made perfect. In this body we have failed; in that body we shall love and obey God without fault. In this body we have been weak and helpless, full of troubles; in that body we shall be free from all such limitations and defects. So shall it be in the resurrection of the dead.

In the closing verses of our study Paul gives another answer. A literal transliteration of the adjectives in verse 44 would be, "There is a psychic body, and there is a pneumatic body." Right now, you and I are living in a "psychic" body. In heaven we are going to live in what Paul calls a "pneumatic" body.

The natural or psychic body is governed by the soul; of that body Paul says, "I keep under my body." It is a body that has to be mastered, kept in subjection, for in it are all the latent possibilities of sin. "Who shall deliver me from the body of this death?" he cried, speaking of the downward drag of the physical frame in which he lived. If you do not keep this body, with all its natural inclinations, in subjection, it will lead you into endless sin and trouble, defeat and failure.

There is also a "pneumatic" body; that comes from the Greek word meaning "spirit." It is therefore a spiritual body, governed by the Spirit, no longer under the mastery of the animal life, but under the complete control of the Holy Spirit of God.

Now here is the miracle: I sow in death the "psychic" body; God raises in the resurrection the "pneumatic," or spiritual body. I sow in death the natural; God raises that which is supernatural. I sow in death that which is of sin; God raises that which is of victory. The two are essentially different, but the one comes out of the other.

Think of Jesus after His resurrection, as He walked along the Emmaus road, when He came to the Upper Room. There had never been a resurrection from the dead until then. You may say, "But what about Lazarus?" He was not resurrected from the dead, he was revived from the dead, and because he still had a body that was weak and decaying, he went back to the tomb.

When Christ arose, He was beyond all the limitations and weaknesses of the human body. Doors need not be opened, He came through them. He could make Himself known or unknown as He wished.

How was Jesus Christ brought out of the grave a resurrection body, free from every taint of mortality and weakness? "The first man Adam was made a living soul; the last Adam was made a quickening spirit" (15:45). The first Adam was made a living soul: natural, earthly, flesh and blood, and became mastered by sin. The last Adam, Christ, was made a quickening spirit, life-giving, spiritual, heavenly. As we have borne the image of the earthly, so we are to bear the image of the heavenly.

The Lord Jesus bore the image of the first Adam in His flesh; then He brought out from the grave a resurrection body with no limitations. First Christ, in His mighty redemptive power, lived in a natural body; He had to do that in order to redeem us. In that natural body He never sinned or failed; His was the only perfect "psychic" body, and He put it in a tomb. But on the third day He rose again, and now out from the natural has come the supernatural, the spiritual.

You and I have borne the image of the earthly indeed, with all its sin, failure, frustration, pain, suffering, sorrow, heartbreak. As we have borne that image, we can bear the image of the other: "we shall also bear the image of the heavenly" (15:49). By second birth we have received the foretaste of that which is spiritual and eternal. Although we have been made in the image of Adam by our first birth, the Lord from heaven has, in sovereign grace and mercy, stepped into the personality of each of us who has come to Him in acknowledgment of sin, and given us resurrection life, that which is spiritual.

Paul shows us an inescapable conclusion: "Flesh and blood cannot inherit the kingdom of God; neither doth corruption inherit incorruption" (15:50). Of course not! It is of the earth, earthy, living in sin, decay, defeat, and bondage. If, however, the Lord Jesus has come into our lives and we have received the quickening Spirit, we have a foretaste of that which is to be forever.

As we face the future, unless Jesus comes first for us, we know we shall all experience death. What happens then? They will put in a coffin, with much respect, that which is of flesh and blood, that in which we have sinned and failed. On the great resurrection day, out from this, and yet different from it, God will raise up that which is spiritual.

If, therefore, you would bear one day the image of the heavenly, you must possess heavenly life now. Beyond the grave only that which is spiritual can enter heaven, that which has already been through death in Christ. Only that life will remain eternally which has begun with the second birth, when in commitment of my life to Jesus Christ, I received His life into my heart.

There is a logical conclusion to this message, which is not found in these verses except by implication. Paul does not mean that the unbeliever can say, "That is all very well for you Christians, but I am not going to bother. It doesn't matter about me, I'll be left there." Oh, no, you won't! The dead who die out of Christ are not left in disintegration and corruption.

"I saw the dead, small and great, stand before God" says John in Revelation 20:12. Every one of them will be there from every race and nation: murderers, adulterers, whoremongers, unbelievers—all are included. It does not matter whether they have been moral or immoral, religious or irreligious, sinful or comparatively righteous, they are unbelievers. They have never received the Lord from heaven, and therefore they die in corruption, and shall not put on incorruption because they have never established a relationship with God in this period of time. "And whosoever was not found written in the book of life was cast into the lake of fire" (Revelation 20:15).

There is a resurrection of the believer, and that is what we are going to be like when we get there. But there is a resurrection of the unbeliever, too. Therefore I must ask you, in the name of the Lord Jesus, are you still in Adam, or has there been a day in your life when the image of the Lord Jesus was implanted into your heart, and you received Him, the second Adam, and a new birth of that which is spiritual? If so, you are able to say, "Though I walk through the valley of the shadow of death, I will fear no evil: for thou art with me" (Psalm 23:4).

CHAPTER 30

THE FINAL VICTORY

I Corinthians 15:51-58

I SUPPOSE that to the casual observer the royal route to heaven ends as does every other way of life, in death. The language of such a person would be, "If the end is just the same for all of us, why should I bother about being a Christian, especially the kind of Christian depicted in these messages?"

Of course, it is perfectly true that unless there is real assurance of victory at the end of the road, it is pointless to endure everything that is involved in the journey. As Paul has already said, "If in this life only we have hope in Christ, we are of all men most miserable" (15:19). To many people the idea of our earthly bodies, which moulder into dust, or are scattered over the face of the earth, or drowned in the oceans, or exploded into the elements by bombs, being raised and united again to an undying soul seems quite impossible, even fantastic.

But Paul has proved the resurrection of the dead in this chapter beyond all shadow of doubt. He has demonstrated the fact of the resurrection of Christ; he has produced evidence to support it. He has shown its implications for a Christian, and he has declared that Christ is only the firstfruits, and afterwards they that are Christ's at His coming will be raised. In other words, the resurrection of Jesus from the tomb is just the beginning of a great harvest. Within that word "afterwards," are all the hopes, the sighs, the longings, the tears, the disappointments, the tests, the faith and confidence of God's people ever since.

As we have seen in our last two studies, God has equipped us by the indwelling life of His risen Son to bear Christ's image in place of that of the first Adam. Now we will consider the final victory that is to be ours, and may God grant it may be very soon!

I want to point out to you from this portion, in the first place, the victory that confronts us. I have a word to say to the believer, a word to the unbeliever and the skeptic, and also to the one whose heart is heavy with a sense of loss, who longs for that day when he will see his loved ones and the Saviour face to face.

First a word to the Christian: look at this victory that confronts us all. "Behold I show you a mystery" (15:51). This arouses our attention; it alerts all our faculties to discover what he has to say. A mystery is not something that cannot be explained, but something that you will never prove by intellect, something that you will never reason your way into by sheer process of argument. You do not find God that way; you can argue yourself out of blessing and eternity, but never into it.

Here is the mystery which has been revealed to Paul: "We shall not all sleep." What a lovely word that is to describe the condition of those who have departed from this life trusting in the Saviour. They are asleep in Jesus. To be absent from the body is to be present with the Lord, and to be with Christ is far better. They are waiting to be clothed upon with a new body, waiting for your arrival and mine as eagerly as we wait to see them once again. They are waiting for all the purposes of God to be fulfilled; waiting until all those for whom Christ has purchased eternal salvation have received Him and are redeemed through His blood, when the number of the elect is complete and the bride has made herself ready. The dead are "asleep in Jesus," a redeemed spirit without a body waiting for that tremendous moment, that day of resurrection.

Then what will happen? Suddenly, in the twinkling of an eye, the trumpet shall sound and the dead shall be raised incorruptible, and we shall be changed. Notice that we shall not all sleep, but we shall all be changed. There will be a generation which will not die, for in the middle of life, among the ordinary events of human experience, this change will come. They will not go into the valley of the shadow; they will not taste the darkness of death, but all shall be changed. There are no dates given, but it will be at the exact moment which is in the purpose of God. It could happen before this day is out.

In the case of those who have died, corruptible flesh shall put on incorruption, the body that is laid aside in the tomb will be raised a new body. So also, for those who are alive on that great day, mortal shall put on immortality. Corruption cannot inherit incorruption; mortality cannot inherit immortality.

I am reminded of the man who came to Jesus and said, "Good Master, what must I do that I might inherit eternal life?" (Mark 10:17-22). You cannot inherit eternal life. The Lord's answer to that rich young ruler was what Paul is constantly emphasizing: put off the old, put on the new. Put on the new man in Christ and make no provision for the flesh.

You do not inherit incorruption, you put it on. You do not inherit eternal life, you put on the Lord Jesus, and in Him is eternal life. One day the corruptible body shall put on incorruption, because the spiritual body put on Jesus Christ here, forsaking the flesh and its method of life. The Christian has recognized that self-satisfaction, greed for possessions, money, and pleasure, even self-improvement and the desire to be important, have all blocked his view of glory and made him completely earthbound. At conversion these things have been put off. He has repented of them and put on the Lord Jesus Christ, and at that moment there is born in his heart that new nature of incorruption, of immortality.

There comes a day when that incorruptible spirit shall be reunited again with a body that will then put on incorruption, also. The fate of your soul will also be the fate of your body; the two are partners. They separate for a little while, as the body waits for its resurrection. But what happens to your spirit one day happens to your body, also. It is put aside in the grave, but it is raised again incorruptible if it has already, in the course of this life, been the home of a spirit that is incorruptible—the very life of Jesus Christ. Death cannot touch the soul or the spirit of a Christian. It touches the body a bit, for the tent in which we live soon shows signs of collapsing.

Paul uses the same kind of language in First Thessalonians: "For the Lord himself shall descend from heaven with a shout, with the voice of the archangel, and with the trump of God: and the dead in Christ shall rise first: Then we which are alive and remain shall be caught up together with them in the clouds, to meet the Lord in the air: and so shall we ever be with the Lord" (4:16-17).

We talk about sending a space ship to the moon—what an event that will be! But by that time you and I may have bypassed the moon and be in glory. I don't want to be shot up into heaven by a rocket, but I'm looking forward to being called up by a trumpet from the Lord. Not to be propelled up into space by colossal earthly effort, but to be pulled up by the magnetism of my Lord Jesus coming in power and glory—that is my anticipation.

This is the assurance that comforts us. "O death, where is thy sting? O grave, where is thy victory? The sting of death is sin; and the strength of sin is the law. But thanks be to God which giveth us the victory through our Lord Jesus Christ" (15:55-57).

Here is the Apostle Paul daring to laugh at death and the grave! He stands confronting an enemy which has held in its clutches every human being through all history except two: Enoch who went for a walk with God and never came back, and Elijah who was taken up to heaven in a chariot of fire. Death would never have existed apart from sin, however, for if there had been no sin, there would have been no death. Death, I presume, would simply have been translation from earth to heaven, as in the case of Enoch.

The law of God passed sentence of death upon Adam, and it still says to every human being, "The soul that sinneth, it shall die." The law of God cannot be set aside. The dominion of death is universal, and the law is as unchangeable as the God who made it. "As by one man sin entered into the world, and death by sin; and so death passed upon all men, for that all have sinned" (Romans 5:12). Because death has power over the whole human race, if justice is to be maintained in order instead of chaos before the supreme court of heaven—the one place where we know absolute truth and justice prevail—the law of God is unalterable, and some provision has to be made for His love and mercy to act.

Therefore the Lord Jesus Christ has put Himself in our place, and has satisfied every demand that God can ever make upon anybody. Does God's law require the death of the man who breaks it? Very well, He has died for the sinner. Does the law demand that the offender of the law shall die? Very well, He was made sin for us, He who knew no sin, and He bore the penalty of a broken law. Must a man have a perfect righteousness to stand before a holy God? Very well, then by Christ's obedience unto death He has established an everlasting righteousness which is credited to every man who comes to Him as a sinner and receives Him by faith.

Then the sting is taken out of death because sin is cancelled, and the strength of the law to condemn us is removed, because it has been fulfilled in Jesus Christ. Therefore death is no longer an enemy to the Christian, but an instrument of freedom from the reign of sin in his body. There will always be that human fear of entering the valley, unless Jesus comes first. Yet, as I think about death and what it means, I think of it as a friend who comes to me and draws aside the veil which has been hiding the full glory of the Saviour from my eyes. That is death to the Christian. As Paul says, "Thanks be to God which giveth us the victory through the Lord Jesus Christ!"

If you are a believer, then just put your foot on the neck of the enemy and laugh at him: "O death, where is thy victory?" Instead of swallowing you up, praise God, death itself will be swallowed up! Instead of casting you into an eternal hell, death itself will go there: "And death and hell were cast into the lake of fire" (Revelation 20:14). Because of Calvary the tables have been turned. God is just, and yet He is the Justifier of them that believe in Jesus. That is the glory of the gospel; that is the comfort that assures us.

Does that make your heart rejoice? But we have also a call that challenges us: "Therefore, my beloved brethren, be ye stedfast, unmoveable, always abounding in the work of the Lord, forasmuch as ye know that your labour is not in vain in the Lord" (15:58).

I believe that to preach or teach the Bible without applying it to life is sin. The Bible is not a textbook, nor a book of theory and doctrine. It is to be the compass, the chart, the guide for my whole life. If I teach it in Sunday school or preach it from the pulpit, and fail to apply it to my listeners, I am guilty before God of sin.

What is the application of this message? It tells us that we are to prepare for victory on that great day. First, we must give steadfast adherence to the faith and not let anyone rob us of our confidence in God. Hold fast the profession of your faith; don't be moved away from the hope of the gospel.

Then be diligent in the performance of your duty: "always abounding in the work of the Lord." Never be satisfied with just a little bit of service for Him; give yourself wholly to it. Of course, be sure that it is the work of the Lord: ask yourself how much of your service in the past days has been the work of the Lord. He came to seek and to save that which was lost. How much has there been of testimony, of witness, of real earnest endeavor to reach souls that are perishing? How much of it has simply been administration, program work, machinery?

We have the assured promise of reward: "your labour is not in vain in the Lord." Labor means sweat and blood and tears. The Lord is not unrighteous that He should forget your work and labor of love; with His own hand one day He will repay. It is only the man who is really abounding in the work of the Lord who can be assured that his faith is saving faith..

This is the victory ahead for Christians. But may I say to you very solemnly that if you are an unbeliever, death is no friend to you. It is an enemy. If you have never sought refuge in the Lord Jesus Christ, if you have not come to Him out from the curse of a broken law, you are still in sin and therefore must perish. Then death is dreadful. It is just like opening the prison door for a criminal to take him out for execution. For a season your body will sleep in the dust, certainly, but your soul will re-occupy it one day. The body is put in the tomb and the soul goes to the place of the departed dead; but those who have been partners in sin and in rejection of Christ will be partners together in that awful judgment before the throne of God.

But it need not be so. If you would just look to Jesus Christ now, to Him who has fulfilled the law for you, taken away all your guilt by His precious blood; if you would but humble your heart before Him, because He lives, you shall live also. Quit this life of rebellion; put an end to the reign of sin and death. Let Jesus Christ step in and take charge, and He will lead you to final victory!

CHAPTER 31

RESPONSIBILITY TO OTHERS

I Corinthians 16:1-6

THESE OPENING verses might appear an anticlimax to what has gone before. We have been given a glimpse of the glory that awaits us, and an assurance of the victory even over death that is ours through Jesus Christ our Lord. The sound of the trumpet with its call to resurrection has seemed wonderfully real. Surely, anything beyond that must be somewhat reactionary.

"Now concerning the collection." What a coming down to earth! Well, of course—because a Christian is a man whose heart is in heaven, but whose feet are on the ground. Every glimpse of future glory is given to the child of God in order to encourage him to present-day growth in consecration and responsibility. Certainly we do come down to earth here, but I trust we have been refreshed and greatly challenged by all that God has been saying to us in the course of our journey along the royal route to heaven.

As a matter of fact, this chapter is the crown of all the teaching of this Corinthian letter. The epistle begins with the reminder that "God is faithful, by whom ye were called unto the fellowship of his Son Jesus Christ our Lord" (1:9). Because of that, they have also been called into partnership with one another, for through the whole church there pulsates one common life, the life of the indwelling Holy Spirit, flowing through the whole body of the church, whether at Corinth, Jerusalem, Galatia, Macedonia—anywhere.

In both of these relationships, toward God and toward their brethren, the Corinthian church had tragically failed. The whole direction of Paul's teaching in this letter has been to restore their broken fellowship with God, and their broken communion with one another. Once the Christian is right with God, then his relationship with his fellow believer is settled.

These things cannot be interpreted in a local sense, and therefore we find here a fitting climax to this epistle. The whole church comes into view, because the result of our right relationship with God is the glory of that moment when death is swallowed up in victory, and the fruit of our right relationship with fellow Christians is our acceptance of a sense of responsibility to the whole church. Our responsibility is as wide as our fellowship, and our fellowship is as wide as the whole body of Christ on earth. There is no limit to it.

Here, then, Paul refers to the churches in Galatia, Jerusalem, Macedonia, Ephesus, Achaia. Here we find brought to our attention Timothy, Apollos, Stephanas, Fortunatus, Achaicus, Aquila and Priscilla—a world-wide fellowship and a world-wide responsibility.

To get the meat out of this portion, let us look at what I would call "the church and its poverty": "When I come, whomsoever ye shall approve by your letters, them will I send to bring your liberality unto Jerusalem" (16:3). Paul's teaching has been centered upon the church's relationship to the Lord and to one another. Having settled that, he now lifts their eyes to a wider horizon, and asks them to consider their responsibility to the poor church at Jerusalem, the original home base of all New Testament missionary enterprise.

Paul always has a great concern for this church: for instance, "It hath pleased them of Macedonia and Achaia to make a certain contribution for the poor saints which are at Jerusalem" (Romans 15:26). The adjective indicates absolute poverty. They were a penniless crowd at Jerusalem, so far as this world's goods are concerned; there was not a rich man among them. If there had been, Paul would have been saying something to him!

The reasons for their poverty are not far to seek. If you link early church history with the Word of God, you find that they were poor for two basic reasons, one they could not very well help, but the other they could. There had been a famine about that time, which made life very difficult for them on the material level, and they were not responsible for that. The other reason is that they had tragically failed in their obedience to the New Testament commission. The Lord Jesus had charged them to go forth to be His witnesses, beginning at Jerusalem, to Judaea, to Samaria, to the uttermost parts of the earth (Acts 1:8). But they did not go out until they were scattered by opposition. They hugged their privileges, they rejoiced in their position, and when they began selfishly to cherish that which God had given them, they lost their spiritual power. God sent persecution to drive them out to preach the gospel. By that time they were reduced to a state of utter poverty.

Here is a great principle: "There is that scattereth, and yet increaseth; and there is that withholdeth more than is meet, but it tendeth to poverty" (Proverbs 11:24). That statement is true in regard to both life and possessions. The Lord Jesus said, "Whosoever will save his life shall lose it: and whosoever will lose his life for my sake shall find it" (Matthew 16:25).

Maybe you have had opportunity to watch this rule in operation. Just let a man hold back from total commitment to the sovereignty of Jesus Christ, and watch him shrivel up spiritually. See how he becomes a critic of everything that is spiritual in the church, because of the front he has to put up in attempting to justify his position.

On the other hand, let a man scatter his life abroad, fling it away for Jesus' sake, then watch him increase in spiritual stature. You can always equate your spiritual growth or lack of it, your wealth or poverty in the things of the Lord, with your obedience to the Master. Just prove it! Obedient living and overflowing blessing are inseparable. And just as inevitably, disobedient living results in the withholding of the blessings of God.

This is also true in relation to material things. To withhold that which ought to belong to the Lord never leads to a man's material enrichment; but to practice Matthew 6:33, "Seek ye first the kingdom of God, and his righteousness," is to experience the faithfulness of God, who never has broken His promise: "My God shall supply all your need according to his riches in glory" (Philippians 4:19). Here is a principle from which there is no exception. This will always be a reason for the poverty of the child of God, if we have failed to obey the Master and live up to the hilt of His Word. Failure on the part of the church at Jerusalem caused poverty which created a responsibility.

In the second place, I want you to notice what I would call "the claims of the pioneer missionary." Because the lines of communication were very different then from what they are now, the Christians at Corinth could not possibly get to the church at Jerusalem themselves. They could not fulfill their responsibility in person, but they could through their missionary, Paul.

Here you see Paul as a worker, called into fellowship with the Lord and His people, opening his heart to the church at Corinth. There is a glorious uncertainty about his own future in these verses. To those of us who are bound to a program, this is a refreshing breeze from heaven! It would be a wonderful thing if sometimes the Holy Spirit just broke through our little plans and opened our eyes to the far greater purposes of our wonderful Lord. When will we give Him opportunity to do something new in our churches?

Paul did not know when he would get to Corinth or how long he would stay. He did not know when he would leave, nor where he would go next. What a wonderful thing for a missionary to be in a position like that! The one great steadying factor, the source of authority and assurance, was that he was under the command of the Lord: "If the Lord permit."

On the part of the missionary we see here a sacred responsibility that is twofold. First, freedom of action within the will of God: freedom to move here and there, wherever the Holy Spirit may direct, a complete freedom, not from authority, but from machinery. In the second place, he has a sacred relationship with the home base. I believe absolutely in missionary societies, but the most vital relationship is between the missionary and his home church. The society is the agency through whom the missionary is sent and by whose oversight work is maintained on the field. But the home church is the place of fellowship in prayer and support, without which no missionary enterprise would be possible.

Here, therefore, is the double responsibility. On the part of the missionary there is the opening of his heart completely to the home church, his willingness to serve and work and to have fellowship with them. There may be uncertainty concerning the future; yet the missionary is under the sovereign control of the Lord all the time, and he is sharing this uncertainty as well as the blessedness of this sovereignty with the believers at the home base.

On the other hand, here is the sacred responsibility of the church: to receive their missionary and to "bring me on my journey whithersoever I go" (16:6). As I understand it, this means not merely that support in giving which insures his basic needs, but also support in prayer which assures his safety from all the fiery darts of the devil.

Corinth did not face this challenge alone; Paul applied this principle to all the churches. Wherever he went he expected this fellowship from them, and he laid the responsibility on the local believers so that together they had the privilege of seeing that he took a generous offering to Jerusalem.

A truly Christian man became increasingly interested in missions, and at first he prayed, "Lord, save the heathen." Then, "Lord, send out missionaries to save the heathen." Although he prayed earnestly, this did not satisfy him, so he began to pray, "Lord, if you haven't anyone else to send, send me. But if you can't send me, send somebody else." He still was not satisfied until he settled down to this form of missionary praying: "Lord, send whom you will. If it could be me, how I would love it. But if not, then teach me to pay my share of the expenses." I wonder how far you and I have come along that ladder of prayer and consecration.

There is one thing more, the main thrust of this portion of Paul's letter, what I would call "the collection and its procedure." "Now concerning the collection for the saints, as I have given order to the churches of Galatia, even so do ye. Upon the first day of the week let every one of you lay by him in store, as God hath prospered him, that there be no gatherings when I come" (16:1-2).

Because of the principles of fellowship, the situation at Jerusalem created a demand upon all the churches, not only Corinth. They must feel the suffering of their brethren in Jerusalem, and recognize the immense privilege that God had given them to help. How is this responsibility to be met?

They were to *give*. Money had to be sent to Jerusalem, and Paul had to be seen safely on his journey. This giving has several features I would like to catalogue for you.

First, they were to be systematic: "On the first day of the week." It was to be a real part of their worship and thanksgiving on that resurrection day, which the early church was observing in place of the Jewish sabbath.

Then it was to be very personal: "let every one of you." This suggests that each one was to go away alone, and in an act of worship to settle his account with God Himself.

Thirdly, their giving was to be sacrificial: "as God hath prospered you," says Paul. The exact amount is not stated; that was left between the individual and his Lord: according to God's faithful provision there was to be a real dedication of a portion of their goods.

And it was to be spiritual: "No gatherings when I come." That simply means no whipping up of an offering under pressure at the last moment; no giving under compulsion of any human agency, but all as the result of honest, individual facing of responsibility before God.

It is also my sacred task to face you in the name of our Master with your responsibility in this matter. Do you give regularly to the Lord's work, or is your giving only occasional and haphazard? If so, then there is serious failure somewhere to recognize your responsibility as a Christian to the whole church. I am not, of course, speaking only of the local church but of the fellowship of God's people everywhere. Do you give to missions? In one way or another, is your giving systematic?

Then let me ask you, is your giving personal? Do you ever take five minutes alone with the Lord to thank Him for the provision of your material needs, and to ask His guidance as to what to put into the offering plate on the Lord's day? Is there any worship about it? Do you settle the matter with God first?

Is your giving sacrificial? Many people today seem to give in an attitude of tipping God—how dreadful that is! Tithing is good, but sacrificial giving alone is really glorifying the Lord. That is above a tithe, for it is "as the Lord hath prospered."

Is your giving spiritual—not simply responding when an appeal is made, or your emotions are aroused, but out of the love and devotion of your heart to the Lord Jesus Christ? I honestly believe that if every believer gave like that, there would be no problem in maintaining the Lord's work both at home and abroad.

A certain Christian once said to a friend, "Our church costs too much. They are always asking for money."

"Some time ago a little boy was born in our home," replied her friend. "He cost me a lot of money from the very beginning: he had a big appetite, he needed clothes, medicine, toys, and even a puppy. Then he went to school, and that cost a lot more; later he went to college, then he began dating, and that cost a small fortune! But in his senior year at college he died, and since the funeral he hasn't cost me a penny. Now which situation do you think I would rather have?"

After a significant pause she continued, "As long as this church lives it will cost. When it dies for want of support, it won't cost us anything. A living church has the most vital message for all the world today, therefore I am going to give and pray with everything I have to keep our church alive."

"Now concerning the collection"—you see, this isn't putting giving on a low level, pressuring people to give in a hectic moment of decision. It is asking you to settle this matter as consecrated, surrendered Christians, recognizing your responsibilities. The whole missionary enterprise is impossible without a living church to which all of us contribute with our money and with our prayers. Thank heaven for the privilege, but let us be faithful to it. Otherwise our individual responsibility may be withdrawn, and our shame will be great when we meet the Lord face to face.

CHAPTER 32

REASONS FOR HOLDING ON

I Corinthians 16:7-9

I TRUST that, as we have traveled together on the royal route to heaven, we have realized that there is more than one road. Paul made it perfectly clear that there is the road of carnality, and there is the road of spirituality. There is salvation, and there is full salvation. There is the forgiveness of sins, and there is deliverance from s-i-n. These roads are different, and God's purpose is that all of us should travel on the "royal route."

The truth of Scripture often lies beneath the surface, waiting only for prayer and study to reveal it to the hungry heart and open mind. This is clearly true of verses like these under consideration.

News of the sad state of affairs in Corinth has been brought to Paul at Ephesus by members of the household of Chloe (1:11). The letter we have been studying is Paul's reply. In closing, he speaks to them of his future plans, especially his hope of returning to Corinth. As to the time of that visit, he is uncertain, for he is sure that at the present moment he is in the will of God where he is. "I will tarry at Ephesus until Pentecost. For a great door and effectual is opened unto me, and there are many adversaries" (16:8-9).

Paul rejoices in this assurance, because God had opened for him a door of opportunity, *and* there are many adversaries. He is not saying, "But there are many adversaries, and therefore I had better quit," but rather, "and there are many adversaries, therefore I must stay." In other words, the adversaries were simply part of the opportunity, and were just as much a reason for him staying at Ephesus as was the open door.

Now I want to consider Paul's open door and his adversaries with you. On the one hand, many of us talk far too lightly about God's open doors for service without ever realizing what is involved in them. On the other hand, we are apt to become much too easily discouraged by the adversaries and give up instead of holding on. We say, "It is wonderful to be serving the Lord here, but it is so difficult and there is so much opposition that the only thing to do is resign."

I trust that our meditation on this may put courage into some faltering life, strength into some soldier of the cross, and insight into all our hearts as to what an open door is, and what it demands of us.

To get the background of this situation, it is well to remember that the door to Ephesus had not always been open (Acts 16:6). A few years previously Paul was forbidden by the Holy Spirit to preach the word in Asia, and was sent to Macedonia. Later, on his way from Corinth to Jerusalem, he spent one day at Ephesus (Acts 18:19), and told them he would return again if the Lord willed.

Many things happened before that door was opened to Paul. For one thing, the eloquent preacher from Alexandria, Apollos by name, arrived at Ephesus. He met that delightful couple, Aquila and Priscilla, who had come with Paul from Corinth on his way to Jerusalem, and had stayed at Ephesus until he should rejoin them. They took Apollos aside "and expounded unto him the way of God more perfectly" (Acts 18:26). As a result of this, his preaching became more powerful and fruitful; Acts 18 closes by telling us that he "mightily convinced the Jews . . . showing by the scriptures that Jesus was Christ."

If only you and I could see behind the outward tool to God at work! The door to Ephesus shut to Paul; before he went there God sent another preacher to break up the heavy ground in preparation for Paul's arrival. Ephesus was shut to Paul because Ephesus was not ready for him.

Furthermore, I would suggest to you that Paul himself needed some toughening up for the baptism of fire that awaited him at Ephesus. In between, there was the prison at Philippi: the stripes and beatings before the magistrates, the songs in the night, and God's deliverance. There was the uproar in Thessalonica and the scorn of the intellectual populace at Athens. All these experiences were needed to put heavenly resistance and spiritual courage into him.

Now Ephesus is ready, and Paul is ready. It is God's time to strike, and a blow that is struck in the name of the Lord Jesus and in the power of God the Holy Spirit, in His time, is worth a million struck in the power of the flesh. This city was to be the strategic center of missionary enterprise for the Apostle Paul. One outcome of his three years there was the founding of the seven churches of Asia to whom the risen Lord sent His messages which are recorded in the early chapters of the Book of Revelation. Here, therefore, behind the closed door, I discover God's reasons for it.

If only we could see behind some of life's closed doors and witness the omnipotent hand of God in our day, patiently working to prepare the door and the worker for His will, how rebuked we would be for our stubbornness and unfaithfulness. The chaos in Christian work is bad enough as it is: mission fields at home and abroad are suffering because of people who blunder their way into some sphere of service for which God has not given them spiritual equipment. Such people are very sure they have what is needed for a particular work, and they are not prepared to wait God's time. They will just put the thing right immediately, they think, and perhaps somebody who has labored patiently for years has his heart broken and his work spoiled. Therefore, if you try to rush into what you want to do, sometimes God slams the door in your face because you are not prepared to go in and the place is not prepared for you.

In the second place, let us look at this door that Paul calls "great and effectual." Apollos has now gone to Corinth (Acts 19:1). It is interesting to notice these little human factors: here in I Corinthians 16:12, Paul tells us Apollos did not go there when Paul asked him: "As touching our brother Apollos, I greatly desired him to come unto you with the brethren: but his will was not at all to come at this time; but he will come when he shall have convenient time." I get the impression that Apollos was a strong-minded man; he was not going to be pushed around, even by Paul. Yet he was ready to go to Corinth at God's command, for he was submitted to the will of God.

Now Paul, a prepared man, entered Ephesus, a prepared place. It is a thrilling moment when a man steps into the place of service that is God's will for him. The door is open, and now what will it be like? Will there be overwhelming blessing, mighty revival? No, as a matter of fact, at Ephesus it was a battle from beginning to end. After it was all over, Paul's comment was, "I have fought with beasts at Ephesus" (15:32).

Let us survey this battlefield a moment, and look at the adversaries. To Paul this was a strange city with a huge population, whose methods of thought and culture and background were entirely different from his own. What can he possibly do to stem the tide of sin in that city? What can be done to change the habits of the people spiritually, morally, and socially, and get them to thinking about God? The thing is absolutely impossible; Paul saw that when he faced this great city of Asia.

In Ephesus there was a vast system of organized idolatry in the temple of Diana. The image of Diana had apparently been an early space traveler, supposedly dropped out of the heavens from the god Jupiter, and now was enshrined in a temple (Acts 19:35). "Great is Diana of the Ephesians!" was their slogan, and lavish were the gifts and ceremonies of her worship. In that same chapter of Acts we read of the great trade going on in replicas and charms which every visitor could buy to take home as a memento of his visit to the shrine of Diana. It was a superstitious thing, supposed to preserve them from evil. How could the gospel break into that?

Still further, there was a crowd of wandering Jews who practiced magic, invoking names supposedly potent over people possessed with evil spirits. So deeply rooted were prejudice and superstition in Ephesus that before people made any important decision they consulted these magicians. It is no easy task to turn a savage tribe from confidence in witchcraft and medicine-men to God. But I tell you it is even harder to neutralize the poison of superstition and vice and profit in a city like Ephesus—or Chicago.

But the worst adversary of all was the Jewish synagogue, representing the ancient tradition of the people of God in their unbelief. What trials were to befall Paul by "the lying in wait of the Jews" (Acts 20:19)!

This was God's open door. Was it eager for the gospel? Not a bit of it! Filled with heathenism, idolatry, superstition, demon possession, religious prejudice—such was the open door!

As Paul settled to his trade alongside Aquila and Priscilla, because he worked his passage all the time as a tent maker, he looked far beyond the workshop to victories for the Lord in that great city. How he prayed and how he agonized! Just as William Carey, the great pioneer of modern missions, while he cobbled people's boots and shoes in a little place in England, wept and prayed over a map of the world he kept before him as he worked. If you would step into any work for God, just remember that you will never accomplish anything until God has broken your heart over it.

Are our open doors any different today? I don't think so. Society may be more civilized, with more veneer on the surface, but the adversary is basically the same, even though his manifestations may vary.

If in your experience God has slammed tight the door and you are wondering why, perhaps a little light has fallen on your path. Maybe the place is not ready for you, and you are not ready for that service. The day may come when you are ready, and the place is ready for you; when those two things are timed in the will of God, you step right in. You will then find that you are meeting a similarly tough situation; have you got what is required to meet it?

In the goodness of God, He gives us here some principles for victory. Was Paul what he said he was, more than conqueror in all these things? Turning again to Acts 19:8, you will notice that after three month's conflict with the Jews Paul did what he often did: when he first went into a city he would tackle the Jews, and if they would not hear him, then he would move off and preach to the Gentiles. So now he moved his headquarters to the schoolhouse of Tyrannus and taught there every day. The result was that he continued for two years, "so that all they which dwelt in Asia heard the word of the Lord Jesus, both Jews and Greeks."

Furthermore, the silversmiths who produced the little images of Diana acknowledged that their trade was in danger; they were being put out of business! People were turning from the worship of Diana to the true God. The magicians also were baffled by Paul's miracles of healing. Many brought all their books of magic, confessed their sin, and burned the rubbish in the market place.

The exorcising Jews began trying to use the name of Jesus, only to find themselves answered by the demons—and I can imagine the shock they got! "Jesus we know, and Paul we know, but who do you think you are?" And the man with the demons in him attacked them, making them turn tail and run for their lives, even leaving their clothes behind.

"In all these things we are more than conquerors," says Paul. What a rebuke this is to our utter ineffectiveness; I do not know of anywhere on earth where such things are happening today. There have been periods in history when a city's life has been completely transformed by the preaching of the gospel. There have been days in the Puritan era when whole towns were moved for God, but not now. In spite of all the big evangelistic campaigns, the city is just the same twelve months after. Its life is not deeply touched, and in spite of the testimony of the Christian church today, social, political, and moral evils just go from bad to worse.

Yet Paul says that in all these things we are more than conquerors. What is the reason? Let us get behind the scenes and look into Paul's private life. What has he to say for himself? You will find records of his battles in several places. For instance, "We should like you, our brothers, to know something of what we went through in Asia. At that time we were completely overwhelmed, the burden was more than we could bear, in fact we told ourselves that this was the end. Yet we believe now that we had this experience of coming to the end of our tether that we might learn to trust, not in ourselves, but in God Who can raise the dead" (II Corinthians 1:8-9, PHILLIPS). And again, "Every day we experience something of the death of the Lord Jesus, so that we may also know the power of the life of Jesus in these bodies of ours" (II Corinthians 4:9, PHILLIPS). The source of victory in that open door was not in Paul, but in God; "In all these things we are more than conquerors through him that loved us" (Romans 8:37).

Do you think as Paul faced all that in Ephesus, he overcame his enemies with ease? No, but here is his secret: he was living in daily union with the Lord who loved him and who, because of the life Paul lived, because of the crucifixion of the flesh, because of the renouncement of self, poured into his soul heavenly wisdom, faith, and power. Paul's only concern was lest anything should cut him off from his loving, living Lord. "Shall anything separate me from the love of Christ?" he cried. That was all that mattered to him in his ministry. If nothing could separate him from the love of God in

Christ, then nothing could interrupt his supplies of the Lord's strength and power.

That is Paul's secret of victory in the open door: the eternal love of God coming into a crucified life through Jesus Christ. That is the secret and the only hope of the Christian today in any place. But what is the church doing about it? Often demanding more years at the university, raising the standard of education, making men more intellectual. I would not decry such a thing; I am quite sure that the greater education a man can get, humanly speaking, the more he is going to be equipped for the open door in one sense. But I am saying the peril is that in raising these standards of mental ability and understanding, we are forgetting the whole principle of death and self-crucifixion. For it is upon the man bearing his cross for Jesus' sake that God pours out His love, His strength, His grace.

Can anything separate us from the love of God in Christ? Yes, sin can and does. It does not hold back the love of God, for He loves the sinner. But if there is one thing that holds back heavenly supplies of wisdom, strength, ability, power and grace from the Christian, it is man's dependence upon his own ability and education to meet the need of his day. Oh, for grace to repent before God, to receive anew His inexhaustible supplies!

CHAPTER 33

FINAL COUNSEL

I Corinthians 16:10-20

OF ALL the churches to which Paul wrote in the New Testament, there was none in such trouble as Corinth, none so sinful, none that had failed so badly. None of them received such rebuke as he gave to this church, and yet none of them received such loving counsel. They must have wilted under the scorching fire of his rebuke, but must also have been wonderfully refreshed and restored as this great preacher opened his heart to them and showed them that the way of victory in all things is the way of love.

Now he comes to these closing words of counsel: "Watch ye, stand fast in the faith, quit you like men, be strong. Let all your things be done with love" (16:13-14). In other words, "You have many temptations to face, therefore watch. You are going to hear false teachers who would turn you from the truth, therefore stand fast. You will have many trials, therefore behave like men, be strong. There is a lot of contention among you, therefore let everything be done with love."

Paul relates his counsel and advice to the needs of this little fellowship that he knew so well. As we have traveled along what we have called the royal route to heaven in this epistle, I think many of us have found this letter has a great deal to do with our own needs, and therefore we are going to investigate also these closing words of loving pastoral advice which Paul gives to his converts.

I would group Paul's admonitions into three very simple statements as I take these texts in their context, which is the only fair way to deal with Scripture. In the first place, he says there should be a recognition of real Christian fellowship: "Watch ye." They were going to face many temptations, particularly the one of becoming very indifferent and thoughtless of the needs of other people.

Paul introduces some names here that I find most interesting. First of all he speaks about young Timothy, and says, in effect: "Timothy is going to come and see you shortly. He might very well be afraid of all you very clever, intellectual people, but just put him at his ease. Look after him, and send him on his way to me." Paul had written to Timothy, "Let no man despise thy youth." What he really said was, "Don't let your youth be despicable" (I Timothy 4:12). Now he writes to the church at Corinth, "Don't despise this young believer. He is as much a worker of the Lord as I am." I think one of the wonderful things in the New Testament is this relationship between the aged Paul and young Timothy. It reminds us, and I think we need to be reminded, that old age and youth can get along and can work together in the Lord's service.

Then Paul mentions Apollos: "I wanted Apollos to come and see you, but he didn't want to come." I can imagine Paul saying, "Now, Apollos, I do wish you would go to Corinth. If you went, perhaps you could put a stop to all that party spirit and hero worship. I think your presence there might cure them of saying, 'I am of Paul, and I am of Apollos.'"

I think of Apollos turning to Paul and saying, "I don't think it would stop anything at all; I think it would only make matters worse." So they agreed to differ, but they still loved each other: Paul says here, "Brother Apollos." Though Paul didn't get his own way, he knew how to disagree with another Christian and yet to love him just the same.

Then Paul introduces to us three very delightful people, although we know very little about them. One of them was called Stephanas, and he had a little family; at the very beginning of his ministry at Corinth Paul had baptized them (1:16). And then two others, Fortunatus and Achaicus, evidently Christian gentlemen. These three brethren had visited Paul, and he says of them, "They have refreshed me greatly." Indeed, it seems that these people were renowned for their wonderful hospitality, because Stephanas and his household are mentioned in this chapter, that they "have addicted themselves to the ministry of the saints" (16:15). It simply means that they kept

open house; everybody was welcome in their home all the time.
What lovely people!

And now Paul says, "Acknowledge these people, recognize them
for the gems they really are. Watch that you do not slip into the
temptation of not recognizing the gifts and fellowship of other
Christians." What wonderful ministries are an open home and the
refreshment of the saints. As a Christian duty, as a matter of Christian
ethics, we must all watch our fellowship, our responsibility to others,
and watch our reaction when we disagree with another Christian,
avoiding the peril of party spirit.

It sounds very delightful, doesn't it, to have a little group of people
like this who are always being friendly? If your house is open for the
ministry to the saints, and if you have such a love as Paul had for the
young people, what a difference it would make! Christian fellowship
is such a lovely thing.

But how do I practice it? What is the power behind it? Look at
Paul's second piece of pastoral advice: "Stand fast in the faith." It is
impossible to do any of these things as a Christian should unless our
behavior stems from Christian principles and Christian doctrine.

Elsewhere Paul says, "Stand fast therefore in the liberty where-
with Christ hath made us free" (Galatians 5:1). He says, "Stand
fast in one spirit" (Philippians 1:27), and "Stand fast in the Lord"
(Philippians 4:1). Here, when he writes to the church at Corinth,
"Stand fast in the faith," though he is saying this important thing,
"See that your belief is sound," he is also saying, "See that your
belief is applied in your life."

For to stand fast in the faith means to stand fast in the liberty
with which Christ made us free: "Ye shall know the truth, and the
truth shall make you free" (John 8:32). If His truth has dawned
upon my mind and gripped my heart, it will set me free from the law
of sin and death.

"Stand fast in one spirit," recognizing that a man does not understand his Bible by intellect; he only understands it as the Holy Spirit,
the One who has come that he might lead us into all truth, illuminates
his mind and guides his heart and life on the track of holy Scripture.

"Stand fast in the Lord, that in all things he may have the pre-
eminence." Sound belief is the only key to sanctified behavior. If I
let the one slip, inevitably I become slack in the other. As the Apostle

John says, "Who is he that overcometh the world, but he that be-lieveth that Jesus is the Son of God?" (I John 5:5).

The New Testament standard of Christian ethics is only possible in the life of a man whose sound doctrine has been applied to every detail of his experience. It is doctrine that leads a man to submit to the will of God, and it is submission to the will of God that enables that man to be anointed with the power of the Holy Spirit for daily conduct.

If you turn aside from the principles of the Word of God in just one thing, what happens? You cease to delight in communion with the Lord. You become soured in your fellowship with others. When the Book speaks to your heart and truth comes alive, and the Spirit of God has said something to you from the Word, if you say "no" to Him at any point, if you refuse to apply the doctrine to your ex-perience, immediately your fellowship with the Lord becomes dull and formal, your fellowship with other Christians spoiled. Once you turn away from the Lord Jesus Christ, that in all things He may have the pre-eminence, immediately you hinder all progress in sanctification.

Your growth in knowledge of the Lord Jesus and in likeness to Him is the goal of all Christian experience. Therefore your gracious-ness in Christian fellowship, which is the outcome of that growth, is dependent upon your constant submission to the truth of holy Scripture. To grow more like the living Word means constant sub-mission to the authority of the written Word.

This is one piece of advice which Peter, out of the bitter experience of his own failure, also gives us, "Be sober, be vigilant; because your adversary the devil, as a roaring lion, walketh about, seeking whom he may devour: Whom resist stedfast in the faith" (I Peter 5:8-9).

So may I just put these two things together in your mind: to stand fast in the Lord is to keep your eyes upon the Lord Jesus—that is the greatest source of strength for standing fast in the faith. To stand fast in the faith is to stand fast in submission to the Spirit who is in you to guide you into all truth. To stand fast in one Spirit is to stand fast in the liberty with which Christ has made us free.

Are you failing today in your recognition of fellowship with one another, in your love to others? Are you failing in your responsibility to the faith? I wonder if you have loosened your hold on your Bible

—not that you don't read it, but that you've been saying "no," and therefore you have renounced its authority. Remember that this Book does not simply contain the Word of God, it *is* the Word of God, the only thing by which we can live. Looseness in Christian behavior, coldness in attitude to others, lack of desire for fellowship with God's people—all these things go directly back to a depreciation of the authority of God's Word. Stand fast in the faith!

But the third piece of pastoral advice that Paul gives to this church at Corinth is, "Quit you like men, be strong"—be ready to take up the fight.

His complaint against this church at Corinth was, "I could not speak unto you as unto spiritual, but as unto carnal, even as unto babes" (3:1). But now they should have grown up. "If you are grown up, don't behave like babies." Why? Simply because all who *will* live godly in Christ Jesus *shall* suffer persecution (II Timothy 3:12).

Here is a principle of spiritual life which comes down right into your heart and mine. Satan says we may guard our relationships and friendships, and watch our outward course of action and conduct, if we slack off as far as the pre-eminence of the Lord Jesus and the authority of the Bible are concerned. We can go to any length to be thought a wonderful fellow, as long as we refuse submission to the Word of God. To relax there means that we can go anywhere and do what we like. On the other hand, we may hold on to the pre-eminence of the Lord Jesus and the authority of the Bible as long as we don't let it affect our conduct and our contact with others. But the moment we put watching and holding fast, belief and behavior together, at that moment we draw the fire of the enemy.

We draw the fire of worldly Christian people and of the unbeliever who cares nothing for the things of God. We cease to be regarded by any of them as a delightful person—no good socially, you know, because we refuse to do the things that are contrary to our Bible.

"Therefore," says Paul, "you'd better be ready for the fight. Be strong, be mature, behave like men." What does that mean? As a man, you will not, as a child would, allow yourself to deviate from what you know to be God's will. As a man in Christ, you will examine every suggestion that is put to you, no matter how fascinating it may be, and compare it with what the Word of God says. In every situation you will resolutely refuse to follow a line of conduct that is contrary to the Word of God.

That is the fight. You have to face it, and so do I, every day. The moment you *will* to live godly in Christ, you find ridicule and scorn, and perhaps most subtle of all, the whispering of Satan, "Don't take your Christianity too far—don't be narrow." From my own experience, I have found that the only answer to these constant suggestions of Satan is the continual soaking of my life in the Scriptures.

There is no short cut to holy living. Whatever suggestion or decision is put to me by friend or foe, before I take action it must be referred to the absolute authority of the Word of God. If I am prepared to do that, I shall be strengthened in the fight: "Quit you like men, be strengthened," is the word.

I want to be very careful that you don't misunderstand what I am talking about. But it is not until a man in his will determines to live godly in Christ that he can claim to be a Christian. If you are not drawing the fire, perhaps it is simply because you are not in the battle at all. And if you are not in this battle, is it because you have never willed to live a godly life? If you have never willed to live a godly life, you are not saved, because that involves turning to God from sin.

I am concerned that we have known so much and experienced so little. Tell me, have you had fascinating suggestions made to you recently? And something has whispered into your mind, "What is the harm in it?" What have you done? Have you gone along with what everybody else does, or have you referred it to the Word of God? And when you did, and the Word of God said "no," did you also say "no," even though you faced the sneers of your friends? God bless you!

Or did you refer it to the Word of God which said "no," but you said, "I think I'll go ahead." What has happened to you since? Your quiet time has died out and your fellowship with God has ceased, because the Word of God is no longer your authority. You have turned aside from the battle.

The people who are really fighting this battle, constantly regarding the Word as their final authority for life, will agree with me that this battle is not a brief one; it is lifelong. Often we are tempted to give way to fear and discouragement, but we have to learn to say with Paul, "None of these things move me, neither count I my life dear unto myself, so that I may finish my course with joy" (Acts 20:24).

Whatever may be your views on eternal security (and I think you know mine), remember it is "he that endureth to the end shall be saved" (Matthew 10:22). It is a mark of reality when you see the sign of endurance in a Christian's life. I believe in the perseverance of the saints because I believe in the perseverance of the Lord Jesus Christ.

The greatest force to inspire us in relating our behavior and our belief together is the thought of verse 14: "Let all your things be done with love." It is good to have plenty of zeal, and it is good to have plenty of courage, but they aren't everything. It is very easy for a spirit of bitterness to get hold of us. The Word says we are not to render evil for evil, but on the other hand, blessing.

Perhaps you have discovered that the foes in life are the foes of your own household. Your submission to the authority of God's Book has brought unhappiness in the most precious relationships in life. And you may have gone along with your husband or wife in some issue and compromised for the sake of peace. But there is no peace in your heart—there never is, when you take that policy. Or you may have resisted, but in an unkind spirit. Often the battle will demand that you obey God rather than man, but if you show a bitter spirit you lose the battle, even though you do what you think is God's will. Somehow we have to learn to take up the cross meekly, to bear it patiently, to bless God that we are counted worthy to suffer for Christ, remembering that the Lord Jesus prayed for His enemies. May all things, even our battle, be surrounded by the sweet warmth of love.

The Lord enable you to determine to live a godly life, and to relate what you believe to your conduct, as the evidence of a genuine Christian experience. The Lord give you victory in the battle that must follow when these two things are put together, and enable you to do all things with love.

CHAPTER 34

THE VITAL ISSUE OF LIFE

I Corinthians 16:21-24

As was Paul's custom in concluding all his letters, he takes the pen in his own hand and writes a farewell greeting. This will receive, from those who get the letter, more attention than anything else. Don't you find yourself, sometimes, looking at the end of a letter before you start it? Perhaps you want to know whom it is from or what he or she really thinks of you. Frequently, what the writer wants to emphasize is contained in the last sentence, possibly even in a postscript.

Now what has Paul to say? How will he sum up his teaching to these Christian people at Corinth? What will he desire that they should remember above everything else? "If any man love not the Lord Jesus Christ, let him be Anathema Maran-atha. The grace of our Lord Jesus Christ be with you. My love be with you all in Christ Jesus. Amen" (16:22-24).

Thank you, Paul, for sending us your love. Thank you for praying that the grace of the Lord Jesus may be with us. We shall certainly need every bit of that as we walk along the royal route to heaven. But this other verse seems rather an ugly tone with which to finish a letter.

Let's look at those two unfamiliar words just a moment. *Anathema* is a Greek word, not even translated into English here. You sometimes find it translated, as in Romans 9:3, when out of the passion of his heart for his Jewish people, Paul exclaims, "I could wish myself accursed from Christ for my brethren's sake." This is the word: "If any man love not the Lord Jesus Christ, let him be accursed."

The second word is really two words in the Aramaic language, which possibly was the language of Paul's youth. *Maran*—"the Lord"; *atha*—part of the verb "to come." Dr. Ironside says that a free paraphrase of this verse might be: "If any man love not the Lord Jesus Christ, he shall be condemned at the coming of the Lord." Paul is just stating an inevitable fact.

Isn't it harsh to consign to judgment and destruction a man who perhaps is not guilty of any gross sin, and maybe has quite a bit of the form of religion, and yet is destitute of the power of the Christian faith? But how else can you interpret this verse; indeed, how else can you interpret the whole revelation of the Christian gospel?

The unique feature of the Christian faith is that it requires a resolute adherence and a constant devotion to the Lord Jesus Christ. Of course, it doesn't stop there, but it is out of personal devotion to the Lord Jesus, and out of that alone, that there spring all the implications of the Christian life. It is out of a personal devotion to Christ that there arises the social gospel as well as the holy life. That is why Paul emphasized in I Corinthians 13 that if I "have not love, I am nothing."

Merely to use a title, to call Him "the Lord," and yet have no personal love or affection, to show no regard for Him in your life, is the worst form of hypocrisy. To love Christ is to put Him before everybody and everything else, and to delight in His presence above all. It means, to use the language of the Apostle, that we count all things but loss for the excellency of the knowledge of Christ Jesus our Lord. It means that we say with David, "As the hart panteth after the water brooks, so panteth my soul after thee, O God" (Psalm 42:1). And again, "Whom have I in heaven but thee? and there is none upon earth that I desire beside thee" (Psalm 73:25).

When a man truly loves the Lord Jesus, his delight in His presence is always matched by readiness to obey Christ. It was, if you remember, by this criterion that the Lord Himself taught us to judge the reality of Christian experience: "He that hath my commandments, and keepeth them, he it is that loveth me" (John 14:21).

So this is what Paul would underline: the secret of a happy life, a holy life, a victorious life, a Christian life, is a passionate devotion to the Lord Jesus. If you do not have that, you have nothing, and you will stand condemned on the Judgment Day.

As we have been traveling along this royal route to heaven, constantly the burden on my heart has been, "Has the Word had any effect? Has it reached hearts and produced a deeper devotion to the Lord Jesus Christ?" We have been brought back, time and time again, to ask that question. But what matters more than anything else, the thing which is going to be decisive on that Judgment Day, is, "If any man love not the Lord Jesus Christ, let him be Anathema Maran-atha."

I would not discourage the weak, on the one hand, but neither would I confirm the nominal Christian or the hypocrite in his delusion that as long as he has orthodox "religion," he is going to heaven. Let me give you three reasons from the Word of God why not loving the Lord Jesus Christ is so exceedingly sinful, and that if such an attitude is maintained, it brings separation from the presence of the Lord and everlasting destruction.

First, not to love the Lord Jesus Christ means that in my heart I am in rebellion against the highest throne in all the universe. God has spoken in these last days in His Son, and God has nothing more to say. Everything He has for me of blessing is in Jesus Christ. He has commanded us to hear Him in an audible voice that spoke from heaven, "This is my beloved Son, in whom I am well pleased; hear ye him" (Matthew 17:5). God intends us to regard the Lord Jesus with reverence, with affection, and with obedience. And the Lord Himself said it was intended "That all men should honour the Son, even as they honour the Father" (John 5:23).

Are we at liberty to set aside this word of authority from heaven? Indeed not! The essence of all sin is arrogance, setting up the little puppet-god of self on the throne of my heart instead of its rightful ruler, the Lord Jesus. The essence of salvation is the collapse of the regime of self altogether, and the enthronement of another King. There is no New Testament salvation without submission: "If a man love me, he will keep my words: and my Father will love him, and we will come unto him, and make our abode with him" (John 14:23). The Holy Spirit will not enter a heart that is arrogant and self-righteous; He will only come in when there is willingness for the new regime in which Christ is Sovereign. "Not every one that saith unto me, Lord, Lord, shall enter into the kingdom of heaven; but he that doeth the will of my Father which is in heaven" (Matthew 7:21).

This note which I seek to strike has almost entirely disappeared from gospel preaching today. The word "believe" is so abused that it means little more than an acceptance of truth, which still leaves us uncommitted when it comes to applying that truth to our lives. To declare that the gospel of Jesus Christ demands submission to Him is to be dubbed a bit peculiar, one of the "deeper life" sect. But this is the gateway to life, at the cross where self is crucified and Jesus is enthroned. There is no salvation apart from that.

The road that takes a man to hell is not only "skid row," not just the indifference of millions of people in this country to the truth—those who never darken a church door. It is much more subtle than that: the road that takes a man to hell can be the path that brings him into church membership without the puppet of self having been dethroned. That is Satan's most clever device.

This principle seems to be utterly strange to this generation. Do you know why? Because it is strange in every relationship of life today.

The Scripture says, "Wives, submit yourselves to your husbands in the Lord." In the New Testament, this is the loveliest picture imaginable, drawn for us by the Holy Spirit to illustrate the submission of the Christian to his Saviour. To enter into that precious experience with Christ—I would not say it is impossible, but it is a thousand times more difficult when that principle of submission in married life is ignored. Submission one to another is the key to a happy home life. When that principle is refused, what happens? It is not long before the bride says, "I don't see why I should do what he wants; I don't agree with him." And the bridegroom says, "Listen, you've got to do what I tell you." They get into conflict and run away to the divorce court to escape the tangle. If I would refuse to submit to an earthly bridegroom, how can I ever bring myself to submit myself to One whom I have not seen?

Again, "Children, obey your parents." That is not taught or practiced in many homes today. Lack of discipline will produce children who have never learned to obey their earthly father, so how can they be expected to obey their heavenly Father? The careless, slipshod bringing up of children has led not only to unhappy homes and juvenile delinquency, but to shallow Christian living. When a child goes out from the shelter of the home in which he has been pampered and spoiled, and he is called upon to submit to the King of kings, do you think he will? All of us are selfish, despicable, wretched creatures unless the grace of God gets into our hearts through submission to Christ's sovereignty. He is the *Lord Jesus Christ*, and to fail to love Him is to rebel against the highest throne of all the universe.

In the second place, not to love the Lord Jesus is to reject the loveliest character of all creation. In Christ is every possible beauty; He is the altogether lovely One. There is nothing lacking in Him that could be for the glory of God and for the blessing of my life. "For in him dwelleth all the fulness of the Godhead bodily" (Colossians 2:9). The great outcome of love for the Saviour is that the Holy Spirit comes to dwell within our hearts, that we might know the love of Christ that passeth knowledge, that we too might be filled with all the fulness of God. In other words, to love Jesus is to become like Him.

There is a question in Psalm 115:2: "Wherefore should the heathen say, Where is now their God?" And that is exactly the question people around us are asking. The heathen's god is made of silver and gold; he has eyes that see not, a mouth that speaks not, ears that hear not, a nose that smells not, hands that handle not, feet that walk not. And "They that make them are like unto them; so is every one that trusteth in them" (Psalm 115:8). The heathen becomes like the god he worships.

"Where is your God, Christian? Where is this Lord you say is so wonderful?" they ask. And the Christian has to hang his head in shame, because he has failed to be like Him. Oh, what a rebuke! When an unbeliever sees a Christian, he should be thinking, "There is God, walking in that man, talking through him, living in him, loving through him." That is to be our witness to our God, who is incarnate within our redeemed personality.

To fail to love Christ is to reject this possibility. If I love Him, I worship Him, and if I worship Him, I grow to be like Him. To reject His loveliness is to prefer to be mean and selfish and ugly. It means to become like the material things I worship: cold, ruthless and powerless.

Of what use do you think it is to have a religion that is theologically correct, doctrine that is fundamentally sound, a big Bible that you believe from cover to cover and carry around with you, and yet you are mean and selfish and unlovely? When you are not recognized you resign and walk out—but the trouble is that you come back again. What is the value of a religion like that? Do you love the Lord Jesus? Do you worship Him? Are you growing like Him? Or have you been saved, so you say, for twenty years or more, and you are still as irritable and resentful as ever?

"If any man love not the Lord Jesus Christ, let him be Anathema." Why? Because, thirdly, it is a refusal of the greatest Lover of my soul. Just reflect a moment on what Jesus has suffered for us: "Who, being in the form of God, counted it not a thing to be grasped after to be equal with God: But made himself of no reputation, and took upon him the form of a servant, and was made in the likeness of men: And being found in fashion as a man, he humbled himself, and became obedient unto death, even the death of the cross" (Philippians 2:6-8). Have you watched Him coming down the stairs from glory? "Though he was rich, yet for your sakes he became poor, that ye through his poverty might be rich" (II Corinthians 8:9). And again, "But God commendeth his love toward us, in that, while we were yet sinners, Christ died for us" (Romans 5:8).

Can there be a creature on earth who does not love Him for that? Can you think of His lowly birth in utter poverty, all the toil and labor in His life, the pain and suffering of His death as He was made sin for us, the constancy of His intercession for us at the throne ever since—can you think of it all and not love Him?

Yes, we can, and it stamps upon our character such utter baseness, and it makes the language of our text speak to us with heavenly authority: "If any man love not the Lord Jesus, let him be accursed." When I think about that, I have it in my heart to say, "Amen, Lord. You couldn't do anything else. Hell is no more than we deserve."

In the early days of the church, when the Roman Empire was trying to stamp it out, the Christians had a sign, a fish, because the Greek word was similar to the name "Jesus." And they had a watchword; wherever they went they spread it: "Maran-atha!" Those little groups, harried and chased as fugitives from place to place, scattered by persecution, would follow the sign of the fish, and as the Roman soldiers sought them out, they would encourage each other, "Maran-atha! Hold on, be brave, the Lord is coming!" It was the word of fellowship—"We cannot carry on without Him; we cannot give in." That early church triumphed in spreading the gospel across North Africa and around the Mediterranean world.

Have you been saying to yourself, "But I cannot love Him as I ought"? No, none of us can. But you can ask Him to light the flame of His love within your heart today. Submit to the will of God and the sovereignty of Christ; seek for His character, His righteousness; surrender to this great Lover of your soul. If you do, the love of God will be shed abroad in your heart by the Holy Spirit, and even years of bitterness and heartache, coldness and cynicism—all these things that have gone with so much of nominal Christian profession—will be taken out of your life by the inbreathing of the love of God.

Do you love the Lord Jesus? I'm not asking what your mind says you believe. I'm asking you what your heart says. If you don't, that is rebellion, refusal, rejection of the Lover of your soul. Make this submission that His love may come in, that your life may be transformed, and that the sweetness of His presence may become a precious reality to you. All along our royal route to heaven, God has said to us, "If any man love not the Lord Jesus Christ, he will be condemned at the coming of the Lord."

If this were my last word to preach this side of meeting my Lord face to face, I would say to you that there is no heaven for any of us without that love for the Lord Jesus. There is no new birth without surrender, no salvation without submission. But there is such joy when His love and life and power are breathed into my heart by the Holy Spirit, so that I may reveal His love to others.